Why Christianity
Happened

Why Christianity Happened

A Sociohistorical Account
of Christian Origins (26–50 CE)

James G. Crossley

Westminster John Knox Press
LOUISVILLE • LONDON

Scripture quotations, unless otherwise indicated, are from the New Revised Standard Version of the Bible, copyright © 1989 by the Division of Christian Education of the National Council of the Churches of Christ in the U.S.A., and are used by permission.

Book design by Sharon Adams
Cover design by Lisa Buckley
Cover illustration: © *John Foster*

First edition
Published by Westminster John Knox Press
Louisville, Kentucky

This book is printed on acid-free paper that meets the American National Standards Institute Z39.48 standard. ♾

PRINTED IN THE UNITED STATES OF AMERICA

06 07 08 09 10 11 12 13 14 15 — 10 9 8 7 6 5 4 3 2 1

Library of Congress Cataloging-in-Publication Data is on file at the Library of Congress, Washington, D.C.

ISBN-13: 978-0-664-23094-4
ISBN-10: 0-664-23094-6

For Pamela Crossley, Richard Crossley,
and Caroline Watt

Contents

Preface

The overall approach I have advocated over the past few years has led to a fair share of predictable hostility. Most outstanding for me have been attempts by a certain NT scholar to get me to remove the key parts of chapter 1, a chapter that challenges the ideological makeup of the discipline of NT studies. I was informed that NT studies *is* a faith-based discipline and that I just have to accept that. What's more—and this I find both staggering and revealing—I was informed that NT scholars probably won't care less about the discipline of history, so I should not bother discussing it! Thankfully and predictably, no one I know was even remotely persuaded by these views. But undeterred by the unsurprising failure of a nonargument, said scholar resorted to dirty tricks, including an attempt at discrediting me through the usual means: hot air, condescension, unsubstantiated opinion, innuendo, and slurs. It has been an unedifying piece of scholarly behavior that I hope will never happen again. If scholars follow the route of the insular religious separatist, then biblical studies will not deserve to be taken seriously as an academic discipline. I cannot help but think that in just about any other academic subject an argument suggesting that it would be healthy to have a greater mix of non-Christians and Christians would hardly be the most controversial suggestion.

For these reasons I am doubly thankful for some very decent people in my life who have been more than encouraging. A variety of people have provided some sort of input, comments, discussion, or support over the past few years (some of whom I expect would take a radically different stance to me), right up to the last minute and my introduction to the Department of Biblical Studies at the University of Sheffield. These people include Loveday Alexander, Andy Angel, Richard Bell, David Bryan, Alison Bygrave, Philip Davies, Diana Edelman, Gill Fogg, Elizabeth Harris, Maddy Humberstone, Seth Kunin,

Will Lamb, Mary Macneill, Glenn Mahaffy, Callum Millard, Thelma Mitchell, Steve Moyise, Rebecca Mulhearn, Wendy Sprosdon North, Jorunn Økland, Hugh Pyper, Rafael Rodriguez, Aurelio Casado Sanchez, Rob Thorne, Glennis Watt, Mike Watt, and Keith Whitelam. I would also like to thank Philip Law of WJK for his support of this project and the WJK staff for the extremely efficient way in which the publication process was handled. Thanks are also due to anonymous readers for their feedback. In some cases chapter 1 went against their personal convictions, but virtually every reader was prepared to engage with it in an academic fashion. Steph Fisher must also be thanked for reading huge chunks of the manuscript at very short notice.

My recent arrival at the University of Sheffield's Biblical Studies Department has even managed to leave its stamp—particularly through interaction with some seriously historically minded scholars and a great social life—even though this project was effectively completed by the time I arrived. That said, Diana Edelman still managed to provide me with some important critical comments and helpful suggestions at various points in this book.

Maurice Casey has consistently been a good man as well as a top scholar. He has always supported my academic work and has proven to be genuinely open-minded about different ideas. Off-the-field, so to speak, he isn't bad either. In particular, I'll never forget a pretty spectacular run of Monday evenings in the first four months of 2004 at some eating place or other.

Whether he likes it or not, David Horrell has been a very important influence on the way I have approached earliest Christian history. He also manages to be a particularly decent human being (no mean feat for an academic). I happily recall good times with David when I was associated with the ever-friendly Department of Theology at the University of Exeter, not to mention the company of Carrie Horrell and their children Emily (no one else could *ever* get away with calling me "Jamesie") and Katharine.

Since my last book, my brother Richard Crossley has undergone a miraculous transformation. No longer does he sit on his arse all day playing a certain football-management game. This is due in no small part to my kind-of-sister-in-law Gill Turner, the now mother of my nephew Francis James Crossley, both of whom now have the dubious pleasure of Richard as the loving father and doting kind-of-husband. Alas, this has led to a decline in our discussions of Bleu de Gex, Gevrey Chambertin, and Carlos Torano Exodus 1959 (still, I always have Andy Mathieson, Iain Wright, and my new cousin, Mal Lingard, for this). Yet I challenge any reader to top Richard's twelve years of retirement from the age of seventeen onwards after bravely enduring an epic three (yes, *three*) months of employment in that *place* (I'm being polite), the shipyard.

Pamela Crossley has always read through whatever I put in front of her. Her views on religion are as sane as anyone I have ever come across. I thank whomever for both parents not laughing too much at what I've (sometimes) ended up doing for a living.

I would also like to pat myself on the back for having to put up with Caroline Watt (who also happened to read much of the manuscript). My work has doubtlessly suffered, as she has dedicated the past few years of her life to general enjoyment. Many a time have I endured patiently and without grumbling as she tried to remember that obscure pub name or house number, or made my work take a back seat as she thought up some absurd holiday or wanted to eat somewhere or other. Throughout all this I have gone beyond the call of duty by not complaining and being wholly supportive.

To ruin the pleasantries, I should add that I am of course entirely responsible for the contents of this book.

Introduction

In a previous book I provided a chronology of the changes in law observance in earliest "Christianity,"[1] from the historical Jesus through the early Pauline mission and the Jerusalem council to Gospel redaction.[2] There is no evidence that the historical Jesus overrode any commandment, and there is no evidence that Jesus was indifferent to any biblical law. Jesus may well have clashed over the *interpretation* of biblical laws with opponents such as the Pharisees, but such clashes were certainly within the boundaries of first-century Jewish legal debate. After Jesus' death, Christianity remained a largely law-observant movement until the early to mid-40s CE, when more and more Gentiles were becoming associated with the movement (surely no coincidence), something which almost certainly provoked the Jerusalem conference of c. 50 CE to try and find answers. This not only meant that the first Gentiles attracted to Christianity were law observant (at least in the presence of Christians) but also that Paul, in practice at least, was law observant in the 30s and did not at that time openly suggest that Gentiles did not have to observe major commandments. One implication of all this is that the reasons Christianity included people who were no longer observing major commandments were largely social—as opposed to an individual genius like Jesus or Paul finding "something wrong" with Jewish law. But these social reasons for the shift from a law-observant movement to one that included people no longer observing the law require a full explanation. This book is an attempt to do just that.

In general the approach adopted here is an unashamedly secular one that I hope contributes in some way to advancing the prominence of secular critics and criticisms, following the leads of specialists in (significantly?) the Hebrew Bible and early Judaism, such as Philip Davies and Jacques Berlinerblau.[3] What I would want to add are the very down-to-earth social, economic, and historical reasons for the spread of earliest Christianity as opposed to a grand theological explanation associated with many of the works that come under the bizarrely named genre "New Testament History."[4] This does not mean the impact of early Jewish and Christian ideology has been abandoned. On the contrary, these ideologies justified reactions to socioeconomic conditions faced by Jesus and the earliest Christians. But it is true that I have downplayed the role of individual genius in favor of broader social, economic, and historical factors to explain the spread of earliest Christianity.

The use of social-scientific criticism in NT studies has blossomed since the 1970s and has thus provided the possibility of applying a range of secular methods to the old question of shifts in law observance among the earliest Christians. Some of the methods and approaches used in this book will be familiar to some readers; others, perhaps not. From my experience, scholars interested in the interdisciplinary approaches used here while not being widely read in the relevant areas have found it of benefit that I have outlined such approaches in some detail. Where the use of social-scientific methods is (as far as I am aware) particularly new is in the deliberate adaptation of established approaches to provide a broad-ranging explanation for the change in legal practices among the earliest Christians and ultimately for why a new religion emerged from Judaism. This too required more detailed outlining of my methodology at certain points in the book.

For those with little time on their hands or the just-plain-lazy, here is a summary of the main arguments of this book. Chapter 1 outlines the need for a secular approach to Christian origins grounded in the humanities. Comparing NT studies with the discipline of history and locating it in its modern historical context, the first chapter argues that the dominance of Christians in NT studies has (1) prevented important advances in the historical study of Christian origins and (2) focused too heavily on history of ideas rather than trying to find a range of down-to-earth social and economic *causal factors* that led to the spread of earliest Christianity. This emphasis may well continue if things do not change. The remaining chapters provide a secular approach to Christian origins and shifting patterns of law observance that is grounded in social and economic causal explanations, although the significance of ideas and theology is not wholly downplayed.

Chapter 2 provides a socioeconomic explanation for the emergence of the Jesus movement in Galilee, Jesus' particular take on the law, and his concern for the rich to repent before it was too late. Chapter 3 builds on this explanation by arguing that Jesus' mission to sinners was a crucial link to the emergence of a notable association with Gentiles after Jesus' death because (structurally) perceptions of Jewish sinners were very close to perceptions of Gentiles. Chapter 4 provides some suggestions about how macrosociological insights into the rise of monotheism in agrarian societies may be linked to the spread of a universalistic and monotheistic Jewish movement in the ancient world, with a shift towards a greater emphasis on fictive kinship. This shift also required accommodation of initially law-observant Gentiles in this new religious movement, and it is argued that this issue is reflected in early editing of Gospel traditions ("Q" and Mark 6–8).

Chapter 5 then explains the crucial part: how we get from a law-observant movement to a nonobservant movement. Here interdisciplinary analysis of conversion and studies of the spread of new religious movements through social networks are employed. What is particularly important is how changes in key beliefs emerge when a religious movement has to adapt to new social settings. This methodology is applied to conversion through households in earliest Christianity to see how observance of the law was modified in conversion through examples from early Christian and Jewish texts. Once Gentile friends of friends of friends started to join the Christian movement and had little care for issues of the law, then there would have been a pool of people connected to the emerging Christian movement not being justified by works of the law. The scene is thus set for someone to come along and deal with this social problem. Thus we get the emergence of a Pauline mission. The conclusion looks for potential ways forward for secular approaches to Christian origins with a particular stress on macrohistory and macrosociology, suggesting also that there might just be too much stress on exegesis in historical approaches to Christian origins.

For abbreviations used throughout this book, see *The SBL Handbook of Style* (Peabody, MA: Hendrickson, 1999).

1

Toward a Secular Approach
to Christian Origins

The Use of the Social Sciences
in New Testament Scholarship

There is nothing unethical about a given scholar having religious beliefs. Things become potentially objectionable when a scholar in question studies these very same religious beliefs in his or her capacity as a scholar. The tendency of so many exegetes to come to conclusions that perfectly conform to their preexisting creedal convictions is something that members of our discipline will need to think about.[1]

Biblical scholarship is viewed by most of its practitioners, and nearly all nonpractitioners, as a theological discipline. The common habitat of the subject is the seminary or theological department of a college or University. In secondary schools, it is taught in Religious Education and rarely in literature classes. The majority of biblical scholars are Christians and many of them are clergy. It is not surprising that the 'ancient Israel' to which biblical scholarship is in the habit of referring is a homogeneous entity, an embryonic church, thinking religiously, sinning but ultimately justified by its 'faith' in God (this God being the God of scholars, of course). . . . My quarrel is not with individual fellow travellers but with the structure of the discipline which Christian theology has built and which binds us together in what I see as an enterprise that falls short of being seriously critical. . . . So long as the discipline remains theological, much of what has been said in this chapter will be unacceptable.[2]

This book is an attempt to explain the rise of Christianity with a particular focus on the crucial issue of law observance. How did what I described in the introduction as a law-observant Jewish movement turn into a Jewish and Gentile movement with notable numbers no longer observing key aspects of the law? The arguments in this book will provide an explanation that is thoroughly secular and sociohistorical. Put differently, this book attempts to explain the rise of Christianity by downplaying (but not wholly discarding) theological factors and without privileging Christianity in any particular way other than choosing it as the object of analysis. This should be an obvious thing to do. However, the history of Christian origins is dominated by *theological* agendas that all-too-often explain the rise of Christianity in pristine terms of the history of ideas rather than the dirtier world of social history. We even get explanations of the rise of Christianity unthinkable in nontheological academic disciplines, such as the impetus provided by the supposed bodily resurrection of an actual historical figure, as recently argued by N. T. Wright in his enormous book on the resurrection of Jesus.[3]

I am not saying that the approaches I advocate are inherently superior discussions of the past in comparison to the supposedly more-slanted Christian approaches of (say) an Anglican bishop. On the contrary, this chapter will argue that it is absolutely essential that more and more different interest groups participate in NT studies and force greater interaction. This in turn should provide advances in historical research that may otherwise be impossible. It is, I think, clear when one compares NT studies with the academic discipline of history that the study of Christian origins has been impoverished by a lack of non-Christian interest groups—including those wishing to explain Christian origins in a more secular and nontheological way—and that significant advances have been made by individuals who have not fitted the traditional molds of Christian scholarship. This will set the tone for the social-scientifically informed historical argument of the rest of the book.

As much of this chapter concerns social sciences and history, two brief comments ought to be made, one definitional, one apologetic. First, there are often attempts to distinguish between social history without much care for models, on the one hand, and the explicit use of models and theories, on the other.[4] While this is a useful distinction for surveys of scholarship, it is not one I will (usually) use here because in many ways both approaches are two sides of the same coin, a point echoed by biblical scholars and historians alike.[5] Besides, historians who have written some of the most-famous social histories from below have been strongly influenced by theoretical insights from, for example, anthropology, sociology, and Marxism (see below).[6]

Most important for present purposes, the more-social-historical approaches and the more-theoretical-model-based approaches effectively rise, fall, and rise again simultaneously in the history of NT studies. Thus when I refer to "social-scientific approaches" or the like, I usually mean both social-history and model-based approaches. Second, an apologetic: the relatively large number of quotations in this chapter is unfortunately inevitable, as my primary material is not on the whole ancient literature but modern scholarly literature, mostly from the discipline of history. Much of it will be unfamiliar to many who study the NT; thus more extensive quotation is required to make the argument more comprehensible.

EXIT SOCIAL SCIENCES

One puzzling aspect of the history of the study of Christian origins is that there was a virtual absence of social-scientifically informed approaches between approximately the 1920s and the 1970s. Before the mid-1920s there were contributions to the social context of early Christianity from scholarly heroes such as Adolf Deissmann, Ernst Troeltsch, and Adolf von Harnack.[7] There were even contributions to the study of Christian origins from the prominent Marxist figures Friedrich Engels and Karl Kautsky.[8] In the United States in the 1920s and early 1930s the "Chicago School" in particular investigated the social context of early Christianity—most notably in the works of Shirley Jackson Case—and F. C. Grant produced what was for many years the standard work on the economic background to the Gospels.[9] Although there were occasional notable contributions, such as E. A. Judge's *The Social Pattern of the Christian Groups in the First Century* (1960), after the 1920s interest in the social context of early Christianity began to wane significantly. Case's academic interests were diverted elsewhere, and the Chicago Divinity School began to focus on philosophy of religion, with its NT focus more on textual criticism.[10] Grant's 1926 book on the economic context of the Gospels was still the standard work on the subject at the time of its second edition in 1973, despite all the advances made in economic theory and economic history since the first edition. But in the 1970s—and, as David Horrell points out, in distinction from the early twentieth century—there were new developments particularly marked by creative use of social-scientific methods, models, and theories.[11] This should raise the obvious question: Why did the rebirth—albeit with a slightly different body—take so long?

One of the usual reasons given is the influence of Karl Barth and dialectical theology after the First World War. Here, in contrast to the "social gospel" of liberal Protestant theology, the importance of the radical otherness of the gospel was crucial while social context and social influence on the gospel wanders off into the sunset. This is tied in with a related reason for the decline of social context: Rudolf Bultmann and the rise of form criticism. At first sight this may seem strange as one of the key mantras of form criticism was *Sitz im Leben*, the setting in life. But in reality it was the *Sitz im Glauben*, the setting in faith, that dominated, as Bultmann emphasized an existential hermeneutic with theological truth supposedly found in the seemingly transcendent Gospel of John.[12] Yet the option for social context was certainly available at the time. In addition to the early attempts at social-scientifically informed approaches to early Christianity already noted, Oscar Cullmann famously commented on the rise of form criticism, with the suggestion that it would have to interact with a specialized form of sociology devoted to the analysis of laws governing the growth of popular traditions.[13] Philip Esler wonders if putting Cullmann's suggestion into practice might have led to different results.[14] A different question may be added, and one that is not properly tackled in surveys of social sciences in NT studies: *Why* was Cullmann's suggestion not put into practice?

Here we need to look at the context in which form criticism emerged, namely, Germany at a time when antisemitism was rife. From this context emerges antisemitic history by prominent NT scholars, something that is gradually becoming more widely recognized.[15] Walter Grundmann is a notable case. Grundmann was a member of the Nazi Party and a supporting member of the SS who argued what would almost inevitably follow from this perspective, namely, that Jesus was more likely to be racially Aryan and not Jewish at all.[16] Another important example must be noted: the openly antisemitic Gerhard Kittel. Kittel was an editor of the still-standard *Theological Dictionary of the New Testament* (*TDNT*), with the early contributions, such as those by Grundmann, being riddled with anti-Judaism and antisemitism.[17] Kittel was a member of the Nazi Party who published an antisemitic pamphlet, *Die Judenfrage* (*The Jewish Question*) and wrote for the official Nazi publication *Forschungen zur Judenfrage* (*Researches into the Jewish Question*).[18] Of course, Rudolf Bultmann (an early contributor to *TDNT*) and many other German Christians were opposed to Nazism but, as is now widely recognized, especially due to E. P. Sanders's devastating critique, there is a profoundly anti-Jewish tone in much of Bultmann-influenced pre- and postwar scholarship. This should not be so surprising given the general sociopolitical context from which early form criticism emerged.

To see just how embedded Christian anti-Judaism was in NT scholarship, the notorious example of Bultmann's student Ernst Käsemann should suffice. Käsemann was famously a trenchant opponent of Nazism and rumored to have been a supporter of the German Green Party, so it could never be claimed that his motivations were like those of Kittel. But in the 1960s Käsemann claimed in print but originally on radio that Paul was firing at "the hidden Jew in all of us, at the man who validates rights and demands over against God on the basis of God's past dealings with him and to this extent is serving not God but an illusion."[19] As Daniel Boyarin argues, such a statement by a German writing in the postwar period would be bad enough in itself but given that ideas associated with hidden Jewishness was part of Nazi ideology and German anti-

semitism makes such a statement in postwar Germany particularly repug-
nant.[20] In this general context we can now see why form criticism failed mis-
erably in providing a genuine setting in life. If German form criticism had
done otherwise, it would have to locate a great deal of Gospel traditions firmly
within the everyday social setting of Palestinian and Diaspora Judaism, and
this would hardly have been to the liking of the dominant German Protestant
NT scholarship, whether Nazis or their opponents.[21]

ANNALES AND THE MARXIST HISTORIANS

To understand the uncomfortable extent of the lateness of social-scientific
approaches to the historical study of Christian origins, we must compare it
with an analogous discipline, namely, history, a discipline that has witnessed
many scholars working with the social sciences and writing social histories
throughout the twentieth century. Bear with me here because there will be a
lot of listing of various scholarly works. This listing is necessary because only
through this comparison with a particular focus on what types of social sciences were being practiced will we be able to provide a fuller explanation for
the near absence of social sciences in NT studies throughout the decades of
the mid-twentieth century.

The French-based *Annales* movement advocated a multidisciplinary
approach to history focused around the journal *Annales*.[22] The founding
fathers, Lucien Febvre (1878–1956) and Marc Bloch (1886–1944), who worked
with one another at Strasbourg, were profoundly influenced by developments
in areas such as geography, sociology, economics, and social anthropology; by
movements such as Marxism; and by figures such as Emile Durkheim. In 1924
Marc Bloch published a book with a surprisingly contemporary feel concerning the belief that kings, from the medieval period through to the eighteenth
century, could heal skin disease by touch.[23] People returned, evidently not
cured, but their faith in the power of the monarch to heal was not diminished.
The Royal Touch, influenced as it was by diverse figures such as Charles Blondel,
James Frazer, Lucien Lévy-Bruhl, and Emile Durkheim, reflects insights from
the social sciences and explores issues such as the idea of royal power, ritual,
and the psychology of belief. As Peter Burke comments, the book may be
described "as an essay in historical sociology or historical anthropology,
focussing on belief systems and the sociology of knowledge."[24] Febvre was con-
tinuously concerned with the Renaissance and Reformation throughout his
career with particular emphasis on collective psychology and social history:
indeed Febvre linked the emergence of these two major historical periods in
European history with the demands of the bourgeoisie.[25] Furthermore, the

Annales journal that Bloch and Febvre founded, initially fully entitled *Annales d'histoire économique et sociale*, was first issued on 15 January 1929 and boasted an editorial board that included a sociologist, an economist, a geographer, and a political scientist, in addition to historians. The effect of the developing *Annales* movement was increasingly felt, and by the mid-1930s both founders had left Strasbourg for distinguished chairs: Febvre, at Collège de France in 1933, and Bloch, at the Sorbonne in 1936.

After the Second World War the *Annales* revolutionaries had followed that time-tested pattern and had become the establishment, at least in French historical circles, with their influence also felt and respected beyond the French borders.[26] The heir to Febvre's throne (Bloch had died in 1944; Febvre in 1956) was Fernand Braudel (1902–1985) who continued pioneering interdisciplinary research in his professional life as a historian (1949–1972) and beyond. In 1949 Braudel published his huge (600,000 words) *The Mediterranean and the Mediterranean World in the Age of Philip II*.[27] Here it was famously argued that historical events such as battles or actions of a leader were only of small significance as compared to deeper structures of society. For Braudel, human actions and events were like the ocean froth. Below this almost superficial surface were broad socioeconomic trends, such as the changing circumstances of the nobility, the middle classes, and the poor. These slow-moving trends placed heavy restrictions on human ability to dictate events as humans were swept along. At the bottom of the ocean is the slowest movement of all, labeled "geohistory," the relationship between humans and their environment (climate, landscapes, agriculture, travel routes, etc.). Other interdisciplinary influences have been detected, such as that of Marcel Mauss on Braudel's chapter on Mediterranean civilization.[28] By the 1960s, then, we have another major interdisciplinary *Annales* work, and one widely regarded as a twentieth-century masterpiece of historical writing.

Marxist historians were also pioneers in social history and their own particular brand of social-scientifically informed histories.[29] Marx and Engels themselves engaged in empirically informed approaches to history in addition to their more famous theoretical approaches, as can be seen in such works as Marx's *Eighteenth Brumaire of Louis Bonaparte, Class Struggles in France*, and *Civil War in France*; or Engels's *Peasant War in Germany* and *The Origins of the Family*. Although Marx and Engels inspired major theoretical approaches in the humanities and social sciences, an empirically based conventional historical practice was just as crucial for them. As Engels put it in a letter to Conrad Smith in 1890,

> nor, today, has the materialist view of history any lack of such friends
> to whom it serves as a pretext for *not* studying history. As Marx said of
> the French Marxists in the late seventies: "Tout ce que je sais, c'est que
> je ne suis pas Marxiste" ["All I know is that I'm not a Marxist"]. . . .

> Our view of history, however, is first and foremost a guide to study, not
> a tool for constructing objects after the Hegelian model. The whole
> of history must be studied anew, and the existential conditions of the
> various social formations individually investigated before an attempt
> is made to deduce therefrom the political, legal, aesthetic, philosoph-
> ical, religious etc. standpoints that correspond to them.[30]

As is often pointed out in the overviews of social-scientific approaches to the
NT, Engels also wrote on Christian origins, penning articles not only on Revelation but most notably "On the History of Early Christianity" (1894). The
prominent Karl Kautsky also wrote a Marxist history of Christian origins titled
Der Ursprung des Christentums: Eine historische Untersuchung (1908).

The next generation of Marxist historical writing produced some twentieth-
century classics, such as Leon Trotsky's massive three-volume work, *The History of the Russian Revolution* (1932). Antonio Gramsci's (1891–1937) analysis
of, for example, folklore, anthropology, class, and hegemony would, as Har-
vey Kaye shows, influence subsequent Marxist historians, not least the Communist Party Historians' Group (1946–1956), of early postwar Britain.[31] The
formation of the Communist Party Historians' Group (from now on CPHG)
in 1946 brought together some of the biggest names in postwar history writing.[32] In 1952 members of the CPHG launched the major social-history journal *Past and Present*, which has consistently included an editorial board of both
Marxists and non-Marxists, including non-Marxist social scientists, and interactive contributions from both Marxists and non-Marxists (or, in the case of
those such as Geoffrey Elton, anti-Marxists). There were other more interdisciplinary links: in the 1950s, for example, Eric Hobsbawm was in discussion
with social anthropologists such as Myer Fortes and Max Gluckmann.

By the mid-1960s, scholars associated with the CPHG had already produced important and classic works of Marxist history, social history, and history from below, such as A. L. Morton's popular *A People's History of England*
(1938); Christopher Hill's *The English Revolution 1640* (1940); Rodney Hilton's
work on peasantry and class in the medieval period, including the popularity
of the Robin Hood legends in English folklore (1958);[33] Eric Hobsbawm's
studies of labor history, eventually collected in *Labouring Men* (1964), and his
study of banditry and rebellion in *Primitive Rebels* (1959), a work now well
known to many NT scholars; and of course E. P. Thompson's famous *The
Making of the English Working Class* (1963). By the mid-1960s Marxist history
writing had been broadly applied: from medieval Europe (Rodney Hilton)
to black slavery in the United States (W. E. B. Du Bois); from the English
working class between 1780 and 1832 (E. P. Thompson) to individual
lives (e.g., Dona Torr on Tom Mann, Isaac Deutscher on Trotsky and Stalin,
and E. P. Thompson on William Morris); from the transition to capitalism

(Maurice Dobb) to the role of the crowd in the French revolution (George Rudé); from banditry and primitive rebellion (Hobsbawm) to revolution after revolution after revolution (e.g., Trotsky on the Russian revolution; Hill on the English revolution/civil war; Rudé, Albert Soboul, and Georges Lefebvre on the French revolution); and so on.[34] A good indicator of Marxism's dominance over social-scientific approaches to history is given by Keith Thomas—who was to pioneer non-Marxist social history in Britain—in a 1963 edition of *Past and Present*:

> If . . . many historians now subscribe, if only implicitly, to a brand of vulgar Marxism, this may be taken to indicate less the seductive effects of that particular doctrine than their acquaintance with any other theoretical attempts to effect that interrelation and mutual explanation of social facts they would much like to see. . . .[35]

So why were so many prominent historians working with the social sciences and producing classic and influential works while NT scholars were busy washing their hair? It might be argued that talk of class, capitalism, and labor struggles has a decidedly modern feel to it and so it might be inferred that Marxism, so deeply associated with social-scientific approaches to history before the 1970s, would not be a particularly useful tool for studying earliest Christianity. What was Marx but an analyst of capitalism? But history from below does not have to be a work of overtly theoretical Marxism. Furthermore, Marxist or Marxist-influenced approaches to the ancient world are now known, such as the 1975 edition of the classics journal *Arethusa* (vol. 8) dedicated to "Marxism and the Classics" and the work of G. E. M. de Ste. Croix.[36] As we have seen, the earliest Marxists, including Engels himself, had already analyzed Christian origins and, even before the impact of liberation theology, Marxist and Marxist-influenced works are found. But such works are rare in the canon of Western NT scholarship, hence the novelty factor implied in the title of the 1976 English translation of Milan Machoveč, *Jesus für Atheisten* (1972): *A Marxist Looks at Jesus*.[37]

Yet with all its talk of money, poverty, landownership, power, the oppressive rich, and role reversal of rich and poor, it might be thought that the NT almost invites social-scientific analysis of a Marxist bent. Indeed, as Luise Schottroff put it in a different context but one particularly apt for present purposes, "God's revolution . . . is certainly just a little older than the concept of the leading role of the working class in Marxist revolution."[38] Whether or not we agree with Marx, Marxism, and/or Marxist theory, we cannot blame the historical period or the empirical data for the lack of social-scientifically informed approaches (frequently associated with Marxism) in the historical study of Christian origins before the 1970s.

This point is important because it would suggest that a fear of or hostility to Marxism may be part of the problem for a Christian-dominated discipline such as NT studies (see below).[39] It is not difficult to equate Marxist criticisms of the bourgeoisie and the anesthetizing power of religious authority with Christian academics in the universities.[40] But there is an even more primal fear. In general terms Marxism itself is problematic for the Christian scholar because its manifestations tend to be atheistic, militantly so in certain cases, and can pose a stark alternative belief system to that of Christianity. Concerning social-scientific approaches to the NT, compare Stephen Barton's warning, echoed by others, of a "more fundamental" problem than reductionism and imposition of models, namely, "the *danger* of using methods and models and remaining unaware that their philosophical roots lie in Enlightenment epistemological atheism [my italics]."[41] For all the problems of Enlightenment epistemology, it is surely unlikely that atheism would be a *danger* for any other study of history and society in the humanities outside theology and religious studies. Furthermore, if there is a lack of awareness in NT studies of atheism at the roots of certain social-scientific methods, then Marxism is surely an obvious exception.

While there were Christians who identified themselves also as socialists or card-carrying communists, it remains that there were consistent anticommunist tendencies reflected in many official lines of churches or attitudes of prominent individuals. They are not difficult to find. The Vatican, for example, has long been famously hostile towards things associated with Marxism, particularly in the Cold War period, from the ruling of Pope Pius XII in 1949 that Catholicism and communism are effectively incompatible, to the Second Vatican Council (1962–1965) openly expressing condemnation of atheistic communism, or from John Paul II's personal fight to rid the world of communism to the hostility shown towards the Marxist-influenced liberation theology emerging from Latin America. To take another relevant example, German Christians who had resisted Hitler, and thus hugely credible figures in the postwar period, were then confronted with the presence of Soviet communism in German territory. Heavyweights such as Martin Niemöller could openly express that the hope for German Protestants lay in the hands of American Protestants, a view reciprocated in the American Lutheran community. After the war, Otto Dibelius was once again made bishop of Berlin-Brandenburg, a see that he lost under the Nazis in 1933. Dibelius held views of the old aristocratic right and, as Owen Chadwick puts it, thought "sociology was a form of atheism and that all modern evil started with the French Revolution," something that made for a combustible mix in a diocese partly in the Russian zone.[42] This great ideological divide was naturally enough reflected not only in the United States but also in the United Kingdom. Compare Adrian Hastings's comments on English Christianity in the early postwar period (1945–1960):

> The challenge of Communism abroad contributed to a conservative
> hardening of the ecclesiastical line at home. . . . English Christianity
> was certainly not widely McCarthyite, theologians could still insist
> that Christians and Communists had some things—important
> things—in common. . . . Nevertheless with very few exceptions Chris-
> tians were agreed as to where the danger lay. The consequence was
> something of a closing of ranks in a conservative direction. This was
> in a fair measure of consensus between Catholic and Protestant such
> as had not existed in pre-war days.[43]

Given these factors, it is perhaps unsurprising to find that there has been
what may reasonably be called a fear of or hostility to Marxism running
throughout NT scholarship since the time of Karl Marx himself. Gerd Theissen argues that the period he designates as the first period of research into the
social context of earliest Christianity (1870–1920) is not only closely linked
with liberal Protestantism's critical attitude towards church and state and
increasing scholarly interest in historical perspective but also an apologetic
tendency in dispute with the labor movement and Marxism.[44] Probably
the most notable example of this was the establishment of the Lutheran
Evangelisch-sozialer Kongress in 1890, whose leading lights would include
Adolf Deissmann and Adolf von Harnack.[45] The Kongress was to combat the
issues of industrialization in Germany and the increasing popularity, particularly among the working class, of the Marxist Social Democratic Party, which
boasted Karl Kautsky as one of its major intellectual figures. The Kongress
would develop their own Lutheran social gospel to appeal to the masses,
although much of the work associated with the influence of the Kongress
focuses more on history of ideas or religious thought than hard socioeconomic
questions.[46] A crucial debate was the nineteenth meeting in Dessau, 1908,
where Deissmann delivered "Das Urchristentum und die unteren Schichten"
("Primitive Christianity and the Lower Classes"), which included attacks on
Karl Kautsky and Albert Kalthoff and emphatically stressed that Christianity
is absolutely not in any way to be understood as a revolutionary proletarian
movement aiming to restructure society. These views are echoed elsewhere in
Deissmann's work.[47] Yet it was argued that early Christianity did, to an extent,
have its origins among the lower classes. This is no coincidence of course. The
battle with Marxism for hearts and minds of the working class was central for
the future of the church. Why else would Deissmann write the following
romanticizing comments on his discovery of a kind of laboring-class apostolic
succession—laboring classes described as only the archetypical broadsheet
reader can?

> Even when Christianity had risen from the workshop and the cottage
> to the palace and the schools of learning, it did not desert the work-

shop and the cottage. The living roots of Christianity remained in their native soil—the lower ranks of society—and regularly in the cycle of years, when autumn had gathered the topmost leaves and the dry boughs had snapped beneath the storms of winter, the sap rose upward and woke the buds from slumber with promise of blossom. . . . Jesus the carpenter and Paul the weaver of tent cloth mark the beginnings, and again at the most momentous crisis in the history of later Christianity there comes another *homo novus* in the person of Luther, the miner's son and peasant's grandson.[48]

But what is peculiarly striking is that in subsequent scholarship a fear of Marxism has all too often been more imaginary than real. Luise Schottroff noted in 1985 that NT scholarship repeatedly stresses that a Marxist understanding of Christian origins as a revolutionary social movement must be rejected even though such analysis from Marxist historians is virtually nonexistent, at least in "mainstream" scholarship. Thus, she argues, the specter of a Marxist interpretation of Christianity as a social revolutionary movement is a "product of Christian-bourgeois polemic."[49] Schottroff gives the example of Edwin Judge, who claims that given there is a belief in class struggle it is then easy (but mistaken) to invent a working-class protest movement among the Galilean peasantry, not to mention the irreverent things that can be done once a community of goods is identified in formative Christianity.[50] She along with Wolfgang Stegemann, their co-written book *Jesus von Nazareth, Hoffnung der Armen* (1978), and Fernando Belo received sharp criticisms from Eduard Lohse for coming to their conclusions on the radical role of the poor in the early church by way of the classical Marxist view of history.[51] This, Schottroff retorts, has Marxism functioning as a disqualifier.[52] Put another way, Marxism is just plain wrong.

These points on the perceived threat of and hostility to Marxism are crucial and must be briefly expanded. Numerous more examples could be given but constraints of space mean they will have to be restricted. Besides, the assumptions made in the following examples should be enough to illustrate the point. Günther Bornkamm, in his book on the historical Jesus, discusses the parallels between Bolshevism and Jesus' views on eschatology before stressing a fundamental difference:

> These revolutionaries, when they wanted to claim Jesus as an ally in the struggle for a new world or social order, have had to learn again and again that they could not rely long on this ally, and that the kingdom of God which he proclaimed would not square with their own expectation. It is, therefore, not surprising that today this alliance, often enough attempted in revolutionary movements in the West, has apparently been definitely renounced, and that this completely secularised Marxist doctrine of salvation has replaced that of Jesus.[53]

Clearly Marxism/Bolshevism and Jesus are ultimately incompatible for Bornkamm, but it is a little odd, to say the least, that this discussion turns up in the middle of a book on the historical Jesus. Bornkamm points out that his aims here were not to identify the devil but "merely to indicate the contemporary relevance of the first thrust of Jesus' preaching."[54] Fair enough, but the choice of a dramatically contrasting example is striking as is the need to clarify his aims in such a light.

But there is more: at the end of his book Bornkamm provides an appendix on the exposition of the Sermon on the Mount where he rejects the ideas of "Kautzky and others" of Jesus the revolutionary leading the suppressed and underprivileged towards a new social order. Yet, he says, "It is easy enough for us to recognise in all these utterances the frequently horrible and grotesque misrepresentation of Jesus' person and message."[55] Clearly, for Bornkamm, then, this kind of analysis is absurd. Yet at the same time, more space is devoted to this exegetical tradition and its precursors than any other in an appendix that also includes brief discussions of the more usual suspects, namely, Albert Schweitzer and the general Lutheran tradition, the latter unsurprisingly regarded as the most plausible. This is an interesting example also because such claims attributed to Jesus by Bornkamm's revolutionaries are now in vogue in certain scholarly circles, whereas the Lutheran view has taken a battering in some recent NT scholarship. When Bornkamm was writing, however, this was obviously not the case; it is thus particularly significant that he can dismiss such views so disparagingly. It is also telling that he felt he had to.

This fear of Marxism or related views was so deeply embedded in NT scholarship it continued into and well beyond the 1970s.[56] In his recent book on the historical Jesus, James Dunn argues that "Jesus' call to and teaching on the poor are not reducible to some class-war dogma" and recommends that certain hard sayings (e.g., Mark 10:25) should not be treated "woodenly."[57] Dunn is a good example because his scholarly work is consistently well referenced and consistently interacts with a variety of scholarly views. But in this instance there is no reference to and no indication of any particular scholar Dunn has in mind. So why do we need to be told that Jesus' sayings are not reducible to class-war dogma? Who said they were? If there were no fear of Marxism in NT studies, at least in the old West German context, with its own interesting particularities, Gerd Theissen would not have to put a comment such as the following in a footnote defending social-scientific approaches to the NT in the 1970s, just when such approaches were starting to gain some momentum:

> I must therefore limit myself to a few remarks which I wish were
> unnecessary. . . . (2) Anyone who learns from Marxism and finds it
> stimulating as a result to apply theories of conflicts in society to the

interpretation of social and religious processes is not necessarily a
Marxist. Remember Rolf Dahrendorf![58]

The fact that Theissen even has to defend Marxist *influence* and stress that it
does not equate to being a Marxist speaks volumes about the interests and fears
of NT scholarship.

There was also, rightly perceived or not, the problem of intellectual restriction and association with totalitarianism, which no doubt contributed to the
lack of sympathy for Marxism in NT circles. Indeed, religious liberty was a key
theme for churches in the context of the Cold War, or better a certain form of
religious liberty, that is, the very liberty to practice religion behind the Iron
Curtain.[59] Furthermore, Christian scholars were (and are) well versed in the
history of the fight to study the NT in a critical manner and knew of present-
day difficulties with some of their more controversial results (cf. J. A. T. Robinson, David Jenkins, etc.). Interaction with the Marxist tradition, which had the
perception at least of scholarly constraints dictated from the equivalent of the
church, would hardly have been appealing for the more critically minded
Christian scholar. Scholarly constraints are evident in the crucial example of
the CPHG. Although the CPHG held open and creative debates and produced groundbreaking work on the past, there was a problem of constraints,
particularly for the modern historians. There was restricted debate in key areas
of recent history, such as the twentieth-century British labor movement, the
Soviet Union, and notably the Hitler-Stalin pact.[60] There were disagreements
between the party leadership and the CPHG over the writing of the history of
the Communist Party of Great Britain, with the leadership edging towards a
glorious history of past victories, if indeed it should be written at all, whereas
the CPHG naturally tended towards a more critical history.[61]

But there was a much-more sinister association that would have caused serious problems for many scholars and that was Stalin. As Matt Perry points out,
there should be a distinction drawn between the crimes of the Stalinist regime
and many of the rank-and-file Communist Party members in, for instance, the
United Kingdom who were in good faith actively opposing fascism, marching
against unemployment, and providing invaluable help in the trade-union
movement. Yet there was among the CPHG "an unconscious assimilation of
some elements of Stalinism" in areas such as absolutism and bourgeois revolution.[62] To see the extent of such influence we only need look at the man who
was to become scathingly anti-Stalinist: E. P. Thompson. Thompson removed
sections of his book on William Morris for the 1977 second edition (first edition 1955), which had come under Stalinist influence.[63] Providing further
insights into the intellectual reception of Marxism at the time, Thompson
comments in the postscript of the second edition that

it is true that in 1955 I allowed some hectoring political moralisms, as well as a few Stalinist pieties, to intrude upon the text. I had then a somewhat reverent notion of Marxism as a received orthodoxy, and my pages included some passages of polemic whose vulgarity no doubt makes contemporary scholars wince. The book was published at the height of the Cold War. Intellectual McCarthyism was not confined to the United States, although few in the subsequent generations understand its discreet British modes of operation.[64]

Of course, before the dramatic events of 1956–57—Khrushchev's secret speech denouncing Stalin's crimes and Soviet action in the Hungarian Revolution in particular—much of the Soviet/Stalinist influence was innocent to some degree, hence the dramatic breakup of the CPHG and many Communist Party members, including Christopher Hill and E. P. Thompson, leaving the party when these events impacted. But it must be stressed that those historians who remained within the British Communist Party, such as Eric Hobsbawm and Maurice Dobb, were no antidemocratic Stalinist puppets. Quite the opposite: they explicitly condemned the crimes and abuses of the Soviet regime, the distortion of facts, and the support given to the Soviet action in Hungary.[65] The problem is, of course, that mud sticks, as Hobsbawm was to find out subsequently in allegations made against him by Arthur Koestler.[66] It is also significant that even in a 2002 publication a Marxist writer such as Matt Perry still has to stress repeatedly a clear distinction between genuine Marxism and rank-and-file communists, on the one hand, and Stalin and Stalinism, on the other.

Although the extent of Stalin's crimes was not widely known before 1956, we should note that George Orwell's *Nineteen Eighty-Four* (1949) and especially *Animal Farm* (1945) had shown that even some socialists regarded the Stalinist regime as being sinister at the very least. Furthermore, Hobsbawm, who remained a member of the Communist Party, wrote a letter to *World News* in January 1957 that mentioned those who had strong suspicions "amounting to moral certainty for years before Khrushchev spoke" despite shock at the extent of Stalin's mass murders.[67] Moreover, Christians had also suffered under Stalin's atheistic empire in the sometimes physical restriction of religious practice. In 1938 the Russian Christian Iulia de Beausobre, who arrived as a refugee in London in 1934, published a recollection of her time as a prisoner, *The Woman Who Could Not Die*.[68] There were problems on the papacy's doorstep, due to the strength of the Italian Communist Party at the end of the Second World War. This, too, became violent: between 1944 and 1946 fifty-two priests were killed in Emilia, a part of northern Italy where armed bands claimed loyalty to communism and hatred of the Church.[69] Association with Stalinism and violent silencing of belief would therefore have been profoundly problematic for Christian NT scholars even before the events of 1956–57.

An additional and related reason for the neglect of social-scientific approaches to NT history is that it takes us perilously close to explaining away Christian origins in terms of socioeconomic context and moves away from ideas, theology, the divine, and the overwhelming individual influence of Jesus and Paul.[70] On the influence of great individuals, it is worth noting the following comments of Robin Scroggs on Marxist approaches:

> Important advances in sophistication have on occasion been made since Kautsky's book of 1920. *Not* in that category is the volume by Martin Robbe, *Der Ursprung des Christentums* (1967). Working from a traditional Marxist-Leninist perspective, he develops a view of Christianity's emergence purely as social process, as a protest against the class society and its injustice. The importance of the figure of Jesus completely disappears (no Weberian perspective here!); Robbe is not even concerned whether Jesus existed or not. Nothing would have been different had he not.[71]

Scroggs is not hostile to Marxism per se and continues by providing positive evaluations of Marxist Milan Machoveč's stress on the significant influence of Jesus and the importance of human action. While Scroggs is not necessarily wrong, it is telling that the mentioned reason for the stark objection to Robbe is that Jesus' significance is dramatically diminished.

But debates over the limited role of the individual in the historical process are taken more seriously by many historians, including non-Marxists.[72] One obvious example is the rise of Hitler. Whether correct or not, it would hardly be too revolutionary to say that something like what happened in Germany in the 1930s and 1940s would have happened even if Hitler had not been born. The hugely respected French historian Fernand Braudel, who often made use of the metaphor of the individual as a prisoner of environment and mind, made extravagant comments such as the following on the role of people and events already alluded to in this chapter but now worth an extensive quoting:

> . . . surface disturbances, crests of foam that the tides of history carry on their strong backs. A history of brief, rapid, nervous fluctuations, by definition ultrasensitive; the least tremor sets all antennae quivering. . . . We must learn to distrust this history with its still burning passions. . . . The historian who takes a seat in Philip II's chair and reads his papers finds himself transported into a strange one-dimensional world . . . unconscious of the deeper realities of history, of the running waters on which our frail barks are tossed like cockle-shells. A dangerous world, but one whose spells and enchantments we shall have exorcised by making sure first to chart those underlying currents, often noiseless, whose direction can only be discerned by watching them over long periods of time. Resounding events are often only momentary outbursts, surface manifestations of these larger movements and explicable only in terms of them.[73]

This more deterministic view of history is hardly accepted by all historians—indeed Braudel has been heavily criticized on this very point—but, as Peter Burke put it, "the debate over the limits of freedom and determinism is one that is likely to last as long as history is written."[74] The supreme importance of the figure of Jesus in Christian theology does not need repeating, but to reduce his role in history, not to mention that of Christian heroes such as Peter and Paul, to general nontheological socioeconomic "forces" is almost bound to produce a negative reaction in a Christian-dominated scholarly field. It is no coincidence that the Weberian charismatic leader has proven to be one of the most popular sociological approaches in NT scholarship right up to the present day.[75] Indeed, Bruce Malina (negatively) categorizes the Weberian approach of charisma and routinization in the "Received View" of Christian origins.[76]

That many of the big names in post-1970 social-scientifically informed approaches to Christian origins make it clear that theology and ideas are *not* going to be rejected, often following Scroggs's famous image of bringing body and soul together,[77] is particularly noteworthy. The message: there is nothing to fear. To some extent this is also found in the social sciences. One of the most emphatic statements I have come across is by Peter Berger—whose work on the sociology of religion has proven to be one of the more popular interdisciplinary approaches borrowed by NT scholars—when he says it "is *not* implied that any particular religious system is nothing but the effect or 'reflection' of social processes."[78] It is no coincidence that such sentiments—and it must be stressed that I am *not* criticizing their validity—are extremely frequent and even more explicit among practitioners and reviewers in NT studies.[79]

However, many prominent practitioners of the social-scientific study of the NT go further. Holmberg devotes the final chapter in his book on sociology and the NT titled "Finding the Body—and Losing the Soul?" to connecting the "soul" (theology) with the "body" (social-scientific approaches).[80] Philip Esler grants some space in his introduction to an edited volume on social-scientific approaches to the NT to argue that it is crucial for contemporary theological appropriations of biblical texts to be understood in the light of sociohistorical exegesis and provides such a synthesis through the use of the Christian theology of George Lindbeck.[81] One of the most openly concerned is Stephen Barton who, as we saw above, makes it clear that the epistemological roots of much social-scientific methodology lie in Enlightenment atheism and so,

> awareness of this genealogy should also act as a safeguard against unwittingly allowing the agenda of interpretation to shift in a secularizing direction, away from evangelical imperatives native to the NT itself and central to the concerns of those who read the NT with a view to growing in the knowledge and love of God.[82]

The reason that these sorts of arguments are made is obvious. Such interpreters are, as Theissen openly admits, "theologians," forming "a leading group in the modern churches . . . who have a decisive responsibility for the church's communication with society as a whole."[83] Again, this is not to say of course that any of the above views are wrong, but the frequency and force of defense is striking and most obviously accounted for by the need to make sure that Christianity is not explained away purely in human terms.

Indeed, it is particularly interesting that social sciences are clearly used to defend the importance and superiority of Christianity among the early pioneers. For example, one of the criticisms sometimes raised against Harnack's *The Mission and Expansion of Christianity*, and one that could be raised against many present-day works of NT scholarship, is that it explains the success of earliest Christianity in terms of its superior message over its rivals.[84] To split the idea of social-scientific approaches from social history for one moment, it is also striking that the pioneers of social-scientific approaches placed the emphasis on social context rather than on explicit social-scientific models, the exceptions including, significantly, two famous Marxists outside the discipline of NT studies: Engels and Kautsky.[85]

But what of the *Annales* movement? Why did it not have an impact on NT history? There are several reasons. Before the 1970s translations of books from the *Annalists* were rare (Braudel's *Mediterranean* was translated into English in 1972–73). Peter Burke recalls that those like him who had supported the *Annales* movement in the early 1960s felt like a heretical minority.[86] But, as ever, distrust of Marxism also provides a key. Although the *Annales* movement was not a Marxist movement and in some ways an obvious alternative to a Marxist approach, the influence of Marxism was present from the beginning. To add to its unattractiveness for many NT scholars, alliances were formed with the Marxists in the fight against a perceived common enemy of traditional conservative history. British Marxists such as Eric Hobsbawm and Rodney Hilton recall cooperative and friendly relations and found their interests overlapped with the *Annales* movement.[87]

Although Fernand Braudel has had one work described as being "in some ways a profoundly conservative, nationalist text" particularly when discussing purity of French blood,[88] and another labeled (by two Marxists) "great and anti-Marxist,"[89] he also had some respect for Marx and Marxism even if he tried to keep his distance.[90] Hobsbawm notes that not only does the title of Braudel's *Capitalism and Material Life* (London: Weidenfeld and Nicolson, 1973; French orig. 1967) provide a link to Marx but Marx is referred to more than any other author, even French authors. "Such a tribute from a country not given to underestimate its national thinkers is impressive in itself," he adds.[91] There was also a perception that Braudel could be lumped together with Marxism, not least due to the broad overarching view of history that was associated with Marx. This can be seen in comments on Braudel and Marxism in a 1968 *Times Literary Supplement* review article: "The influence of Marx is very perceptible, and is much avowed, but so far the new French orthodoxy has avoided the dogmatism and overschematization of Marxism in favor of a more empirical and critical attitude."[92]

In addition to this, it is also worth noting that by the early 1960s the most celebrated attack on antitheoretical and empiricist historians, coupled with advocacy of sociological approaches to history (and vice versa), was provided by E. H. Carr, who famously concluded "that the more sociological history becomes, and the more historical sociology becomes, the better for both. Let the frontier between them be kept wide open for two-way traffic."[93] But Carr had some dubious associations, to say the least. He was a supporter of appeasement in the 1930s and was accused of being a Hitler apologist before accusations of being a Stalin apologist in the 1940s and 1950s. Carr, a major historian of the Soviet Union, was not a Marxist but was influenced by Marxism. Although not uncritical, he was also sympathetic towards the Soviet Union from his days as a cheerleader for Stalinist Russia during World War II to his view at the end of the 1970s that the Soviet Union remained an important representative of human progress.[94] One perspective on Carr's career is found in an infamously damning obituary/review/article by Norman Stone that appeared in a 1983 edition of the *London Review of Books*:

> Carr's *History* is not a history of the Soviet Union, but effectively of the Communist Party of the Soviet Union. Even then, much of it is the kind of unreconstructed Stalinist version that would not see the light of day in Russia itself.[95]

Carr's most widely known book on the nature of history—*What is History?*— from which I quoted Carr's hope of sociology and history intertwining, was damned more with faint praise by Stone. Most important, however, note the crucial connection: "it may count as his most successful book, for there is a keen appetite in schools for this boring subject [!]. . . . In places, it read like a Marxist *1066 and All That*. It does, however, begin well, perhaps even brilliantly."[96]

THE 1970S AND SOCIAL-SCIENTIFIC
APPROACHES TO THE NT

So why did things change in NT studies by the 1970s? Most surveys of scholarship rightly point to the various social changes in the 1960s, such as the protest movements, the "spirit of 1968," the increasing influence of sociology in the universities, declining church numbers and the perception of secularism, and the impact of decolonialization.[97] Social upheavals of the 1960s are usually simply stated as a reason, often with caution, but without being backed up by surveys of the literature.[98] Some evidence should be mentioned as it is explicit in some cases. For instance, in a recent book edited by Wolfgang Stegemann, Bruce Malina, and Gerd Theissen—*The Social Setting of Jesus and the Gospels*—the dedication, written by Malina, is to John Elliott. It recalls the origins of the social-scientific approaches advocated by the international, though largely North American based, group of NT scholars called the Context Group. And it is a classic piece of rebellious 1960s rhetoric:

> Jack Elliott takes pride in his career of liberal activism. In the 1960s, he protested the Vietnam War and marched in Selma, Alabama. Finding that he shared intellectual interests with a number of protesters—many of them from Berkeley—Elliott met with them off the streets to explore the intersection of politics and theology. They called themselves the Bay Area Seminar for Theology and Related Disciplines—BASTARDs. Searching for new theological perspectives to deal with the political situation, he began reading widely in sociology and political science. He asked many of the same questions as the liberation theologians active at the time, but he found that they were not systematic or rigorous enough in their analysis.[99]

It is also of some significance that by the mid-1960s a self-consciously non-Marxist social historiography was emerging. In 1963 Keith Thomas, who was to go on to publish one of the most-famous works of non-Marxist social history, *Religion and the Decline of Magic* (1971), published an article on history and anthropology in the journal *Past and Present*. It openly advocates the need for non-Marxist anthropological approaches to history:

> Marxism has many beneficial effects, and the possibilities latent in the explanation of social facts by their relation to economic ones are by no means exhausted. But economic wants are themselves culturally determined, and it is only some form of anthropology which holds out the hope of providing that sociological explanation of economic life which the economic interpretation of social life has come to require.[100]

Thomas's hope began to gain momentum in the 1960s, and such ideas began to make their way into the *Times Literary Supplement* in the mid-1960s' editions, thereby providing an important platform for an open announcement of non-Marxist social history. As Marxist historical writing was arguably the dominant social-scientific approach to history, this new development of an openly non-Marxist historiography in the mid-1960s shows how lacking in social-scientific approaches—with the honorable exception of the *Annales* tradition, of course—the discipline of history would have been without Marxism before the 1960s—perhaps similar to, although not quite to the same extent, the study of Christian origins.

Most crucially for present purposes, however, the emergence of "new ways in history" made it possible for social history or social-scientifically informed history to take off free from the sometimes imaginary specter of Marxism and communism. This argument is supported by an important intellectual reason for the rise of non-Marxist social-scientific approaches to history in the 1960s: the influence of Max Weber. The first translations of Weber into English were in the 1950s and 1960s. Lawrence Stone believes that this

> probably did more to influence the writing of history in the 1960s than any other single influence from the social sciences, particularly since he offered an alternative to vulgar Marxist economic determinism . . . to Marxist theories of class . . . and to vulgar Marxist theories of change in the means of production as the prime generating force for change in other aspects of society.[101]

Non-Marxists could now continue to fill the gaps with a heavyweight of modern critical thought who, like Marx, was also partial to a bit of historical study. In addition to the fact that Weber was also turning up in German NT scholarship (see below), it is no coincidence that by 1980 Weber was regularly used in major publications in English applying social-scientific approaches to earliest Christianity, such as those by John Gager, Robin Scroggs, Bengt Holmberg, John Schütz, and Howard Clark Kee.[102] Geza Vermes's seminal work on Jesus included what would turn out to be an influential chapter on "Jesus and Charismatic Judaism," where Jesus the healer, exorcist, and holy man was compared with Jewish "charismatic" figures such as Hanina ben Dosa and Honi the Circle Drawer. And this book came out in . . . 1973. Vermes's work is not the kind to be usually considered in discussions of social-scientific approaches to Christian origins, and there is no reference to Weber in the 1973 book, but it is revealing that Vermes's study appeared when it did. Indeed Vermes's 1993 book on Jesus includes a section on "The Charismatic Authority of Jesus" headed by supportive quotations from Weber.[103] Vermes's charismatic Jesus and Weber's charismatic leader are clearly compatible.

Weber was of course already available in German. But here there are different reasons for the emergence of social-scientifically informed approaches. The influence of and subsequent reaction to Nazi ideology in twentieth-century German historiography can also help explain why social-scientifically informed approaches to Christian origins did not take off properly until the late 1960s in the country that dominated biblical scholarship up to that point. Richard Evans, with example after example, argues that the postwar West German historians were regaining power and status lost in the political turmoil of the early twentieth century and the anti-intellectual assaults of Nazism. These historians made a conscious effort to distance themselves from verifiable distortions of Nazi historians and placed great value on "objectivity." The cult of the individual under Nazism was rejected and reflected in a marked shift from biography to histories of people, groups, and trends. Evans also argues that the social upheavals of the 1960s also coincided with the maturing of the postwar German historians, who by the end of the 1960s were beginning to use various social-scientific approaches from North America, especially neo-Weberian sociology, which eventually became dominant in German historiography. This too was done to avoid the dangerous subjectivity that marked the historiography of Nazi Germany.[104]

Of course dropping the individual out of Christian origins was not going to be as easy for German (or non-German, for that matter) NT scholars. We might note, however, that the movements in West German historiography discussed by Evans also seemingly coincide with a greater appreciation of social-scientific approaches, including those of a more home-grown Weber, to Christian origins in German scholarship. Martin Hengel, who also produced a major work on Jewish social history by the end of the 1960s, wrote on Jesus the charismatic leader, inspired of course by the Weberian approach.[105] By the end of the 1970s Gerd Theissen had become one of the major practitioners of social-scientifically informed approaches to the NT, with various works on wandering charismatics and the shift from rural Palestine to urban centers, that also included clear nods in the direction of Weber.[106]

The importance of the impact of social-scientific approaches to the NT should now be obvious. It is no coincidence that there has been a robust Christian defense of these approaches against charges of reductionism and secularism, and it is no coincidence that the prominence of Marxism was an important reason for the late return of social-scientific approaches in NT studies. This is partly because they have the potential to provide methods with which to explain the rise of Christianity in nontheological human terms; indeed, some will be adapted in this study for that very purpose. The above history of social sciences and NT studies shows that neglect of such approaches has proven to be profoundly detrimental. But does this not leave my approach open to charges of a non-Christian bias, and is it not just as loaded as a history-of-ideas-based Christian approach? My answer to both would be a qualified "Yes." This obviously needs defending, and it is to the issue of bias that we must now turn.

THE SIGNIFICANCE OF PARTISANSHIP

In an important book on objectivity and historical scholarship, Peter Novick uncovered the biases and prejudices that crept into the works of American historians.[107] Thomas Haskell, in a sympathetic but critical response, objected to Novick's near equation of objectivity and neutrality. Unlike the striving for neutrality, being an advocate of some ideological position or other is not a dishonorable thing but needs to be guided by respect for the ascetic self-discipline of detachment in order to achieve

> some distance from one's own spontaneous perceptions and convictions, to imagine how the world appears in another's eyes, to experimentally adopt perspectives that do not come naturally—in the last analysis, to develop . . . a view of the world in which one's self is not at the center, but appears merely as one object among many.[108]

A crucial point arises from this: "preaching to the converted" with no respect for outside views is not the way forward, unlike, for example, "the powerful argument—the text that reveals by its every twist and turn its respectful appreciation of the alternatives it rejects." Such a text is so compelling because "its author has managed to suspend momentarily his or her own perceptions so as to anticipate and take account of objections and alternative constructions."[109]

In a similar manner, Eric Hobsbawm gives the example of genetics, where significant advances were made with aid of the partisanship of its practitioners, from antidemocratic elitists such as Francis Galton and Karl Pearson to communists such as J. B. S. Haldane.[110] As an aside to anticipate potential criticisms, what Haskell and Hobsbawm show is that perspective and partisanship do not lead to hyperrelativism, which is often, though frequently unfairly, attributed to postmodernist thinkers. Self-criticism is vital, and no matter to what extent the individual is manipulated by perspective and partisanship, the validity of arguments will ultimately, as Richard Evans points out, have to "conform to the rules of evidence and the facts on which they rest, by which they must stand or fall in the end."[111]

Here we can now see the importance of the above discussion on social-scientific approaches to the NT: NT scholarship has not always benefited by being dominated by Christians, largely white, middle- or upper-class ones,[112] and has sometimes gained benefits when it has included insights from non-Christian and nontraditional perspectives. Of course, white, middle- or upper-class Christian perspectives also provide insights of their own—I am certainly not denying that—and within the circle of Christian scholarship there have been multiple Christian perspectives. Here Haskell's important approach can be modified. It is true that Christian scholars do not "preach to the converted" in the sense that (say) liberal Christians engage with conservative Christians, and at times they persuade each other of the validity of some of their arguments. The charge of nonengagement could be made if we do not take an intra-Christian view and take Haskell more literally: despite all differences among Christians it is effectively Christian preaching to Christian.

As it stands presently, NT scholarship will always get largely Christian results, be they the nineteenth-century liberal lives of Jesus, the Bultmannian dominated neo-Lutheranism, or the results of smaller subgroups, such as the social reformer/critic Cynic Jesus associated with the Jesus Seminar: all different but all recognizably Christian.[113] As Maurice Casey points out,

> many institutions, such as major British universities and *Studiorum Novi Testamenti Societas* itself, genuinely operate academic criteria in decisions about appointments and membership. But when some 90 percent or more of applicants are Protestant Christians, a vast majority of Christian academics is a natural result. Moreover, the figure of Jesus is of central importance in colleges and universities which are overtly Protestant or Catholic, and which produce a mass of books and articles of sufficient technical proficiency to be taken seriously. The overall result of such bias is to make the description of New Testament Studies as an academic field a dubious one.[114]

In September 2000 the annual British New Testament Conference, held in Roehampton, opened with both a glass of wine and a Christian prayer, the perfect symbols of middle-class Christianity, some might say. The glass of wine I can accept, but should an academic meeting that explicitly has no official party line really hold a collective prayer at its opening, particularly when some of the participants are certainly nonreligious and some possibly from non-Christian faiths?[115] Leaving aside the moral issue, the fact that there is an overwhelmingly Christian presence in British NT scholarship is surely the reason that this could happen. Would other contemporary conferences in the humanities outside theology and biblical studies even contemplate prayer? Would the participants of nontheological conferences even *believe* that other academic conferences do such things?[116]

A particularly significant example is a subgroup of biblical scholarship associated with social-scientific approaches because, as we saw, they often require defenses against accusations of reductionism and secularism. Philip Esler closed his introduction to a collection of essays first presented at Context and Kerygma: The St. Andrews Conference on New Testament Interpretation and the Social Sciences held in St. Andrews (29 June to 3 July, 1994) with the following comments:

> Then we too may reach Emmaus, having had the experience described
> in words from the Scots version of Luke's Gospel as read at the liturgy
> concluding the Conference where the essays below were first deliv-
> ered: "Wisna the hairts o us lowin in our breasts, as he spak wi us on
> the gate and expundit the Scriptures til us?"[117]

Naturally enough the conference participants consisted of scholars with different views, from members of the Context Group to their critics, such as
David Horrell. Yet, crucially, all the differences were ultimately harmonized
under the umbrella of Christian faith. More explicit still were the comments
of Stephen Barton noted above. Recall his warning against "unwittingly
allowing the agenda of interpretation to shift in a secularizing direction, away
from evangelical imperatives native to the NT itself and central to the concerns of those who read the NT with a view to growing in the knowledge and
love of God."[118] But we must not forget about those NT scholars who have
no evangelical imperatives, or those who care little about reading the NT in
order to grow in the knowledge and love of God, or indeed those who merely
wish to provide a nontheological explanation for the rise of Christianity.
Minority though they may be, they do exist! Yet clearly comments such as
Barton's, which are hardly radical—and again I am *not* saying they are inherently wrong—are made possible by the Christian dominance of his scholarly
audience.

It is because of this scholarly context that some quite peculiar academic
arguments can be made and most frequently in what would seem to be historically unlikely cases, such as the resurrection and virgin birth. It is only in
the world of NT scholarship and theology that when Jesus' resurrection is
studied, the major historical debates focus around whether or not these supposed events are beyond historical enquiry or if the "spiritual meaning" is
more important than the literal understanding. In this context, major propo-
nents (e.g., Gerd Lüdemann and Michael Goulder) of the bodily resurrection
not happening are often regarded (rightly or wrongly) as mavericks. Only in
this context can this author be legitimately placed on one extreme of biblical
scholarship for arguing that a bodily resurrection from the dead did not take
place.[119] A 1997 book edited by S. T. Davis, D. Kendall, and G. O'Collins, *The
Resurrection*, has a misleading but revealing subtitle: *An Interdisciplinary Symposium on the Resurrection of Jesus*. The contributors are not from the world of
ancient history, history, sociology, or anthropology as this subtitle might suggest but largely from Christian theology, philosophy of religion, and biblical
studies and include figures such as an Anglican archbishop and the editor of
the *Tablet*. It is no surprise then that the contribution by Gerald O'Collins can
make arguments that could be criticized as being historically naïve. He asks,

> What are we to make of the moral probity of Mark in creating such a fictional narrative (and one that touches on an utterly central theme in the original Christian proclamation) and of the gullibility of the early Christians (including Matthew and Luke) in believing and repeating his fiction as if it were basically factual narrative?[120]

This is far too rooted in modern concepts of truth and ignores the well-known fact that people in the ancient world created fictional stories of past events, including ones that are utterly central for their beliefs: for example, *Joseph and Aseneth* on table fellowship between Jews and Gentiles or *b. B. Mesi'a* 59b on rejecting the legal authority of the wonder-working and divine-voice-supported R. Eliezar.[121] These are serious issues for the Jews involved, but no historian thinks the stories really happened, no historian should think the original audience were especially gullible, and no historian should criticize ancient authors of immorality simply on the general point of inventing historical scenarios.

But could we assume that those Christians who argue in favor of the historical reality of the bodily resurrection would treat non-Christian religions with the same degree of openness to the evidence?[122] In N. T. Wright's book on the resurrection, when he discusses a chat between the Roman emperor and Gamaliel II's daughter (*b. Sanh.* 90b–91a), he can say it is "no doubt fictitious"[123] and most would agree. But nowhere in Wright's enormous book are NT texts treated with this degree of skepticism, not even the story of people rising from tombs after Jesus' crucifixion (Matt. 27:52–53), not even the resurrection stories of Jesus, with all their talk of a bodily resurrected man who goes around eating and drinking. It would be fair to say that for many nonbelievers and for many mainstream historians outside biblical studies and theology, some lass talking to an emperor is far more historically plausible than dead people rising from tombs. Notwithstanding the unethical feel to these arguments,[124] it should be clear that Christian stories can be treated differently because of Christian dominance, which allows the more literalistic advocates to make such claims.

The recent arguments of Wright on the resurrection require much more careful consideration than can be given here, but given the dramatic claims he makes, there is a crucial point that needs to be stressed: Would another discipline in the humanities seriously consider as historically reliable something as spectacular as someone literally rising from the dead but also argue that it provided a catalyst for the rise of a major new movement? That is surely unlikely. Notwithstanding Wright's learning and irrespective of whether he is right or wrong, it is almost certainly the context of a Christian-dominated scholarly community that has allowed his views of the bodily resurrection to be published as a major book in the study of Christian origins and to gain praise from some of the most famous scholars in the field. Certain major reviews contain criticisms of Wright's arguments but not the argument favoring the historical accuracy of the bodily resurrection, something very unusual for many people. One such example is a review by James Dunn, who finishes in illuminating fashion for present purposes: "But in the end what Christian heart could fail to rejoice at such a trenchant defence of Christianity's central claim regarding Jesus?"[125] Indeed.

While Christian perspectives no doubt contribute to knowledge of Christian origins, it is unhealthy for an academic discipline to be so dominated by one group. As this chapter has shown, it restricts Christians from properly engaging with those of different persuasions, and it even allows Christian academics to make arguments that (rightly or wrongly) would hardly be permitted in other academic disciplines, not to mention some extremely weak arguments. The lack of a significant number of non-Christian or even scholars deliberately attempting to see beyond their Christian background has prevented serious secular alternatives to Christian origins being properly discussed. You do not have to be a Marxist to suggest that the lack of sympathy for Marxism in Christian origins (at least before the 1970s) has been to the detriment of the historical study of Christian origins. Many non-Marxists appreciate the positive impact Marxism has had on the discipline of history, particularly in areas such as labor history, religious dissent, history from below, economic history, urban history, and banditry. Similarly, influential Marxist historians such as Christopher Hill, Eric Hobsbawm, Rodney Hilton, and E. P. Thompson have gained widespread international respect among non-Marxist historians.[126]

Since the 1970s some theologians and NT scholars have welcomed the insights of Marxist-influenced liberation theology, which should have sharpened every NT scholar's focus on the asymmetrical socioeconomic relations so abundantly reflected in the Bible. But who knows what the historical study of Christian origins missed out on before the 1970s when Marxist history writing was at its peak? Such comments apply more broadly. Who knows what the study of Christian origins has missed out on without the significant inclusion of nonreligious historians looking for secular explanations? Although obviously a more general problem in higher education, who knows what the study of Christian origins has missed out on by the lack of significant participation of people from, say, the lower and working classes and through the relative ignoring of non-Western exegetes?

Increase the different perspectives, and it will allow greater interaction and force white middle-class Christians to deal with interpretations and explanations that they may otherwise only have to confront in diluted form. Moreover, greater interaction for, say, non-Christians will force them to take seriously more Christian-centered interpretations of Christian origins. As the history of NT studies shows, the advent of what were previously unconventional perspectives (including Christian ones) has had impressive impact, one of the most notable being feminism. The increasing number of women involved in higher education from the 1960s onwards can be obviously linked with the rise in the academic study of feminism and women's history. Even if the correlation between female undergraduates and female postgraduates and lectures in theology and religious studies is far from satisfactory, the impact of an increasing number of women has made feminist interpretation and women's history of NT times a fixed and relatively mainstream aspect of NT scholarship. It has also helped produce some major individual works on Christian origins—most famously Elisabeth Schüssler Fiorenza's *In Memory of Her*—and it has made men and nonfeminists engage with it or, at the very least, acknowledge its presence. And this was all made possible by the increasing number of an interest group partaking in the study of Christian origins. It would be interesting to see how such approaches (not to mention the discipline as a whole) could further develop in the future if more and more people from the working and lower classes were given genuine access to participation in scholarship.[127]

PARTISANSHIP: BIOGRAPHICAL CRITICISM

We have seen autobiographical criticism emerging in recent times, so here is a related criticism that already exists elsewhere and is now given a label that ought not to be taken too seriously: biographical criticism. What I will do here is show how details and biases of a given scholar's life can affect the discipline— in other words, how partisanship can work in practice. When I have discussed the following ideas with people, some have enjoyed the biographical details (I enjoyed finding them) while others have not liked the amount of detail (and I understand their reasons). I think a pattern may emerge as to the interests and mind-sets of these two groups, but that can wait. For now all I want to do is warn certain readers that brief biographies follow. I think the details are important because they provide crucial insights into the ways in which the discipline has been shaped and can be shaped. I also feel a bit naked without them.

The potential of Jewish scholars to have a major influence on NT studies was always there, given the overlapping histories of Christianity and Judaism. One of the most important contributions to Christian origins from a Jewish perspective is Geza Vermes. The biography of Vermes and his "Jewishness" is well known. He was born into a Hungarian Jewish family but was christened into Catholicism in 1931, although the family never forgot their Jewish origins.[128]

Vermes was thus educated as a Catholic and spent time in Louvain and Paris with the Fathers of Notre-Dame de Sion (1946–1957), where he developed interests in the Hebrew Bible and postbiblical Judaism, notably the Dead Sea Scrolls, combined with some concern for Jewish-Christian relations. Vermes's commitment to Catholicism waned, and he would marry. Increasingly, Vermes was becoming more immersed in Jewish society. By 1969 he was formally identifying himself as Jewish and in 1970 became a member of the Liberal Jewish Synagogue of London. It should be pointed out that Vermes also stands in a Jewish tradition wishing to reclaim Jesus the Jew, "distorted by Christian and Jewish myth alike" but who was "in fact neither the Christ of the Church, nor the apostate and bogey man of Jewish popular tradition."[129]

Another crucial aspect of Vermes's ideology and one which is difficult to separate from his Jewish interests must be emphasized, namely, his desire to be a thoroughgoing historian. The 1973 book not only has the subtitle *A Historian's Reading of the Gospels*, but it was also partially a spin-off from the revised version of Emil Schürer's *The History of the Jewish People in the Age of Jesus Christ*, which had led to Vermes wanting to reexamine the Gospels in the context of first-century Palestinian Jewish history and culture.[130] Significantly, the interests of a historian are made explicit in his introduction to *Jesus the Jew*. There is no motivation for "critical destructiveness" but rather a "devout search for fact and reality undertaken out of feeling for the tragedy of Jesus of Nazareth."[131] This reflects a general motif in Vermes's academic life. At Jesuit college Vermes recalls the unexciting study of Paul and the place his interests really lay: not in the expounding of the theological doctrine of the major Pauline letters but the reconstruction of the "real world" of Paul.[132] Related both to his concerns for the Jewishness of Christian origins and his historian's mind-set, Vermes's work is consistently concerned with making a clear contrast with Christian theological embellishment, and at times Vermes is quite explicit.[133] In his autobiography he recalls, "I meant to portray Jesus against his genuine historical background [i.e., first-century Palestinian Judaism], and not in the alien framework of Graeco-Roman culture *and* nineteen centuries of Christian elaboration."[134]

Vermes has of course made major contributions to scholarship in areas related to NT studies (DSS, early Judaism), but for present purposes it is his study of Christian origins that is of immediate concern, and particularly the Jewishness of his Jesus. Clichés are not always helpful, but in the case of "Jesus the Jew" it would be hard to dispute the importance of that particular cliché. Compare Vermes's reporting of the decision prior to the release of his seminal 1973 book: "When Lady Collins and I decided to call my original contribution to the Jesus story 'Jesus the Jew', the title enunciating what should be patent to all still sounded striking and pioneering."[135] While Vermes's learning has made such advances possible, they must also be partially attributed to his Jewish background and historian's mind-set. Vermes's Jewish background and profound knowledge of Jewish sources clearly made it obvious that Jesus was not standing outside Judaism when he used terms such as "son of man" or when he uttered sentiments such as those recorded in the Sermon on the Mount, as the numerous Jewish parallels he cites show. The combination of a Christian and liberal Jewish background, coupled with his concerns to be an "objective" historian, have no doubt contributed to his rounded portrait of a historically particular charismatic Jewish Jesus. Consequently this has also contributed to his ability to avoid both demonizing Jesus and portraying Jesus as some kind of orthodox Pharisee in the mold of Hillel, as is found in some Jewish traditions.[136] Indeed, some of Vermes's distinctive contributions have been extremely influential and so far stood the test of time. In addition to the general view of Jesus the Jew, placing Jesus in the same category of charismatic Jewish holy men such as Hanina ben Dosa has proven to be particularly popular and the overall thesis has not been refuted, even if various details have been challenged.[137]

The next biography shows what might be done if a scholar acting as a historian prepares to take a step outside his Christian tradition and critique its influence. E. P. Sanders, for example, does not put much faith in his "theological heritage" being founded by Christ, as he famously put it in his 1985 book on Jesus.[138] Further details can now be expanded due to an autobiographical publication first delivered at a conference in Sanders's honor.[139] Throughout this autobiographical paper two general interests are dominant: the "nontheological" historically orientated study of religion and a deep interest in Judaism. I will briefly summarize these two key, immediate influences on Sanders that consequently fed into his NT scholarship.

From a young age Sanders was interested in history and religion.[140] Throughout Sanders's subsequent academic career he constantly recalls a distinct interest in a comparative and historically informed "nontheological" approach to NT studies. When studying at Union Theological Seminary in New York in 1963, one of Sanders's key views was this: "Religion is not just theology, and in fact is often not very theological at all. New Testament scholarship then (as now) paid too much attention to theology and not enough to religion." Sanders's developing interest in the study of mysticism (identified as nontheological religion) was to resurface in his study of Paul, mysticism being something Sanders believes was driven out by Protestant NT scholars' obsession with justification by faith. He also enjoyed reading about ancient astrology, which "constituted more evidence of a fairly non-theological form of religion" and saw much of it in the NT.[141] This emphasis on a nontheological approach to the study of the NT is repeatedly recalled throughout Sanders's account of his subsequent academic career. For example, when he was at

Oxford in 1984 he interacted with scholars in what he tellingly labels "other aspects of the ancient world," scholars who may be reasonably described as having similar concerns: e.g., Geza Vermes, Martin Goodman, Robin Lane Fox, Fergus Millar, Angus Bowie, and Simon Price. Sanders modestly adds, "I wanted to be like them. Well, I could never be that clever or learned, but I could go back to non-theological religion and specifically to religious practice."[142] On reflection of his whole career, Sanders claims the books he lists that have influenced him reflect his "long standing interest in works that deal with the nitty-gritty of religion (such as sacrifice) and those that allow us to set religion in a historical and social setting." He concludes by telling off many NT scholars for knowing "far too little about ancient history and . . . ancient sources other than the Bible."[143] So it should now be abundantly obvious that Sanders's interests are clearly those of a historian of religion, with theology— so dominated by the influence of Bultmann and neo-Lutheranism when Sanders started out—on the back burner.

Take Sanders's 1993 book *The Historical Figure of Jesus*, for instance. Sanders makes it clear that he is to discuss "Jesus the human being, who lived in a particular time and place" and that he is to "search for evidence and propose explanations just as does any historian when writing about a figure in history." Though theology was important for Jesus and his followers, Sanders makes it plain that he is not going to try "to square these theologies with later Christian dogma."[144] Theology is only discussed in terms of what Jesus thought, much in the same way, Sanders points out, as historical questions posed concerning Jefferson on liberty, Churchill on the labor movement and the strikes of 1910 and 1911, or Alexander the Great on the union of Greek and Persian in one empire, and what contemporaries thought of such individuals. In fact in his introduction Sanders repeatedly mentions Jesus in comparison with these historical figures—and indeed others, such as Lincoln—with the idea always in mind as to how a *historian* is to evaluate them and claims made about them. This, in principle at least, means that the historical study of any famous figure like a Churchill or a Jefferson should not be hagiographical and if there is dirt there is dirt. So too with Jesus: "I shall not, however, write only about how nice he was, nor shall I ignore the aspects of his life and thought that many of his most ardent admirers wish would go away."[145] In other words, Sanders acts as a thoroughly conventional *historian* studying one aspect of *ancient history*.[146]

The other key influence on Sanders's scholarly work, and one not unrelated to his academic approach to the study of religion, is his concern for and profound knowledge of Judaism. Sanders had positive contacts with Jews and Judaism from an early age.[147] Before starting doctoral work, and with the help of David Daube, Sanders had been to Oxford and began learning rabbinic and modern Hebrew and participated in a class translating Mishnah *Sanhedrin*.

Sanders also went to Jerusalem, where Mordechai Kamrat took him under his wing to teach him rabbinics and develop his Hebrew. At Union Theological Seminary, where Sanders came under the influence of W. D. Davies, a NT scholar with strong interests in rabbinic literature, two of Sanders's views on the field were that the study of religion must be comparative and that the NT scholar ought to study Judaism. At Union, Sanders was also across the road from the Jewish Theological Seminary, where he took some courses. He also recalls being impressed with sympathetic scholars of Judaism such as E. R. Goodenough and George Foot Moore. After starting out his professional career at McMaster, Sanders gained a fellowship to Israel (1968–69) where he worked once more with Kamrat. Here we get clear signs of typical Sanders thought on rabbinic literature:

> I fell in love. The first things I noticed about the Rabbis were their humanity, tolerance, and good humour. I noticed, of course, their academic love of precision. . . . Besides the desire to understand the sacred text, which makes them very much like New Testament scholars, toleration of disagreement was their strongest and most consistent characteristic.[148]

This, Sanders frequently notes, stood in direct contrast to what most Bultmann-influenced, neo-Lutheran NT scholars were teaching about Judaism.

Both these key interests (historical/nontheological and Jewish concerns) are notable for standing at odds with the dominant scholarly tradition in which Sanders found himself, and his partisanship has not only contributed to leaving a distinctive mark on NT scholarship but has effectively changed the tide of studies on both Jesus and Paul. Perhaps the concern for Judaism has been the most obvious. Sanders's 1977 book, *Paul and Palestinian Judaism*, made it absolutely clear that the history of critical scholarship on Paul and Judaism was too often deeply offensive towards, not to mention misrepresentative of, Judaism and was at times even antisemitic. Sanders's reevaluation of Paul and Judaism sparked off what James Dunn was famously to call the "New Perspective" on Paul.[149] Even some scholars who do not agree with Sanders's depiction of salvation in Judaism now make it explicit that even though there are significant differences between Paul and many Jews, this does not mean that Jewish views should be viewed in a derogatory way.[150] Similar concerns to reevaluate Judaism are also found in Sanders's work on the historical Jesus. In this work we also see Sanders's commitments as a historian of ancient religion. Partly due to his learning and commitments, we have one of the most-convincing accounts of Jesus as a very Jewish, law-observant eschatological prophet, the general outline of which has proven difficult to refute and, for most scholars, impossible to ignore. Indeed, Sanders has influenced even those of a much more openly "theological" and evangelical bent, most notably N .T. Wright. Anyone reading Wright's *Jesus and the Victory of God* (1996) will recognize that it would not be the same book if Sanders's views on restoration eschatology were not so emphatically made, and anyone reading Wright's *The Climax of the Covenant: Christ and the Law in Pauline Theology* (1992) will recognize that it would not be the same book had Sanders not launched a full-scale attack on anti-Jewish understandings of law and salvation in early Judaism.

I have chosen the examples of Vermes and Sanders because they both can be seen as standing outside the conventional Christian circles of NT scholarship. Imagine the impact of more and more scholars with such explicit interests and the learning of these two scholars! Imagine the impact if more and more nonreligious, secular-minded historians were to become NT scholars. But if such a hypothetical collection of scholars were to make its impact felt, there must be mutual tolerance and the avoidance, as Thomas Haskell might put it, of preaching to the converted. It would be foolish and arrogant to claim that one approach is inherently superior to opposing ones (a warning to those absolutists emerging from among reception historians of the NT). Richard Evans has pointed out that the history of history is littered with examples of different hegemonic claims by a given historical theory or practice wanting to dominate the world of historical study but usually ending up as legitimate subspecialties.[151] Ditto the history of NT scholarship.

The dangers of a lack of tolerance can be seen in a recent work that also advocates the need for the study of Christian origins to be explained in terms of social context: Burton Mack's *The Christian Myth: Origins, Logic, and Legacy.*[152] Mack stresses the point that there has to be a shift away from the traditional approach in NT studies that has the individual Jesus at the heart of events, effectively inaugurating a new religion. Mack wants a widespread attempt to get behind the spell of gospel mystique that dominates the study of Christian origins and advocates an explanation of Christian origins in terms of social interests thoroughly grounded in anthropology and the humanities. In the "Annex" he also provides details of one such attempt: the Christian Origins Project, a development of a meeting on the theme of "Ancient Myths and Modern Theories of Christian Origins" at the 1995 Society of Biblical Literature conference in Philadelphia. In the short history of the project, discussions have been conducted on themes such as social and political functions of sacrifice, ritualization processes, and other issues of social formation, without recourse to questions of origins. All are happy about dispensing with the quest for the historical Jesus. The traditional social-scientific approaches of NT studies of the Weberian charismatic leader and the quantitative study of religious groups in American society and the attraction of "personal salvation" are no longer applicable and must be replaced with a new (i.e., their) social paradigm based on cultural anthropology. Mack proudly concludes that

> the seminar is poised to make a significant contribution both to early Christian studies and to studies in the theory of myth and social formation. . . . It is of course much too soon to tell whether the guild of New Testament scholars will want to engage with the work of this seminar. But supposing they will, a marvelous chapter of honest intellectual and exciting academic debate can be imagined.[153]

In the abstract, much of this would seem to provide a great hope for the future of biblical scholarship. Sadly this approach is not good enough. Many of Mack's arguments, such as the case for the Cynic Jesus, are incredibly implausible. N. T. Wright carefully demolished Mack's arguments in a prominent 1996 book that could hardly be ignored, yet Mack makes no attempt to respond (Wright does not even get a mention). This must surely be done, as the Cynic Jesus gains virtually no support outside the small influence of the American Jesus Seminar. It is no coincidence that Mack's work does not take into account masses of detailed work, including the Semitic background to the Gospel traditions and European Q scholarship, and he does not engage with conservative scholarship such as Wright's *Jesus and the Victory of God* (1996) or prominent Jewish scholarship on the historical Jesus, such as Geza Vermes's seminal Jesus the Jew trilogy. By not interacting properly beyond his friends, Mack loses out and provides a reconstruction of earliest Christianity almost designed more to cause uproar than debate if Mack's lack of response is anything to go by. If Mack wants a bright future of open intellectual debate and acceptance of the Christian Origins Project, then the academic engagement must be mutual. If it is not, it may be suggested that such an approach will have minimal influence beyond its small North American base. But this does not, of course, render Mack's hope for the future of scholarship invalid. An openly secular approach to Christian origins thoroughly based in the humanities is an honorable dream, but it must take critical Gospel scholarship (conservative, liberal, or whatever) seriously, and it must take its critics seriously. The dominance of Christian scholarship really does need to be challenged, but its insights must not be ignored.[154]

CONCLUSIONS

This book attempts to continue in the tradition of those scholars who have sought to provide a thoroughly (socio-) historical explanation for the rise of Christianity without having to resort to theological reasons. It also comes from what may be deemed, from the perspective of biblical studies, an untypical background. I have not found anything in particular that makes me think Christianity is in any way superior to any other movement, and its rise can be explained in human terms of social context, frequently discussed in theological language in the primary sources. It is no doubt legitimate to criticize me for being a product of my background and upbringing and my argument as being biased by my desire to see a thoroughgoing, nontheological historical explanation. As many NT scholars will now tell you, who can't be criticized for their background and beliefs having too much influence? But the history of NT scholarship has shown that greater interaction with movements, groups, and individuals who are not necessarily white, middle- or upper-class, god-fearing Christian men has made a profound impact on NT historical scholarship. Still, much more has to be done, for Christian dominance of NT studies remains.

We can now see fully the importance of the comparison between NT studies and the discipline of history. Before the 1970s and even to this day, interdisciplinary approaches to history—Marxist and non-Marxist—were effectively associated with Marxism and atheism. The dominance of Christian ideology in NT studies prevented some serious inroads into historical research, as was seen in the academic study of history, and this may continue to be the case if things do not change. The late John Peel, the ever-innovative—and, after his death, ever-popular—radio DJ, once described the impact of U.K. punk music as a welcome breath of foul air in the context of the repetitive pop and progressive rock of the 1970s music scene. In fear of using an unlikely historical parallel (aren't they all?), I suspect something similar may well be required in NT studies for it to change. But I am a bit skeptical as to whether this change can come about in the near future without accompanying social shifts. The reemergence of the political power of the Christian right and its potential influence on biblical studies may make such change an even-more-difficult task. Consequently, this book may be a mere drop in the ocean, but some attempt is absolutely necessary for a variety of voices to be heard in NT scholarship.[155] Only then can it genuinely function as an academic discipline and can questions be raised that might otherwise be ignored. If it does not, NT scholarship might as well pray at its conferences and just admit that it by and large represents academic justifications for the various ideologies of middle- and upper-class Christians.

2

Peasant Unrest and the Emergence of Jesus' Specific View of the Law

"Fallen, fallen is Babylon the great!
. . . and the merchants of the earth have grown rich from the power of her luxury."
. . . And the merchants of the earth weep and mourn for her, since no one buys their cargo anymore, cargo of gold, silver, jewels and pearls, fine linen, purple, silk and scarlet, all kinds of scented wood, all kinds of ivory, all articles of costly wood, bronze, iron, and marble, cinnamon, spice, incense, myrrh, frankincense, wine, olive oil, choice flour and wheat, cattle and sheep, horses and chariots, slaves—and human lives [or: chariots, and human bodies and souls—ῥεδῶν καὶ σωμάτων καὶ ψυχὰς ἀνθρώπων].
—*Rev. 18:2, 3, 11–13*

Jesus' view of the law reflected a key aspect of his general teaching: the immense problems that come with socioeconomic inequality. The relationship between socioeconomic reality and the Torah is quite explicit in texts such as Mark 10:17–22 and Luke 16:19–31. These related concerns are not difficult to find in Jewish law: they are deeply embedded in the Pentateuch, biblical tradition, and postbiblical tradition. But why do such concerns run consistently and densely throughout Jesus' teaching? Why specifically did Jesus' concerns emerge when and where they did? These questions are crucial because Jesus emerged at a time and in a place of socioeconomic upheaval that eventually resulted in full-scale bloody revolts against Rome. If we want to understand Jesus' attitude towards the law and how it subsequently was to be developed among Gentiles, we cannot ignore both this crucial emphasis in Jesus' teaching and the broader socioeconomic context that clearly reflected similar concerns.

35

In case anyone cares (and why should they?), I do not agree with most of John Dominic Crossan's portrait of Jesus and the earliest Christians. I do not agree with his use of primary sources. I do not find the associated Cynic thesis even remotely convincing. But I do think that Crossan has developed a potentially powerful model for locating the origins of the Jesus movement in a precise social context, something usually overlooked by his more vocal critics. Primarily I am thinking of his use of the work of Gerhard E. Lenski and John H. Kautsky to develop a model for peasant unrest in agrarian societies,[1] which I will supplement with the related work of Eric Hobsbawm on peasants and politics.[2] This approach can make a substantial contribution, as I hope will become clear, to an understanding of Jesus' approach to the law, why it emerged when and where it did, and subsequently why it could lead to an inclusion of Gentiles in the earliest Christian movement. Given the importance I have attached to the approaches of Lenski, Kautsky, and Hobsbawm, a detailed overview of the key points is required.

First, a brief but necessary aside ought to be given. Many are still wary about the use of such social-scientific approaches to the NT, particularly those "models" that seem too abstract, are apparently lacking empirical grounding and, even when they are empirically grounded, are from the wrong period and include too-dissimilar societies. The objections are not without merit and should help emphasize the importance of constant care and attention to cultural diversity.[3] Yet, as I will indicate below, Lenski, Kautsky, and Hobsbawm are all perfectly aware of exceptions and blurred conceptual boundaries. Their approaches are not some great monolithic, modernist metanarrative of certain people's imaginations, supposedly lacking appreciation of diversity.[4] Furthermore, the approaches possess further advantages: Lenski's and Kautsky's approaches, for example, are partially based on detailed studies of the right period, the general geographical proximity, and the right type of society. In addition, as Crossan notes, one of the features that gives Lenski's approach "its tremendous descriptive and persuasive power" is that the "model is not built up deductively from theoretical presuppositions but inductively from historical studies and detailed analyses of empirical societies."[5] Likewise Kautsky's generalizations are based on wide-ranging historical evidence,[6] and Hobsbawm's writings are grounded in masses of empirical detail. I hope to show with historical examples that these approaches fit extremely well the context of Galilee at the time of Jesus.

GERHARD LENSKI, JOHN KAUTSKY, AND ERIC HOBSBAWM

Gerhard Lenski's work includes a wide-ranging macrosociological analysis of human societies, covering gathering-hunting, simple horticultural, advanced horticultural, agrarian, and industrial societies.[7] Some five to six thousand years ago in the fertile valleys of the Middle East, agrarian societies began to develop and spread east and west and were firmly established throughout Europe, North Africa, and Asia by the fifteenth century CE. The Roman Empire, which naturally approximates closest to 20s Galilee, was (obviously) one such agrarian society.[8] Agrarian societies are noted for the use of discoveries and inventions that led to significant advances in production, transportation, and communication. Among the most important of these, the iron plough, the harnessing of animal power, and the basic principles of metallurgy are intimately related. Although Lenski does not ignore cultural diversity,[9] he notes common features of advanced agrarian societies, such as the physically superior engineering achievements compared to, for example, those of horticultural societies: the cathedrals of medieval Europe, the pyramids of Egypt, the aqueducts of Rome, the Great Wall of China and so on. Or indeed the massively rebuilt Herodian Temple at Jerusalem, of which it was to be claimed, "Whoever has not beheld Herod's building has not seen anything beautiful in his life" (*b. B. Bat.* 4a).

One of the most important results of these developments concerns economics. Far less human labor was needed to stay alive, and so more human labor was accessible for different purposes. One purpose was brutally simple: exploitation. Furthermore, the development of military technology created a social cleavage because those who controlled the pool of human labor were in a position to benefit the most. Thus "opportunities for exploitation were correspondingly enlarged."[10] In fact one of the most-famous aspects of Lenski's analysis of agrarian societies concerns *marked social inequality*:

> One fact impresses itself on almost any observer of agrarian societies especially on one who views them in broadly comparative perspective. This is the fact of *marked social inequality*. Without exception, one finds pronounced difficulties in power, privilege, and honor associated with mature agrarian economies. These differences surpass those found in even the most stratified horticultural societies of Africa and the New World, and far exceed those found in simple horticultural or hunting and gathering societies . . . we should logically anticipate an increase in social inequality as the economic surplus expands.[11]

John Kautsky is also not one for holding back when describing the exploitative nature of agrarian societies or aristocratic empires. And so we get comments such as "The aristocratic-peasant relationship is such a blatantly exploitative one. . . . One class that does no productive labor lives off the labor of the other class,"[12] and "Aristocrats and peasants function in different political arenas. The aristocracy, of course, interferes in the lives of the peasants by exploiting them. . . ."[13] Lest this be seen as too geographically and chronologically broad, Philip Harland similarly summarizes the agrarian economy of Palestine as being

based primarily on the production of food through subsistence-level
farming by the peasantry. The peasantry, through taxation and rents,
supported the continuance of a social economic structure character-
ized by asymmetrical distribution of wealth in favor of the elite, a small
fraction of the population.[14]

Lenski notes that increasing social inequality can be due to a number of reasons, one being urbanization,[15] an issue to which we return. As he points out,
urban communities were an important characteristic of agrarian societies and
their number, size, permanence, and urban character were all notably greater
than in even advanced horticultural societies.[16] Yet the urban population was
only a small percentage of the overall population: the overwhelming majority
of the population in agrarian societies were peasant farmers. But this imbal-
ance did not stop urban centers from dominating agrarian societies in all
spheres of life, because wealth and political power were usually concentrated
in urban areas. Indeed, urban centers were where the powerful usually resided;
correspondingly, there was "a small leisure class, whose livelihood was derived
from rents, pensions, profits, or political office."[17] While the urban centers
could provide various services in return for rural goods, the nature of the urban
relationship to the rural was essentially parasitic, as might be expected in a relationship of unequal military strength.

Kautsky is much more emphatic on this point. He stresses that the material wealth of the urban elites was overwhelmingly taken from the countryside
and includes, it should be pointed out, examples from the Roman Empire.[18]
Although the debate over the nature of urban/rural relationships in such societies continues, the general asymmetrical model has been advocated by a wide
range of scholars from a variety of perspectives, using a range of models and
generalizations from the social sciences and from various parts of the ancient
world, including first-century Palestine.[19] We will see below that even if the
generalization does not hold elsewhere, it certainly works in first-century-CE
Galilee.

A hugely influential view on urban centers in relation to the countryside,
with the control of the land being in the hands of the urban elites, has been
developed through the seminal work of Moses Finley.[20] From this general view
has emerged the widely used argument that control of the land by the urban
elites led to greater pressure on small landowners and consequently rising
deprivation. Again, if this be too geographically generalizing, we will see that
urbanization and the role of the urban centers Tiberias and Sepphoris in
Galilee were regarded by many first-century Galileans as centers of exploitation. But for the time being here is a quaint and idealized illustration from Sirach on the dependency of the urban on the rural. The importance of reading
between the lines should not need stressing:

The wisdom of the scribe depends on the opportunity of leisure; . . .
How can one become wise who handles the plow,
and who glories in the shaft of a goad,
who drives oxen and is occupied with their work,
and whose talk is about bulls?
. . . So it is with every artisan [τέκτων; cf. Mark 6:3] and master artisan
who labors by night as well as by day; . . .
So it is with the smith, sitting by the anvil, intent on his iron-work; . . .
So it is with the potter sitting at his work
and turning the wheel with his feet; . . .
All these rely on their hands,
and all are skillful in their own work.
Without them no city [πόλις] can be inhabited, . . .
. . . they maintain the fabric of the world. (Sir. 38:24–34)

So we can see that the agrarian society in which Jesus lived was likely to be highly exploitative. But what would be so different from previous centuries? Why would this state of affairs explain the rise of the Jesus movement and more particularly his specific view of the law? Clearly, something different needed to have occurred. First, we can turn to some general observations made by Hobsbawm on peasant unrest.[21] Hobsbawm's examples are grounded in much later times (nineteenth- and twentieth-century examples are most frequently used) but, as we will see, his is an independent analysis of peasant unrest that bears striking resemblance to the work of John Kautsky. Hobsbawm is doubtful whether there can be a national peasant movement or national peasant revolt or uprising.[22] Local and regional action is the norm and can turn into wider action through some external force (e.g., natural, economic, political, or ideological) and only when a "very large" number of communities or villages move together simultaneously and in strategically significant areas ("What really worries them [governments in loosely administered states] is insurrection in or in the backyard of the capital"[23]). That we have a general parallel to these kinds of rare events in the general buildup to the Jewish revolt of 66–70 should not be in doubt. Nor should there be any doubt that the Jesus movement would have been affected by the turbulent times that eventually led to the uprising (see below).

We can therefore see the *general* socioeconomic conditions that would have been *broadly* relevant for the emergence of the Jesus movement. But we can be more precise. Despite allowing for the possibility of a widespread peasant uprising, Hobsbawm claims that it would rarely coincide with the area of the state and would hardly be a single, general movement but rather a fragile collection of local and regional movements. In fact, local movements can, obviously, begin as a reaction to a specific change in local circumstances. One example Hobsbawm gives is of the Zapatista movement in Morelos (see also below), commenting that it "began by opposing not all haciendas, but merely the new ones which had been introduced in Porfirio Diaz' time."[24] In his study of peasant land occupation as a particular form of peasant unrest in Peru and elsewhere, Hobsbawm makes the following fairly obvious but nonetheless important point (as we will see below): "The land to be occupied may belong to the peasants, *but have been alienated, legally or otherwise, in a manner which they do not regard as valid.*"[25]

The issues of more specific unrest and changes in socioeconomic conditions have been brought into even sharper focus by John Kautsky. He distinguishes two general types of agrarian or aristocratic empires: traditional and commercialized. Though peasants and aristocrats live in two different worlds, the peasant-aristocrat relationship in a traditional empire is in many ways ruthlessly basic: the aristocrat simply lives off the peasant labor. In commercialized empires, such as the Roman Empire, we start to see an increase in trade, commerce, and towns. In fact, the very existence of large empires over long periods of time "tends to foster commercialization" due to tribute coming in to the ruling aristocracy from a vast number of peasants. The aristocracy can thus surround itself with increasing numbers of servants, artisans, and traders "to serve its insatiable wants for weapons and luxury articles." The new urban population may depend on trade and engage in it. Large empires may further favor the growth of trade because they "constitute large trading areas where exchange and transportation may be facilitated."[26] It is also worth noting that in such agrarian societies there is an increase in the specialization of labor, with certain areas known for their specialities, which "naturally leads to increased trade and business."[27] However, this does not mean that the economy of commercialized empire is dominated by trade[28] but "merely that the aristocracy no longer governed alone and solely in line with aristocratic values."[29] Rather, the traditional aristocratic empires "exclude all the beginnings of commercialization and . . . ignore the dynamic that may produce more of it."[30]

Kautsky notes that certain symptoms accompany his commercializing aristocratic empires. For example, if the landed aristocracy wants to buy products now made available by trade, peasants "must contribute a bigger surplus out of their labor than was needed to support the aristocracy before." A crucial issue to arise from this is that such increasing contribution of peasant surplus can lead to "more extensive and intensive agriculture, to peasant indebtedness, the alienability of land and its sale as a commodity, and the division of the peasantry into landed and landless segments."[31] Or again most relevantly perhaps, "the peasant . . . does not regard the land as capital or commodity" and the land "becomes alienable and a commodity only under the impact of commercialization, as happened . . . in Rome."[32]

Kautsky's distinction between traditional and commercialized agrarian empires such as Rome provides further insight into peasant unrest, uprisings, and revolutions. Kautsky shows that peasant revolts are infrequent in aristocratic empires, but when they do occur it is in commercializing aristocratic empires,[33] or, more particularly, "such rebellions begin to occur in the early stages of commercialization."[34] In fact, Kautsky claims that it is "a striking pattern" that major revolts such as those in classical antiquity "break out only in the aftermath and presumably as a consequence of commercialization."[35] Kautsky lists events likely to happen "if and when peasants become involved in commerce to any substantial degree":[36]

> As peasants produce more and as more luxury goods and services become available to the aristocrat, the aristocrat will demand more payments from the peasantry in order to pay for such goods and services.
> The aristocrat may also demand more labor time from the peasantry so as to increase production, sell more on the market, and increase income.
> With increased demands the peasantry may become increasingly reluctant to part with produce, money, or labor time because these things would improve also the life of the peasant.
> Whether or not the peasant is materially better off due to involvement in a money economy, and whether or not there is a voluntary or forced increase in the production of cash crops, the peasantry comes under increasing pressure. This pressure leads to tensions and a changing relationship between the peasant and the aristocrat, with peasant rebellions being one response.
> With the alienability of the land, the peasant may well fall into debt. This may lead to the selling or mortgaging of land to obtain a loan, and if debts cannot be repaid, the land is lost. The landless peasant may then develop and even become involved in the land taken from them by the few fortunate landowning peasants in the village or urban money makers who become absentee landlords. This becomes obviously upsetting for peasants previously involved with subsistence agriculture on their own land.
> Peasant resistance to these new and unfair circumstances is further emphasized by their new contacts with the towns. Here merchants and artisans have gained enough strength to have a degree of independence from the aristocracy. Although some may eventually become aristocrats or supporters of the aristocracy, anti-aristocratic townsfolk, especially artisans, may provide support or leadership for rebellious peasants in the light of commercialization.
> Peasant parochialism can be reduced in the onset of commercialization because previously isolated villages are brought together into a larger market economy. Common markets allow greater peasant interaction hence greater awareness of shared interests and the possibility of greater organization. This makes peasant revolts increasingly possible in a commercialized setting.

Peasant revolts and even unrest are rare. This may seem odd in the light of obvious socioeconomic inequality. One key reason is that peasant lifestyle is perilously close to starvation, so to resort to violence or resistance could mean that *everything* is on the line and the peasant may well feel that it is not worth the enormous risk. Furthermore peasant unrest affects harvests, so however militant peasants may be, "the cycle of their labours shackles them to their fate."[37] Compare, for example, the inhabitants of Gischala, who needed bandits and John son of Levi to incite them to revolt during 66–70. Usually the inhabitants were, as Josephus cosily put it, "inclined to peace, being mainly agricultural labourers whose whole attention was devoted to the prospects of the crops" (*J.W.* 4.84). This concern for basic survival, along with other reasons,[38] such as military inferiority to the aristocracy, makes it extremely difficult for peasants to envisage the possibility of a radically new, improved world.

But, as we saw with Hobsbawm, a change in circumstances can alter this perception. If peasants (say) have to pay more or lose land, especially if this happens suddenly, "they may consider this wrong and improper and they might even, if other conditions are favourable, rise up in rebellion."[39] Having experienced unfavorable changes, the peasant can now demand favorable ones. Although localized peasant unrest may often be defensive, such as looking to the restoration of the status quo, such peasant revolts can, particularly in the case of revolutions, involve "far reaching demands for equality and the end of aristocratic exploitation."[40] Outside organizers can formulate "more far-reaching programs and demands on behalf of peasants," and they can "visualise achieving a world different from the existing one" (cf. *J.W.* 4.85–86).[41] In fact these changes "may now go far beyond the restoration of older forms of exploitation all the way to communistic utopias."[42] It could be said that a utopian ideal is at least dormant, waiting to be triggered. Hobsbawm points to the frequent peasant myth of the remote king or emperor who would make the peasant world just if only the unjust conditions were known, which "both reflects and to some extent creates a wider framework of political action."[43] If one thinks of this general hope as a broader category, thereby allowing for historical particularities, the obvious comparison would be the impact of the teaching about the kingdom of God in a first-century Galilean context.

Kautsky and Hobsbawm, like other students of peasantry and the ancient world, provide insight into the problem of leadership. As implied and noted above, peasants were not organized and were usually passive until the onset of commercialization, which leads to greater interaction and thus knowledge of shared interests. In turn, the peasantry now have greater potential for organization. However, as is widely recognized, organization usually comes from outside the peasantry, a view often derived from the Marxist Sinai itself.[44] As Kautsky put it, "For uprisings to spread widely and to maintain themselves, such skills and resources of outside leaders are required to overcome the local-ism of peasants."[45] Rare though it may be, townspeople are a possibility for leadership because they have a different environment and different experi-ences, which could mean skills in communication and organization, especially when involving strangers.[46] Similarly, Hobsbawm points to the "importance to peasant movements of locally resident and friendly intellectuals, especially the most formidable of village intellectuals, the primary schoolteacher." Indeed Hobsbawm is inclined to believe that a general peasant movement is unrealistic unless assisted from outside or, better, above.[47]

COMMERCIALIZATION, URBANIZATION, AND UNREST IN ROMAN PALESTINE

On the issue of commercialization in Galilee at the time of Jesus, it may be useful to note that it is reflected in important scholarly studies on Galilean society and economy that do not apply the approaches of Eric Hobsbawm or John Kautsky. It is worth starting with the comments of one who has spent much of his scholarly career on first-century Galilee. Sean Freyne, applying T. F. Carney's approach to ancient economics,[48] looks at rapid economic change in Galilee (changes reflecting broader patterns in the Roman econ-omy) under Antipas that would complement Kautsky's category of commer-cialization. Freyne concludes with the following remarks,

> . . . attitudinal changes in production and consumption, increased orga-nizational specialization and monetization of transactions . . . we have been able to identify clear signs of such movement within the society of Jesus' day. The values of a market economy with all the attendant signs of exploitation of the weak and ostentatious living of the wealthy are easily documented; specialization in terms of more intensive har-vesting of produce both from the land and lake, as well as production of goods for inter-regional trade in addition to domestic use were occurring; and there are clear signs of the extension of monetization as a means of exchange with the production of native Galilean coins for the first time. . . . It seems possible to link these developments with Antipas' foundations of Sepphoris and Tiberias, as symptomatic of the more complex changes occurring within the whole region.[49]

J. F. Strange, one of the major voices on Galilean archaeology, summarizes the insights archaeology has brought to the understanding of first-century-CE Galilee, which include a notable emphasis on trade:

> There is a highly developed local trade network upon which the citi-zens of Galilee transported goods and services from village to village,

to town, and to cities, and vice versa. . . . [W]e can deduce by archaeological methods that a pre-second century extensive trade network
existed that connected the villages, towns and cities of Lower Galilee,
Upper Galilee, the rift, and the Golan . . . [and] an extensive specialised
agricultural and industrial production implies a vigorous trade network.[50]

Of course, following Kautsky's warning, we should not overemphasize the role
of trade. But that these scholars recognize its role in Galilee at the time of Jesus
without resorting to Kautsky's generalizations is particularly illuminating.[51]

Perhaps more than anything the evidence of notable commercialization in
first-century-CE Galilee concerns, as the above quotation from Freyne might
imply, the two major urban projects of Sepphoris and Tiberias (Josephus, *Life*
346: "Of the cities of Galilee the largest are Sepphoris and Tiberias") and their
effect on the villages and countryside.[52] There are a whole host of issues regarding the urban center geographically nearest to Jesus' home, Nazareth, namely
Sepphoris. Did Jesus visit there? Did he enjoy the theater and meditate on the
fate of Orpheus? Was Sepphoris a hive of Hellenism, influencing the whole of
Galilee? Was rural Galilee a bastion of a more traditional Judaism in the face of
Hellenistic Sepphoris? To what extent was the Jesus movement rural or urban
based? Important though these and other questions are, they are not directly
relevant for my present purposes and will not be discussed in any detail here.[53]
I will focus primarily on how urban centers such as Sepphoris and Tiberias tie
in with the generalizations and approaches of Lenski, Kautsky, and Hobsbawm.

Sepphoris was sacked and razed by Varus, the Roman governor of Syria, in
reaction to an uprising led by Judah son of Hezekiah after the death of Herod
the Great in 4 BCE (Josephus, *Ant.* 17.271; *J.W.* 2.56).[54] On gaining Galilee,
Herod Antipas refortified and rebuilt Sepphoris. The rebuilding included a
palace and possibly a theater. It is described in grandiose terms in a well-known
passage of Josephus: "Herod fortified Sepphoris to be the ornament of all
Galilee, and called it 'capital' [Αὐτοκρατορίδα (*Ant.* 18.27; *J.W.* 2.511). It was
"situated in the heart of Galilee, surrounded by many villages" (*Life* 346),
which would no doubt go some way to providing the needs and contributing
to the ornamentation of Sepphoris. One such village may well have been
Nazareth, which was only a few miles and a one-hour walk away, so Jesus' parents, and even Jesus himself, would have had fairly direct experience of the
recent and rocky history of Sepphoris.

Tiberias was the other famous building project of Antipas, completed in c.
18–19 CE. It was significantly built in what was known at least to Josephus as
"the best region of Galilee on Lake Gennesaritis" (*Ant.* 18.36), and it produced
a variety of specialized agricultural produce.[55] But it was also built on graves
(*Ant.* 18.38) that provided the most defiling of impurities. It was of course omi-

nously built in honor of the emperor Tiberius and included a royal palace over-looking the city (*J.W.* 2.618), a palace that included idolatrous statues of animals. Inevitably perhaps, it was an immediate target in the Jewish war (*Life* 65–67). Josephus (*Ant.* 18.36–38) provides what for present purposes are some very interesting comments on the populace of Tiberias. There appears to have been forced peasant dislocation and land alienation: "The new settlers were a promiscuous rabble, no small contingent being Galilean, with such as were drafted from territory subject to him and brought forcibly to the new foundation." However, Josephus adds figures that might be described as "retainers":[56] "Some of these were magistrates [τινὲς δὲ καὶ τῶν ἐν τέλει]." It is also notable that those bribed to live in Tiberias were given gifts of land, something that would no doubt be at the expense of another:

> Herod accepted as participants even poor men who were brought in to join the others from any and all places of origin. It was a question whether some were even free beyond cavil. These latter he often and in large bodies liberated and benefited (imposing the condition that they should not quit the city), by equipping houses at his own expense and adding new gifts of land [καὶ γῆς ἐπιδόσει] . . .

In addition to changes in landscape it is impossible to think that there would not have been a significant shift in economic conditions with the building of these two urban centers. These building projects would have required from the local peasantry both labor and goods, including food for the elites among the urban dwellers. If the generalizations of Lenski and Kautsky hold any weight, presumably the rural peasantry would also have contributed to the increase in luxurious goods for the urban elites. This would suggest that there would have been a visible gap between the wealth of the urban centers and the countryside at the expense of the rural peasantry, coupled with an even greater economic burden.[57] The very building of Sepphoris and Tiberias meant this asymmetrical relationship was at times quite literally cast in stone. Furthermore the alienation and reallocation of land (as Josephus describes in the building of Tiberias, for example) would, potentially at least, have dramatic consequences for peasant farmers, presumably resulting in a spiraling socioeconomic status from small landowning to tenant farming and day laboring, and potentially all the way down to beggary and banditry. Somewhat speculative though it may be, the Stegemanns can even speak of "a regular process of pauperization" as being "nothing unusual."[58]

What should also be clear is that these cities were not only centers and symbols of political and economic domination, but certain cultural and religious features were also tied up with paganism, although it is easy to overexaggerate the extent of pagan features.[59] It is highly unlikely that this connection would have been lost on the Jewish populace of Galilee, and the importance of these building projects occurring in the lifetime of Jesus right in the heart of his home region cannot be stressed enough.[60] Moreover, we should not underestimate the effect of introducing these building projects, along with a different set of values from those of the traditional rural Galilean peasantry, in only a matter of years.[61] Given these factors, it is presumably no coincidence that there is no mention in the Synoptic tradition of Tiberias and Sepphoris.

Yet some have read the evidence of urbanization differently. Douglas Edwards, for example, argues that the various material finds in Galilee point to a greater two-way urban-rural economic interaction and that the rural peasantry was not as hostile as is usually believed.[62] Crucially, however, there is some good evidence to back up the position of social and economic unrest in Galilee linked with Sepphoris. Josephus provides plenty of evidence from around the time of the Jewish war of massive discontent among Galileans with Sepphoris and Tiberias. *Life* 66–68 provides some of the more gruesome evidence. Josephus recalls Jesus son of Sapphias, the ringleader "of the party of the sailors and destitute class" who, in addition to looting the rich, massacred all the Greek/Gentile residents in Tiberias and others "who, before the outbreak of the hostilities had been their enemies." This is presumably some indication of a particularly hostile attitude towards the urban center. The following quotations, also from Josephus's personal recollections of the Jewish-Roman war in Galilee, should be given fully in order to give some further indication of the deep-rooted revulsion aimed at Sepphrois and Tiberias, showing that it is more than a scholarly construct:

> I found the inhabitants of Sepphoris in great distress concerning their native place, which the Galileans had decided to pillage because of their leanings towards the Romans and the overtures of loyalty and allegiance which they had made to Cestius Gallus, the governor of Syria. (*Life* 30)

> Sepphoris, by submission to Rome, had forthwith become the capital of Galilee and the seat of the royal bank and the archives. To these and many other disparaging remarks upon King Agrippa, calculated to incite the people to revolt, he added: "Now is the time to take up arms and join hands with the Galileans. Their hatred of Sepphoris for remaining loyal to Rome will make them willing recruits. Now is your opportunity, with ample forces, for revenge." (*Life* 39)

> The Galileans accordingly came in large numbers from all quarters under arms, and entreated me to attack Tiberias, to take it by storm, raze the whole place to the ground and reduce the inhabitants, women, children and all, to slavery. (*Life* 99)

> The Galileans, seizing this opportunity, too good to be missed, of venting their hatred on one of those cities which they detested, rushed for-

ward, with the intention of exterminating the population, aliens and all.
Plunging into the towns, which they found deserted, the terrified
inhabitants having fled in a body to the citadel. They looted everything,
sparing their countrymen no conceivable form of devastation. . . . As,
however, they refused to listen to either remonstration or command,
my exhortations being overborne by their hatred, I instructed some of
my friends around me, on whom I could fully rely, to circulate a report
that the Romans had made their way into another quarter of the city
with a large force. I did this in order . . . [that] I might check the fury
of the Galileans and so save Sepphoris. . . . Thus were the Sepphorites,
beyond their own expectations, saved by this device of mine from
destruction. (*Life* 374–380; cf. *J.W.* 2.574–75; 3.61–62)

Tiberias, likewise, had a narrow escape from being sacked by the
Galileans. . . . For they had the same detestation for the Tiberians as
for the inhabitants of Sepphoris. . . . I was at a loss to discover means
of rescuing Tiberias from the rage of the Galileans. I could not deny
that the Tiberians had sent a letter to the king. . . . So after long and
anxious reflection I said: "That the Tiberians have done wrong I am
well aware, nor shall I forbid you to sack their city. . . . The Tiberians
are not the only persons who have betrayed our country's indepen-
dence; many of the most eminent men in Galilee have done the same."
(*Life* 381–386)

It is, of course, important to highlight that this material is from the time of
the Jewish revolt against Rome and not from the time of Jesus. Clearly by the
time of the Jewish war these tensions reached boiling point. As is frequently
recognized, such concerns were likely to have been grounded in decades of
discontent, right back to the time of Jesus and earlier.[63] We have already
pointed out that it is no coincidence that the rebuilding of Sepphoris and
Tiberias occurred geographically and chronologically close to the emergence
of the Jesus movement, which, as we will see below, reflected a hostile attitude
towards wealth and socioeconomic inequalities. There is also extremely
important evidence of the symptoms of commercializing activity in Galilee at
the time of Jesus. So, for example, the earliest strands of the Synoptic tradition. It may well be significant that there were large estates in Galilee, including the phenomena of absentee landlords, around the time of Jesus, which
would require hiring day laborers or acquiring tenant farmers or slaves, as
implied right across the Synoptic tradition (cf. Mark 10:17–22; Matt. 25:14–30
par. Luke 19:11–27; Matt. 18:23–34 par. Luke 7:41–43; Matt. 13:24–30;
18:21–35; 20:1–15; Luke 12:16–21, 42–43; 15:11–32; 16:1–12). Given the existence of large estates—even if there were only a notable minority of landowners—this meant less land for small freeholders and thus an increase of landless
peasants, as suggested above. The significance of the Synoptic tradition's bearing witness to landless workers (Mark 12:1–12; Matt. 1:10; 9:37–38; 20:1–8;

Luke 13:27; 15:17) cannot therefore be underestimated.[64] We might also look at complementary evidence from Galilean archaeology. Compare, for example, the comments of James Strange:

> Archaeological surveys of the Galilee and other regions of ancient Palestine confirm that large farmhouses, presumably of wealthy land owners, dot the landscape. . . . From archaeological surveys in Galilee it is possible to posit another dimension of social reality. It seems that there are more farmers on small plots of land than those plots will support. This suggests that the small land owner had to work for wages for somebody else at least part of the time, or else develop a speciality on the side which could be marketed.[65]

The Synoptic tradition also bears witness to the shifting situation of peasant life, from poor to poorer along with hostility to urbanization, large landowners, economic exploitation, and general unrest.[66] There is the recurring theme of debt (Matt. 5:25 par. Luke 12:57–59; Matt. 5:40; Matt. 5:42 par. Luke 6:35; Luke 4:18; 16:1–8; Matt. 6:12; 18:23–35). There is also plenty of hostility toward the rich and powerful and toward those with fine clothing and those who live in luxurious palaces (Matt. 11:8 par. Luke 7:25); there is a hostile attitude toward urban institutions (Mark 13:9 par. Matt. 10:17–19 par. Luke 12:11); and there is clear hostility towards a parabolic rich man who will suffer torment (Luke 16:19–31). The Lukan woes also provide explicit hostility toward the rich and those who eat well (Luke 6:24–25), and there is even a modification of the Decalogue with "Do not defraud" for the benefit of the rich man with much landed property (Mark 10:17–20). There is also plenty of concern for the poor and powerless: for those without food, clothing, drink, and community (Matt. 25:31–46); for the poor man Lazarus covered in sores, in need of food, eating what might fall from the rich man's table (Luke 16:19–21); and according to the Lukan version of the Beatitudes at least, blessings for the poor and those in need of food (Luke 6:20–21). Some of the parables exhibit what may seem to some as an uncomfortable use of language based on everyday experiences of basic oppression and class conflict, yet some language within the parables apparently condones this oppression. The parable of the Laborers in the Vineyard has a particularly unpleasant landowner who treats the laborers as he sees fit simply because he controls the finances (Matt. 20:1–15); the parable of the Talents has a harsh master of some property and also requires the slave to reap where he did not sow and gather where he did not scatter seed (Matt. 25:14–28 par. Luke 19:11–25); and the imagery in the parable of the Wicked Tenants has the tenants seriously displeased with the slaves of the absentee vineyard owner (Mark 12:1–9). It is also notable that the Gospels have a concern for widows and children who may have been orphans (Mark 9:33–37; 10:13–16).[67] Of course, much of the language just outlined will be clichéd, particularly the traditional wisdom (e.g., the Lukan woes), but the fact that it occurs so frequently and given that the everyday language of the parables makes assumptions about the socioeconomic situation of Jesus' audience, we should regard it all as an important reflection of Galilee at the time of Jesus.

BANDITS AND THE REACTION TO WEALTH

> I, Tuco Ramirez, brother of Brother Ramirez, will tell you something: You think you better than I am. Where we came from if one did not want to die of poverty one became a priest or a bandit. You chose your way, I chose mine. . . . Now I'll tell you something: You became a priest because you were too much of a coward to do what I do.
> —*The bandit Tuco to his brother Pablo in* The Good, the Bad, and the Ugly *(1966)*

> Here we are. That's Agua Caliente. Yes, I have many friends here. . . . They don't like strangers.
> —*Bandit chief El Indio in* For a Few Dollars More *(1965)*

It is particularly striking that in Palestine from the first century BCE to the second century CE, when it became directly and indirectly connected with Rome, there are a variety of groups and individuals clearly in some kind of protest against the ruling order that ultimately peaked in the two major revolts against Rome. We have seemingly nonviolent prophets such as Theudas leading popular movements out to the desert, recalling the exodus-conquest themes. Theudas was certainly deemed enough of a political threat to cause Rome to act with deadly decisiveness (Josephus, *Ant.* 20.97–99). There were of course many other similar types of figures in this period. There is most obviously John the Baptist, who was also regarded as a political threat; hence he was put to death by Antipas for reasons deemed insurrectionary (Josephus, *Ant.* 18.118).[68] But it is in banditry where the threat of physically violent rebellious behavior in the here and now genuinely lay. Given that my present purposes are to contribute to an explanation of Jesus' view of the Torah in relation to his teaching on rich and poor, banditry is surely the place to look for clues. It is here, unsurprisingly, where such issues can be most explicit and stark.

Banditry is an extremely well-attested phenomenon in first-century Palestine,[69] as it is throughout the Roman Empire.[70] It is often analyzed with help from Eric Hobsbawm's seminal cross-cultural study of social banditry, which has banditry as a kind of pre-political rebellion on behalf of the peasantry. To generalize this detailed work, social banditry occurs in agrarian societies where someone may be outlawed by the ruling classes and become champion of the peasantry and the exploited, fighting for their justice. Hobsbawm's analysis has been challenged, and he has responded, but it is an approach that continues to be popular in understandings of banditry in first-century Palestine.[71]

It is not surprising then that claims such as the following are sometimes made: "Social bandits are . . . distinguished from ordinary robbers in that they remain somehow connected with peasant society."[72] The boundaries between robbing and primitive rebellion are, however, very much blurred. For example, after the dispersal of a popular revenge mission against Samaritans for the murder of Galileans/a Galilean (see below), a mission that included many a bandit (ληστής), many of the avengers, "emboldened by impunity, had recourse to robbery, and raids and insurrections, fostered by the more reckless, broke out all over the country" (*J.W.* 2.234–40). Here there is clearly a problem differentiating between being somehow connected with the peasantry and (presumably) somehow not. It is not easy to claim an analytical or historical difference between the ληστής of Luke 10:30 and the ληστής of *J.W.* 2.234–40 and so frequently elsewhere in Josephus.[73] Moreover, it is hardly going too far to suggest that the very need to steal may itself be analyzed as a form of rebellion and reaction to socioeconomic circumstances.

Indeed, given this context, banditry ought to be partially seen as a result of commercialization and shifting socioeconomic problems of Palestine in the Roman period. Compare also Hobsbawm: "Certain types of rural society tend to produce a larger surplus of unemployed able-bodied men than others, and hence a larger proportion of potential bandits."[74] Applying this idea to first-century Palestine may sound a little conjectural, but there is firm evidence for a link between banditry and symptoms of commercialization and the results of socioeconomic hardship,[75] as is also found elsewhere in the Roman Empire.[76] As is widely acknowledged, it is no coincidence that debt records in Jerusalem were an early target for the Judean bandits in the Jewish revolt against Rome (Josephus, *J.W.* 2.427–48). Under Herod the Great, as Benjamin Isaac points out, bandit leaders included a former shepherd (Josephus, *Ant.* 17.278–84; *J.W.* 2.60–65), a former royal slave (*Ant.* 17.273–77; *J.W.* 2.57–59), and ex-soldiers (*Ant.* 17.270), which suggests "that the Herodian administration had been economically oppressive."[77] Under Herod the Great, the inhabitants of Trachonitis, a region that had been added to Herod's territory in 23 BCE, "no longer," as Josephus's not-too-hidden agenda puts it (*Ant.* 16.271–72), "had the freedom to practice brigandage (ληστεύειν) but were forced to till the soil and live peaceably."[78] However, Josephus lets a crucial piece of information slip: "This was not what they wanted, nor did the soil bring much profit in return for their labour [οὐδὲ λυσιτέλειαν ἔφερεν ἡ γῆ πονούντων]."

Banditry had increased dramatically by the mid-first century CE (see below; cf. *Ant.* 20.124), and this was no doubt assisted by the harsh famine under Tiberius Alexander (46–48 CE).[79] Albinus (62–64 CE), it seems, virtually encouraged banditry and social unrest through his apparently gangster-like rule, and Josephus isn't backward in coming forward in his polemic on this matter. In his official capacity, and in addition to taking bribes, Albinus managed to "steal and plunder private property and burden the whole nation with extra-ordinary taxes" (*J.W.* 2.272–73; *Ant.* 20.215). Josephus says that the insurgents of Jerusalem sprung into action through no small help from the bribing of Albinus in return for immunity. All this no doubt provoked the populace, who were (apparently) dissatisfied with peace and thus numerous bandit groups popped up (*J.W.* 2.274–76). John of Gishala, unsurprisingly regarded by Josephus as "the most unscrupulous and crafty of all who have ever gained notoriety by such infamous means," was, we are told, "poor [πένης] at the opening of his career" (*J.W.* 2.585), and his followers included a notable amount of people who may have been deemed social outsiders: "He ended by mustering a band of four hundred men, for the most part fugitives from the region of Tyre and the villages in that neighbourhood" (*J.W.* 2.588; cf. *Life* 372). Jesus son of Sapphias, ringleader of the "party of the sailors and destitute class" (*Life* 66), was presumably the leader of the second of three factions in Tiberias mentioned by Josephus who were "composed of the most insignificant persons" (*Life* 35). We might also add that Josephus implies a clear socioeconomic distance between himself and bandits in his memoirs (*Life* 175).

As Josephus's comments sometimes might suggest, Jews of Palestine were only too aware of the potential causes of banditry. Knowledge of these causes was such that it could even be predicted with chilling ease. During the Caligula crisis, large numbers of Jews were present at Tiberias to influence the sympathetic Roman legate Petronius in persuading Caligula not to go ahead with placing his statue in the Temple. They neglected their fields and sat down in protest. Aristobulus (brother of Agrippa), along with Helcias the Elder and a variety of power figures, appealed to Petronius "not to incite them to desperation" and to write to Caligula in order that he may know the desperate situation. They advised Petronius to mention that "since the land was unsown, there would be a harvest of banditry, because the tribute could not be met [ὥστε ἀσπόρου τῆς γῆς γενομένης λῃστεῖαι ἂν φύοιντο ἀδυναμίᾳ καταβολῆς τῶν φόρων]" (*Ant.* 18.269–75; cf. *J.W.* 2.199–201; Philo, *Legat.* 249). It does not matter who is precisely responsible for this sentiment, for it should be clear, at the very least, that one Jew in the history of transmission could acknowledge that a major cause of banditry would have included problematic harvests, which could lead to both hunger and an inability to pay taxes. What else could a peasant do but turn to banditry?

It is easy to romanticize banditry (just as it is easy to accuse people of romanticizing banditry). It is sometimes stated that not only do the local peasantry
protect their heroes who fight against injustice but that we are even dealing
with "Jewish Robin Hoods,"[80] "the Robin Hoods of Palestinian Jewish society."[81] In some ways the image of the bandit as Robin Hood riding through
the glen, stealing from the rich to give to the poor, has a grain of truth. For a
start, bandits are often described as being popular. Although the story of the
release of Barabbas (Mark 15:7) is fraught with well-known historical difficulties, it may well reflect popular support for bandits. Josephus gives several
examples related to bandit popularity. *Jewish War* 4.84 *may* imply bandit popularity among farmers in a small town. Here the normally peaceful agricultural laborers of Gischala were more devoted to crops than violence, but when
numerous bandit gangs arrived, "some members had caught the contagion."
Significantly, there is clear evidence from before the war. When Caesar's slave
Stephen was robbed of his baggage by bandits near Bethhoron, the investi-
gating troops got angry as the inhabitants of the surrounding villages refused
to give up the culprits (*J.W.* 2.228–31; *Ant.* 20.113–17).

The bandit Eleazar ben Dinai was finally captured under Felix (c. 52–60 CE)
and sent to Rome, but only after twenty years on the loose (*Ant.* 20.160–61; *J.W.*
2.253). In this context, Josephus mentions the crucifixion of bandits and their
accomplices: "Of the brigands whom he crucified, and of the common people
who were convicted of complicity with them and punished by him, the number
was incalculable" (*J.W.* 2.253). That Eleazar evaded capture for twenty years
may also imply he had popular support,[82] though helped no doubt also by having his home in the mountains (*Ant.* 20.121). Another indication of the popularity of bandits among local peasantry again involves Eleazar. After the murder
of a Galilean (so *J.W.* 2.232; *Ant.* 20.118 has "Galileans," which is presumably
secondary)[83] by Samaritans, the Galileans wanted revenge. The notables went
off seeking retribution for the sake of pacifying the masses to an uninterested (so
J.W. 2.233) or a bribed (by the Samaritans; and so secondary *Ant.* 20.119?)
procurator Cumanus (c. 48–52 CE). Yet when the news hit Jerusalem "the
masses [of festival goers] were profoundly stirred" and fled off to Samaria without generals. Among the masses were "brigands and rioters" who had as their
leaders Eleazar and, mentioned only in *Jewish War*, a certain Alexander. Hitting
Acrabatene they "massacred the inhabitants without distinction of age and burnt
the villages" (*J.W.* 2.232–35).[84] It does look as if there was powerful support from
the peasantry in this instance although it is not quite the idealized honorable
defenders of the poor but rather what might loosely be called popular, gangster-
style justice. If we wanted to push this analogy too far, it might be mentioned
that, like the infamous London gangsters, the Kray brothers, it appears that certain bandits may have "loved their old mums" as the cliché goes (*Ant.* 14.168).

As the events under Cumanus may imply, it is important not to get swept away by the dashing Errol Flynn that is social banditry. There is another side to banditry that should not be ignored, namely, evidence of bandits who are not so well disposed to the peasantry and who do not fit the ideal role of social bandit.[85] On a generalizing level, an analogy with modern-day gangsters might also shed light: the powerless of society may have no choice but to do as the powerful say, official or not.[86] Few ordinary people tell Tony Soprano otherwise and really ought to be grateful for the help, or else . . . On a more empirical level, there are also plenty of references to bandits acting as plain violent robbers (e.g., *J.W.* 2.581–82, 588–89; 4.406–7; *Ant.* 14.159; 17.285; 20.185, 256; Luke 10:30). Even the Essenes, who should probably not be numbered among the wealthy—indeed, they are said to hate riches (*J.W.* 2.122; see also below)—carry nothing on their journey "except arms as a protection against bandits" (*J.W.* 2.125).

Sometimes bandits were in the pockets of the rich and powerful authorities. Albinus, according to Josephus's account, was quite happy to accept bribes for the release of bandits from prison and for the promise of immunity from arrest. This may have led to the following situation that Josephus describes and may reflect a tyrannical attitude towards peaceable peasants, too: "Each ruffian, with his own band of followers grouped around him, towered above his company like a brigand chief or tyrant, employing his bodyguard to plunder peaceable citizens" (*J.W.* 2.272–76). But worse still, Josephus even claims that the procurator Florus (64–66 CE), who is portrayed as being so utterly corrupt he made the villainous Albinus appear "a paragon of virtue," was in cahoots with bandits, and was happy for banditry to continue so long as he got his cut (*Ant.* 20.255–57).[87] In Galilee during the Jewish war there too were some bandits prepared to serve those they should probably not so long as the price was right. In *Life* 77–78 Josephus speaks of paying off bandits to be mercenaries and to refrain from attacking the Romans. Previously, though, Jesus the bandit chief had sold his services to the pro-Roman Sepphoris, which was resisting submission to Josephus, who himself commanded a sizeable group of Galileans at this point (*Life* 104–11).[88] There are other pieces of evidence that are not so strong. In *Life* 206, for example, Josephus recalls the Galilean populace being deeply worried that if he were to quit Galilee they would be easy prey for the bandits. But we should remind ourselves that this is Josephus speaking, and there is more than a hint of apologetic. After all, Josephus modestly adds in *Life* 207 that the large numbers of Galilean men, along with their wives and children, were "influenced, I imagine, as much by alarm for themselves as by affection for myself"!

In the context of social banditry, it should come as no surprise that there is a consistent hostility aimed at the rich that is also often explicitly anti-imperialistic.

Sometimes the motives were clear socioeconomic outrage, as in the case of the burning of the debt records at the beginning of the war, which also functioned "to cause a rising of poor against the rich" (*J.W.* 2.427–48). Josephus mentions "some adventurous young men of Dabaritta" who ambushed the wife of Ptolemy, "the king's overseer," as she traveled across the Great Plain. She was traveling "in great state, protected by an escort of cavalry," but this did not stop the men of Dabaritta from plundering all her baggage. They presented to Josephus at Tarichaeae four mules laden with apparel and other articles, besides a large pile of silver and five hundred pieces of gold (*Life* 126–27). No doubt, as Freyne points out, the woman served as a symbol of Roman oppression and aristocratic domination, issues that would doubtlessly make the temperatures of the socially oppressed rise.[89]

What is particularly significant for present purposes is that the socioeconomic hardships can be easily linked to a concern for Torah and Jewish traditions, alongside, of course, the anti-imperialistic overtones. Josephus even gives us insight, and not always intentionally, into these concerns on the part of his bitter rivals. John of Gischala, whom Josephus describes as "eager for revolution," looked to Josephus's seal of approval to attack the "imperial corn" stored in the villages of Upper Galilee. But he also had legal concerns, as he was apparently anxious that pure oil and not Greek oil was provided for the Jewish inhabitants of Caesarea Philippi, which the Romans had sealed off, so that they could fulfill legal requirements.[90] Josephus puts this concern down to, as Arthur Daley might have worded it, the entrepreneurial flame still flickering rather than legal piety, but note that he is powerless to stop John because of "fear of being stoned by the mob if I withheld it" (*Life* 70–76). Jesus the leader of "the party of sailors and destitute class" who looted Tiberias and set the palace on fire, seeing it had a gold roof (*Life* 66), responded to the rumor that Josephus was about to sell his soul to the Romans through reference to the law:

> With a copy of the laws of Moses in his hands, he now stepped forward and said: "If you cannot, for your own sakes, citizens, detest Josephus, fix your eyes on your country's laws, which your commander-in-chief intended to betray, and for their sakes hate the crime and punish the audacious criminal." After this speech, which was loudly applauded . . . (*Life* 134–35)

An interesting link between law, the wealthy, and banditry is the case of the baggage robbing of Caesar's slave Stephen by bandits. After Stephen was robbed, the troops had problems finding the culprits in the neighboring villages on the public road to Bethhoron. One soldier went too far and burnt a copy of the Torah. This caused such uproar among Jews that the procurator Cumanus had to pacify the masses and so "thought fit to call out the soldier and ordered him to be led to execution through ranks of his accusers" (*J.W.* 2.231).[91] But perhaps one of the most important examples is found in the context of Caligula's attempt to place a statue of himself in the Jerusalem Temple. Not only can Josephus talk of Jews promising a harvest of banditry (*Ant.* 18.269–75) as a result of strike action if Caligula's threat was to be carried through, but he can also add that it was done quite naturally in the context of law observance: "The Jews appealed to their law and the custom of their ancestors, and pleaded that they were forbidden to place an image of God, much more of a man, not only in the sanctuary but even in any unconsecrated spot throughout the country" (*J.W.* 2.195).

Although not technically Torah, it is also worth noting the hostility to wealth and banditry tied in with claims of royalty, possibly including echoes of traditions concerning popular kingship associated with Saul and David after the death of Herod the Great in 4 BCE,[92] something of obvious relevance for the Jesus tradition. Anti-imperialism is naturally enough present. Although not as strongly present in the more generalizing *Jewish War* 2.56, Josephus again lets a crucial piece of information slip in the parallel account of Judas son of Hezekiah the bandit chief in *Antiquities* 17.271–72, where there is not only the implication of some kind of royal/messianic claim but also of hostility towards the rich. In Perea a proud, tall, and handsome (cf. 1 Sam. 9:2; 10.23) former royal slave called Simon "assumed the diadem" and toured around with his collected bandits (*J.W.* 2.57–59; *Ant.* 17.273–77; Tacitus, *Hist.* 5.9). It seems that Simon and his band were particularly keen on attacking places associated with royalty and wealth. In addition to burning various royal places and allowing his followers to take the surviving booty, Simon burnt down the royal palace at Jericho "and many other stately mansions, such incendiarism providing him with an easy opportunity for plunder" (*J.W.* 2.57). He eventually had his head hacked off.

And then there was the powerfully built Athrongaeus, with his four equally strapping brothers, looked down upon by Josephus as a mere unknown shepherd with the nerve to aspire to the throne (*J.W.* 2.60–62; *Ant.* 17.278; cf. 1 Sam. 16:11; 17:20). Josephus claims that their principle objective was to "kill Romans and royalists, but no Jew, from whom they had anything to gain, escaped, if he fell into their hands" (*J.W.* 2.62). Josephus also recalls that they even attempted a siege of a Roman convoy carrying corn and arms (*J.W.* 2.63). In fact Josephus claims that in this period "these men were making the whole of Judea one scene of guerrilla warfare [τότε δὲ λῃστρικοῦ τὴν Ἰουδαίαν πᾶσαν ἐνεπίμπλασαν]" (*J.W.* 2.65). There may be more to the timing of these uprisings than hoping for a new king, namely, possible socioeconomic reasons that may be suggested by some of their actions. We know that Herod was famous in part due to his ruthless handling of bandits, and, as Peter Richardson and Douglas Edwards point out, his dynasty "repeated a constant pattern: accumulation of wealth, land, and power, with deprivation of small landowners and small businessmen" and so the localized uprisings when he died presumably reflect the underlying tensions.[93]

We therefore have an important socioeconomic context intimately associated with commercialization in which Jesus' hostility to wealth/concern for the poor in relation to teaching on the law could emerge. But Jesus himself was not a bandit leader, did not join a bandit group, did not plunder the palaces of the rich, and did not attack rich wives of Roman officials. However, the boundary between prophet and bandit is not always that clear.[94] The bandit kings discussed above have obvious parallels at least with the way in which Jesus was remembered. But Josephus also gives some crucial information suggesting that banditry is an important parallel to the rise of the Jesus movement. Under Felix, for example, there were a variety of prophetic or millenarian-type figures in addition to, but not sharply differentiated from, bandits or indeed from that particularly lethal type of subversive, the *sicarii* (*J.W.* 2.254–68; *Ant.* 20.161–74). "Deceivers and impostors" claiming divine authority were advocating revolutionary changes and persuaded many to go out into the desert for signs of deliverance. A similar fate was dealt to these unfortunate souls as that of Theudas. Josephus claims these figures had "purer hands but more impious intentions, who no less than the assassins ruined the peace of the city" (*J.W.* 2.258). Felix was no less forgiving of the Egyptian prophet and his multitude of followers (cf. Acts 21:38), although the Egyptian was more fortunate than Theudas and others in escaping. But then the degree of overlap between the more prophetic figures and the bandits becomes explicit in Josephus's narrative. "Impostors and brigands" now join forces, inciting numbers to revolt and threatening those who submitted to Rome. Crucially for present purposes, this coalition looted the houses of the wealthy and murdered their owners.

We might also note the role of John the Baptist, one of the most important individual influences on Jesus' life. His message was clearly one that provoked the authorities or more specifically Antipas. As far as we know, his mission was physically nonviolent, but, as with the case of Theudas, he was still deemed an insurrectionist by Antipas, no doubt because the imminent eschatological events about which he preached would have meant the end of the current political powers. But this too was tied up with the issue of Torah observance, hence his criticisms of Antipas's marital arrangements (Mark 6:17–18 par. Matt. 14:3–4) are often regarded as complementing Josephus's account of John as political threat in Antipas's eyes. But, moreover, and if Luke is to be believed, he was also particularly concerned with issues of exploitation, wealth, and poverty (Luke 3:10–14). Jesus' teaching on rich and poor, as with so much of his teaching, was based on the dramatic actions of God in the future, a theme found in Jewish traditions in relation to Torah, hostility to wealth, and concern for the poor. But before we turn to that, and given that we have just been dealing with leaders of not too dissimilar movements to the Jesus movement, some points of clarification need to be made regarding peasant unrest and socioeconomic protest.

LEADERSHIP AND CLASS

Lenski's and Kautsky's understandings of class, which have been applied to first-century Palestine, are of some relevance here, in particular Lenski's "priestly class."[95] Although boundaries of social class are inevitably blurred and ambiguous, two distinct classes may be identified: upper and lower. To generalize, the upper class included the ruling class, governing class, retainer class, merchant class, and priestly class whereas the lower class included peasants, artisans, degraded class, and expendables. This is important because before we look at the influence that commercialization had on Jesus' teaching and more specifically Jesus' teaching on the law, the view of outside nonpeasant leadership in situations of peasant unrest must be addressed. We may add to these arguments with reference to the particular situation of first-century Galilee and in particular the leadership of Jesus. The following argument is also significant for those such as Crossan who wish to define Jesus as a peasant[96] in the deliberately diverse sense of "exploited agriculturalists."[97]

Kautsky notes an exception to his "rule" that peasants need to be represented by an outsider, namely, the Mexican peasant movement led by Emiliano Zapata. But Kautsky notes that Zapata was no ordinary peasant, as he could read and write, had been to Mexico City, and was in contact with politicians and intellectuals.[98] Assuming for the moment that Jesus can be classed as a peasant, then comparable comments could possibly be made about Jesus (and perhaps many more Galilean peasants). Alan Millard has argued that literacy was notably high in Palestine of Jesus' day, which raises the possibility that Jesus could at least read.[99] It is also the case that Jesus and other Galilean Jews went to Jerusalem, at the very least for some religious festivals in their lifetimes. Moreover, there is some evidence that the Jesus movement was not localized, at least not simply based in Lower Galilee. Jesus had been in contact with the Baptist movement and one of Jesus' followers was Judas Iscariot, whose name may literally mean "Man of Kerioth," Kerioth being in southern Judea. Contrary to the assumption in Sir. 38:24–34 (cf. Cicero, *Off.* 1.150–51) that the artisan cannot be counted among the wise, educated, and learned, it also appears that Jesus has a detailed knowledge of what might be called intellectual traditions. I have argued elsewhere that his knowledge of halakah appears to have been very detailed.[100] Moreover, there is the possibility that

Jesus had some fairly precise knowledge of the views of the Qumran group (e.g., Luke 14:13, 21; cf. 1QS VI, 4–5; 1QSa II, 17–21).[101] If Jesus were a peasant, or at least if he were a village dweller (as he doubtlessly was), then such historical peculiarities mean that he should perhaps be explained slightly differently from peasantry in a cross-cultural sense.[102]

Kautsky is sensitive to other possible exceptions and notes a Rodney Hilton article on peasantry in medieval Europe.[103] Hilton is perfectly aware of the numerous examples of leadership from outside the peasantry in medieval Europe but questions whether it entitles us to make it "a rule that peasant movements cannot throw up their own leadership."[104] Hilton claims that artisans were not far removed from the peasantry, not least village artisans, who were often tillers of the soil. Peasant families of varying degrees of socioeconomic status could occasionally provide members of the lower clergy. Hilton also notes occasions in medieval European social history where peasants were assumed to be leaders, although he does add that "the leading peasants were almost certainly drawn from the ranks of the village rich."[105] This may be helpful for those not keen on defining Jesus as a "peasant," although it should be recalled immediately that Crossan (following many others) would include artisans under the general term "peasant."[106] An interesting piece of evidence for Jesus being of a slightly different socioeconomic status to at least his immediate circle of followers is Mark 2:23–28. It has been argued that the disciples were following the Peah regulations for the poor as found in Leviticus 19:9 and 23:22. But it is noticeable that Jesus was not plucking grain. One explanation for this could be that the passage reflects the master's responsibility for disciples.[107] However—and this is not a mutually exclusive explanation—as Mark 2:23–28 may reflect the taking of Peah, the fact that Jesus does not pluck grain may well have been because "he was not poor enough to do so."[108]

But in some ways it may not matter whether or not Jesus is to be defined as a peasant, or at least not for present purposes, because there is another class that may structurally function as outsiders, namely the so-called priestly class. Lenski broadly expands what he calls the priestly class, usually drawn from the privileged leaders of organized religion—i.e., those who mediate between the divine and humanity—to include "monks, ministers, rabbis, imams and all other religious leaders whose livelihood and status in society were dependent primarily on their leadership role in the religious system." The function of the priestly class can vary from that of simple teachers with little power to those who control the official channels of salvation. They are, then, a very broad group who can be seen to serve and recruit either ends of the social spectrum. The priestly class could consequently be very dangerous.

On the one hand, they could contribute to the stability, legitimization, and continuation of the system of inequality, or, as Lenski put it, many members "were grasping, mercenary, self seeking, cruel, tyrannical, and exploitative."[109] On the other hand, they could also provide opposition to injustice and oppression and support the needs of the weaker elements of society, not least by preserving an ancient redistributive ethic.[110] Lenski significantly notes such principles deeply embedded in the Law and Prophets in the Jewish tradition and points out that the prophets, though not technically priests and very critical of the priestly class, were a part of his "priestly class" by being the basic transmitters of the divine concern for the oppressed.[111] Such a dangerous class with access to the divine would be ignored by the ruling class at their peril. And there should be no doubt that Jesus belonged to this class, particularly that more associated with the prophetic critique of social injustice.

DEATH TO THE RICH

That a concern for social justice in strands of the "priestly class" in Jewish traditions would have clashed with commercializing activity should be clear. Not only was the land of Israel ultimately God's, there is also profound concern for social justice massively attested in Jewish writings from the Bible to rabbinic literature.[112] This is all important and obviously relevant, but I want to focus on a closely related tradition available to Jesus that ties law and hostility to wealth together and one that is echoed throughout the Synoptic tradition. Jewish literature had developed a language of resistance against Gentile occupiers and their willing Jewish cohorts, and it was based on economic inequality. Given the evidence discussed above, this may partially reflect some of the harsher economic realities from the time of Jesus although some will no doubt reflect a pious, more aristocratic tradition (see below). Given the scriptural background, it was almost inevitable that a language of a future reversal of fortunes was going to be used by some Jews.[113] In fact, it is extremely well attested. It was already present in biblical tradition, and the Targumim further emphasize it (e.g., *Tg. Onq.* and *Tg. Ps.-J.* [Gen. 13:13]; *Tg.* [1 Sam 2:5]; *Tg. Isa.* [5:17; 27:10; 30:20; 33:4]; Obad. 17). Examples from *Targum Isaiah* highlight some of the key themes:

> And he shall deliver the wicked unto Gehinnam, and those that are rich in possessions which they have obtained by violence unto the death of destruction, that those who commit sin (חטאה) may not be established, nor speak deceits with their mouth. (*Tg. Isa.* [53:9])

> Then shall you see, and be lightened, and shall fear and your heart shall be enlarged for fear of sins [חטאין]: for the wealth of the west has been transferred to you, and the riches of the peoples shall be brought into your midst. (*Tg. Isa.* [60:5])

Between the Hebrew Bible and the Targumim, this language or role reversal of rich and poor was present at the time of Jesus. Judgment on the oppressive rich is a particularly common theme in *1 Enoch* 92–105 and appears to have some thematic overlap with the Gospel tradition.[114] In Jewish texts from the Second Temple period such sentiments were usually tied up with issues of law observance (or at least this was assumed) and oppression of (true) Israel by Gentile oppressors, general sinners, or indeed Jews perceived to be apostates:

> And there will be no spirit of error of Beliar any more, for he will be thrown into fire for ever. . . . And those that are in penury for the Lord's sake will be made rich and those who are in want will eat their fill and those who are weak will be made strong. . . . And so, my children, observe the whole of the law of the Lord, for there is hope for all who make straight their way. (*T. Jud.* 25:3–26:1)

> Rejoice, Zion, passionately! Shine with jubilation, Jerusalem! Exult, all the nations of Judah! Open your gate[s] continuously so that the wealth of the nations can be brought to you! Their kings shall wait on you, all your oppressors lie prone before you, the dust [of your feet they shall lick . . .] (1QM XII, 13–15)

> "And the poor shall possess the land and enjoy peace in plenty [Ps. 37:11]." Its interpretation concerns the congregation of the poor who will tough out the period of distress and will be rescued from all the snares of Belial. Afterwards, all who shall po[sse]ss the land will enjoy and grow fat with everything enjoy[able to] the flesh. [blank] "The wicked plots against the just person . . . [Ps. 37:12–13]." Its interpretation alludes to the ruthless ones of the covenant who are in the House of Judah, who plot to destroy those who observe the law, who are in the Community Council. (4Q171 II, 9–16; cf. 4Q169, 3, 4, I, 11–12)

> The princes of Judah are those upon whom the rage will be vented, for they hope to be healed but the defects stick (to them); all are rebels because they have not left the path of traitors and have defiled themselves in paths of licentiousness, and with wicked wealth, avenging themselves, and each one bearing resentment against his brother, and each one hating his fellow. Each one became obscured by blood relatives, and approached for debauchery and bragged about wealth and gain. Each one did what was right in his eyes and each one has chosen the stubbornness of his heart. They did not keep apart from the people and have rebelled with insolence, walking on the path of the wicked ones, about whom God says: "Their wine is serpents' venom and cruel poisons of asps." (CD VIII, 3–10)

As these passages show, there is more to criticisms of wealth than role reversal alone. These sentiments are tied up with the issues of covenant, law observance, and, ultimately, salvation. Wealth is therefore potentially very dangerous and can make a person no better than a Gentile. It should perhaps come as no surprise that wealth potentially or indeed inevitably leads to sin and wickedness:

> . . . if one is excessively rich, he sins [ἐὰν ὑπερπλεονάσῃ ὁ ἄνθρωπος, ἐξαμαρτάνει]. (*Ps. Sol.* 5:16).

> . . . Belial's three nets about which Levi, son of Jacob spoke, by which he catches Israel and makes them appear before them like three types of justice. The first is fornication; the second, wealth [ההון/הין]; the third, defilement of the Temple. He who eludes one is caught in another and he who is freed from that, is caught in another. (CD IV, 15–19; cf. 1QS XI, 1–2)

It should be clear that one of the specific sins to which wealth will lead is social injustice (cf. *T. Dan* 5:7; 4 Macc. 2:8), a major sin condemned in biblical thought. But it is also the case that one of the dangers of loving money is that it leads to one of the most roundly condemned sins: idolatry. Compare the *Testament of Judah*:

> I warn you, my children, not to be lovers of money nor to focus your attention on women's beauty, because it was her money and her beauty that led me astray to Bathshua the Canaanite. (*T. Jud.* 17:1)

> My children, the love of money is a sure path to idolatry, because, when led astray by money, men call gods those that are no gods, and it drives to distraction whoever is in its grip. For the sake of money I lost my children; and had I not repented and humbled myself, and had not my father Jacob prayed for me, I should have died childless . . . (*T. Jud.* 19:1–2)

It is clear from these traditions that wealth can too easily be tied up with all things associated with Gentiles and perceived apostates, that is, all things outside the law. It is also clear that observing the law is a key means to avoid going down this road. In this tradition, the law is the sort of thing a good Jew keeps in the face of Gentile and/or "apostate" oppression. This is a crucial point and one all too often overlooked in NT scholarship on Jesus and his criticisms of wealth. These are, after all, the sorts of beliefs available to a Galilean Jew in the 20s CE. The touch-paper almost invites a spark.

It has been argued, and with good reason, that much of the Jewish material on the hostility to wealth reflects less socioeconomic hardships and more pious religious ethical wisdom often associated with the better off in society (e.g., Sir. 13:3–24).[115] This is another reason that it was necessary to discuss the socioeconomic context of commercialization and the rise of banditry. The importance of banditry "is not the purity of its motivations against the rich nor the magnanimity of its benefactions to the poor"[116] but the very existence of stark socioeconomic violence. The issue of banditry in first-century Palestine shows that the cultural context for a vicious verbal attack on the rich was not confined to what may be idealized theology in the literary traditions of the period. We also saw that there was some overlap between bandits and prophets, royal figures, messiahs, and so forth. Given the immediate socioeconomic context of Galilee at the time of Jesus, given that Jesus was regarded as a prophet, and given that Jesus was well versed in his scriptural heritage, we may legitimately bring together these contexts to sharpen the focus on Jesus' teaching on wealth in relation to the law. It is some key Gospel passages on these themes that we must now analyze.

JESUS, THE LAW, AND THE DAMNED RICH

> Commentators have found it difficult to stomach the idea that the rich man suffers just because he has been rich, while Lazarus is compensated simply for having been poor.[117]

As I have argued elsewhere, and will keep stressing, the historical Jesus was a law-observant Jew.[118] I think this point can now be developed further. I would suggest that Jesus' concern to uphold the law, like that of other Jews, was in part a reaction to the perception of Gentile/Roman-endorsed wealth and exploitation, alongside a reaction to the commercialization of Jesus' Galilean surroundings. This comes out in several passages in the Synoptic tradition, particularly when viewed as a whole. These passages must now be discussed in more detail.

In a recent article, which I now summarize, I argued that Mark 10:17–31 is an important passage that stresses the importance of the commandments and their relationship to a concern for social justice, a view rooted in Scripture.[119] Such concerns are quite explicit in the opening of the passage (Mark 10:17–22) where the rich man has observed the listed commandments but needs to supplement this by selling his properties, giving the proceeds to the poor, and following Jesus: like the conclusion to Rich Man and Lazarus (Luke 16:31), Torah must be observed and understood in the light of social justice. What is particularly noticeable is the prohibition of defrauding (μὴ ἀποστερήσῃς) among the commandments (10:19). This phrase is famously not in the Decalogue (cf. Exod. 20:17 par. Deut. 5:21) and, like the underlying Semitic words, has strong implications of not withholding workers' wages and not engaging in economic exploitation (see, e.g., Deut. 24:14–15; Mal. 3:5; Sir. 4:1; 1Qap Gen^ar [20:11]; *Tg. Onq.* [Lev. 5:21]; *Tg. Ps.-J.* [Lev. 5:23]; *Tg. Neof.* and *Tg. Ps-J.* [Deut. 24:14]; *Tg.* [Mal. 3:5]; *Lev. Rab.* 12.1; *Pesh.* [Mark 10:19]; Pesh. [Deut. 24:14–15]; Pesh. [Mal. 3:5]). Given the socioeconomic background just outlined, even if we cannot be precise, the reason for this change is to suit a rich person who had properties. Yet in the Markan passage the rich man had not even done what many rich people were deemed all too able to do: oppress and/or take advantage of and/or deny wages. Given that this rich man had observed the commandments, surely he was being rewarded through his "many [landed] possessions" (10:22)! But this view of reward theology is rejected by Jesus, so we get a powerful rejection of wealth as reward in Mark 10:23–25, a reversal of fortunes which causes amazement among the disciples (Mark 10:26).

Although Mark 10:27 may seem to modern readers to downplay the radical teaching on wealth, it certainly did not to earlier readers, as the textual variants of other verses in the passage show (Mark 10:24–25). Indeed, to see 10:27 as qualifying a tough saying is misleading. It would run contrary to Peter's words in 10:28 and Jesus' response in 10:29–31. The answer to the problem is to be found elsewhere, namely, reward theology. There was of course a long tradition of observing the commandments leading to a prosperous life down here on earth (e.g., Deut. 28:1–14; Job 1:10; 42:10; Isa. 3:10; Prov. 10:22; Tob. 12:9; Sir. 3:1, 6; 25:7–11; 35:13; 44:10–15; 51:27–30; Bar. 4:1). With such an authoritative tradition of wealth theologically justified, a view that subverts this idea by saying the wealthy are as good as damned would have the potential to hit hard and cause puzzlement among Jesus' followers.

But was it *that* subversive really? That is a matter of perspective, for there is another tradition of the virtual equating of wealth with wickedness as noted above (see, e.g., CD IV, 15–19; 1QS XI, 1–2; *Ps. Sol.* 5:16), which is clear elsewhere in the Gospel tradition. You cannot serve God and Mammon (Luke 16:13 par. Matt. 6:24). But the biblical tradition of earthly reward was too strong to be simply ignored, and there are Jewish polemics against people who think they are blessed with riches (*1 En.* 96:4; 103:5–8); hence there were doubts attributed to Peter and the disciples. Jesus or his first interpreters never thought that here was a rejection of the *principle* of reward and punishment. Reward and punishment were in fact reapplied to the eschatological future (cf. Mark 10:29–31), a view of course echoed elsewhere in Jewish literature (e.g., Dan. 12; 2 Macc. 7; *1 En.* 92–105). The eye of the needle saying (Mark 10:25) should be taken as strongly as possible: it is *impossible* for the rich to enter the kingdom. The obvious must not be avoided: in a world of extreme social and economic inequality Jesus damned the rich. The Torah must be understood in the light of this for Jesus.

Major issues that come out of Mark 10:17–31 are the virtual equation of wealth/landowner with economic oppression, the reversal of rich and poor in the life to come, the extension of reward theology to include the life to come, and the interpretation of the Torah from the perspective of the economically poor. These are key aspects of the teachings of the historical Jesus as attested across the Synoptic tradition, so even if there are secondary elements in and different sources behind Mark 10:17–31, we are probably dealing with a *theme* close to the historical Jesus' heart (e.g., Matt. 6:24 par. Luke 16:13; Luke 14:16–24 par. Matt. 22:1–14; Luke 12:13–21; Luke 16:19–31).[120] It is hardly a coincidence that this approach to the Torah emerges at the same time as notable socioeconomic change. And Jesus got a lot more graphic than the views remembered in Mark 10:17–31.

Luke is famously concerned with issues surrounding almsgiving, wealth, and poverty. Consequently he retains some of the most-famous and most-important traditions, notably in Luke 16. One of the most devastating attacks on wealth is Luke 16:19–31, the parable of the Rich Man and Lazarus, a parable that generally echoes (and no more than that) broader folkloristic motifs in Jewish, Egyptian, and Greco-Roman literature.[121] In this passage, the rich and poor are, quite clearly, absolute opposites. The rich man dressed in purple (cf. Prov. 31:22), which can be a color associated with wealth, royalty, (sometimes oppressive) power (Judg. 8:26; Esth. 8:15; 1 Macc. 8:14; 1Qap Gen[ar] (20:31); *1 En.* 98:2; Rev. 18:12), and fine clothing. Crucially, in noticeable contrast to the needs in the Lord's Prayer, the rich man ate very, very well (cf. Jas. 5:5). In fact the rich man is as good a symbolic representative of the beneficiaries of commercialism in 20s Galilee as could be asked for, just as Lazarus is of the victims. In contrast to the nameless rich man, the poor man Lazarus lay at the rich man's gate, hungry and sore. Even the unclean dog licked his sores (cf. Lev. 11:27). He even had to eat the food that fell from the rich man's table. In fact he is as good a symbolic representative of the lowest in the social scale, the expendables, as could be hoped for.[122]

The contrast could not be starker: these people are at the complete opposite ends of the social scale. So, it should be obvious: the rich man has got exactly what he deserves. Not the wealth he might think he deserves, but fire-induced pain in Hades, which a writer such as that of *1 En.* 92–105 also thinks he deserves. Lazarus too got exactly what was coming to him: he would get what he could never get in his natural life. The role reversal could not be made clearer nor the reasons blunter. There is no attack on the misuse of wealth, on unfairly gained wealth, on neglecting charity, or on any specific immoral behavior, nor is there emphasis on Lazarus being particularly pious.[123] None of these reasons are assumed and are neither implicit nor explicit in the text. The only reason is given by Abraham in answer to the rich man: "Child, remember that during your lifetime you received your good things, and Lazarus in like manner evil things; but now he is comforted here, and you are in agony" (Luke 16:25). Now the rich man was dependent on the whims of Lazarus. The rich man realizes what he has done wrong and needs to warn his brothers. But it should, of course, be perfectly clear why the rich burnt so: the

Torah and Prophets say so! Of course this was not obvious to all, and so Abraham, one of the greatest possible authorities, has to make it clear in the parable. Scripture *must* be interpreted through the eyes of the exploited poor.

The general thrust of this passage quite obviously critiques the idea of wealth as a sign of divine favor, and there are further specific indications. Lazarus's condition on earth reflects what might be regarded as divine punishment: "covered with sores [εἱλκωμένος] . . . even the dogs would come and lick his sores [τὰ ἕλκη αὐτοῦ]" (Luke 16:20–21). Compare the similar use of language in one of the punishments inflicted on Pharaoh's Egypt:

> So they took soot from the kiln, and stood before Pharaoh, and Moses threw it in the air, and it caused festering boils [ἕλκη/שְׁחִין] on humans and animals. The magicians could not stand before Moses because of the boils [τὰ ἕλκη/הַשְּׁחִין], for the boils [τὰ ἕλκη/הַשְּׁחִין] afflicted the magicians as well as the Egyptians. (Exod. 9:10–11; cf. Deut. 28:35; Rev. 16:2)[124]

Note also the rich man received proper burial in contrast to Lazarus, who, we are told, was carried off by angels (Luke 16:22). There is no mention that Lazarus had a burial. In the well-known Jewish folkloristic parallel to the story of the rich man and Lazarus, the Torah scholar of Ashqelon "was not properly mourned," due to one minor error, in contrast to the tax collector bar Maayan, for whom "the whole town took time off to mourn," which was his reward for once being nice to the poor (*y. Sanh.* 6:23c; *y. Hag.* 2:77d). While there is no evidence of such reasoning in the case of Lazarus, the polarized contrast in the rabbinic story and the Gospel parable suggests that the lack of a burial may have been in mind in Luke 16:22. A lack of a burial too was seen as a sign of punishment or disfavor by some (Jer. 7:33; 22:19; Ezek. 29:5; *1 En.* 98:13; Josephus, *J.W.* 4.317, 331–32, 359–60, 381–82). The example of Deuteronomy 28:15, 25–27, 35, which immediately follows a major passage on the prosperity as a sign of proper behavior (Deut. 28:1–14), has a lack of a burial alongside the punishment of boils:

> But if you will not obey the LORD your God by diligently observing all his commandments and decrees, which I am commanding you today, then all these curses shall come upon you and overtake you: . . . The LORD will cause you to be defeated before your enemies; you shall go out against them one way and flee before them seven ways. You shall become an object of horror to all the kingdoms of the earth. Your corpses shall be food for every bird of the air and animal of the earth, and there shall be no one to frighten them away. The LORD will afflict you with the boils of Egypt [בִּשְׁחִין מִצְרַיִם/ἐν ἕλκει Αἰγυπτίῳ], with ulcers, scurvy, and itch, of which you cannot be healed. . . . The LORD will strike you on the knees and on the legs with grievous boils

[בשחין רע/ἐν ἕλκει πονηρῷ] of which you cannot be healed, from the sole of your foot to the crown of your head.

On the other hand, burial was, as is well known, what a good person should receive (e.g., Deut. 29:26; Jer. 8:1–2; 16:1–4; Ezek. 29:5; Tob. 1:16–2:10; Josephus, *Ag. Ap.* 2.211).[125] But lest we forget that Jesus was not the only Jew advocating seemingly subversive beliefs, recall the warning of *1 En.* 103:5–6 quoted above.

Given what we have already discussed about Jesus' views on wealth, the story of the Rich Man and Lazarus makes excellent sense in the context of Jesus' teaching. But it also makes excellent sense in the context of Lukan theology,[126] although it lacks a great deal of Lukan vocabulary.[127] One reason sometimes given against its historicity is the conclusion:

> Abraham replied, "They have Moses and the prophets; they should listen to them." He [the rich man] said, "No, father Abraham; but if someone goes to them from the dead, they will repent [μετανοήσουσιν]." He said to him, "If they do not listen to Moses and the prophets, neither will they be convinced even if someone rises from the dead." (Luke 16:29–31)

The Jesus Seminar labels Luke 16:29–31 "black" (i.e., "Jesus did not say this; it represents the perspective or content of a later or different tradition"[128]), commenting,

> The second part of this story (vv. 27–31) concerns the characteristic early Christian theme of the Judean lack of belief in the resurrection of Jesus. The concluding line (v. 31) seems clearly to refer to Jesus, and the testimony of Moses and the prophets is appealed to in vv. 29 and 31 in the same way Luke does in the later resurrection story in 24:27, 44. Over 90 percent of the Fellows of the Seminar were persuaded by this evidence to vote this part black.[129]

However, what is particularly noticeable is that not only is there absolutely no mention of "the Judean lack of belief in the resurrection of Jesus" in the parable, the person coming back from the dead is *not* in fact Jesus but Lazarus! It is an answer to the rich man's request: "Father, I beg you to send him to my father's house—for I have five brothers—that he may warn them, so that they will not also come into this place of torment" (Luke 16:28). As Bauckham shows, this should be read in the general context of sending someone back from the afterlife to warn someone living (cf. 1 Sam. 28:7–20; *Eccl. Rab.* 9:10.1–2).[130] This is supported by the notable textual variant in 16:31: instead of ἀναστῇ, which is most likely to be used of a more physical resurrection, απελθη is used. Moreover, in 16:30–31 εγερθη, which again would point to a raising from the dead, is found in P^{75} as an alternative. As both ἀναστῇ and ἐγερθῇ suggest an attempt to bring the sentiment in line with christological convictions, it looks as if the earliest version would have included ἀπελθῇ and an emphasis on sending back as a more temporary visit in (say) a dream or vision, as we get in the Jewish and pagan parallels.[131]

As for appeal to Moses and Prophets, it is worth noting that this is also part of pre-Lukan tradition (e.g., Matt. 11:13 par. Luke 16:16; Mark 9:4). We should also note another important aspect of Jewish culture here, namely, repentance (μετανοήσουσιν). Repentance is most frequently tied up with Jews (and very, very rarely Gentiles) returning to God and practicing the law in Jewish literature,[132] and here we have the same emphasis of a Jew being told to return to the law with the additional bonus of it being tied in with the definitely pre-Lukan early tradition of choosing between wealth and God. This is hardly the creation of a church with concerns for Gentiles. Crucially we now have a detailed independent attestation of Jesus' Torah hermeneutic of the exploited poor and at the very least the parable of the Rich Man and Lazarus is essentially pre-Lukan. Moreover, collectively the above arguments on the parable of the Rich Man and Lazarus would suggest that it is surely close to the teaching of the historical Jesus.

Various other sayings and traditions that point in the direction of a reversal of rich and poor suggest a context of reward theology even if the Torah is not explicitly mentioned. The stark choice involved with wealth is unambiguously repeated in the famous Q saying on the choice between loving God and mammon (Matt. 6:24 par. Luke 16:13). In the economic context outlined above, this choice was between supporting the commercial and exploitative might of Roman-backed power or the will of God. To love God is a manifestation of Jewish identity and is grounded of course in the Torah. When Jesus was asked about the greatest commandment he gave a standard answer in terms of Jewish law, namely, loving God, followed by loving your neighbor (Mark 12:28–34).[133] This was a known Jewish view. The idea that love of mammon rather than God leads a Jew away from the path of the law is a view echoed, for example, in the *T. Jud.* 18:2–6. Then of course there are other general themes denoting the stark difference between rich and poor, as found in the Beatitudes coupled with the Lukan woes (Matt. 5:3–12; Luke 6:20–26) and the parable of the Great Banquet (Luke 14:12–24; Matt. 22:1–14; cf. *Thom.* 64), for example.

Luke 16 contains other polemics against wealth, and there is some evidence that Jesus' rejection of this worldly reward theology may have caused controversy within Judaism. Luke 16:14–15, which comes after some strong attacks on wealth, has the following: "The Pharisees, who were lovers of money, heard all this, and they ridiculed him. So he said to them, 'You are those who justify yourselves in the sight of others; but God knows your hearts; for what is prized by human beings is an abomination in the sight of God.'" First, Luke's claim that the Pharisees were lovers of money is editorial and obviously polemical. Any statement like this from a rival group should automatically arouse suspicion as to its concrete accuracy. Actually there is evidence that there would have been Pharisees who agreed with Jesus' sentiments. Hillel and Shammai, for example, were remembered for their lack of concern for wealth. Compare also the following: "He [Hillel] would say, 'Lots of meat, lots of worms; lots of property, lots of worries; lots of women, lots of witchcraft; lots of slave girls, lots of lust; lots of slave boys, lots of robbery" (m. 'Abot 2.7). However, it does look as if someone has indeed ridiculed the teaching of Jesus in Luke 16:14–15. And the reasons for this ridicule? Well, these may be deduced from Jesus' reply: "You are those who justify yourselves in the sight of others . . . what is prized by human beings is an abomination in the sight of God." This is exactly what the basic form of reward theology entails: visible rewards on planet earth. It is not difficult to see someone having difficulty with that.

It is quite explicit in certain biblical texts that God himself advocates an earthly reward theology, even if this was to be reinterpreted by certain Jews. It was also a view that would have been accepted by some Pharisees, hence comments such as the following that may echo such a viewpoint: "When R. Elazar b. Azariah died wealth [העושר] departed from the Sages" (m. Sotah 9.15). If Jesus was perceived to be rejecting biblical thought, even if Jesus and other Jews thought the opposite, then surely there would be some complaints. This dispute may not go back to the historical Jesus, and it could easily be attributed to a Lukan hand, but it does show the potential for a dispute in Jesus' ministry because it suggests that someone somewhere had a problem with Jesus' teaching. Moreover, while I remain agnostic on the issue of the historicity of this dispute, there is nothing implausible about Jesus and the Pharisees engaging in fierce polemic over interpretation of Scripture.[134] But there is something deeply worrying about taking such polemic as literal truth by readers, ancient or modern.

Jesus' attack on wealth reaches a dramatic climax in the incident often referred to as the "Cleansing of the Temple." The work of Craig A. Evans in particular has shown that the theme of perceived financial corruption was behind Jesus' action in the Temple.[135] I have developed this important work and stressed that it is also grounded in a concern to observe the law, such as allowing the poor to offer sacrifices, and that for such a perceived neglect Jesus predicted destruction on the Temple.[136] What was at stake was the correct interpretation of the law and for Jesus and some of the earliest Christians the Temple had to be destroyed because of a perceived failure to observe the law. In Jewish thought, the destruction of both the first and second temples was consistently interpreted as a result of nonobservance of the commandments.

Jesus fits neatly into this tradition. As we will see, one of the major transgressions that led to the destruction of the first Temple was said to be idolatry, and this was often tied in with exploitation of the poor. This has some relevance for present purposes. Earlier in this chapter, I noted that wealth could lead not only to social injustice but also to idolatry. Wealth leading to social injustice is clearly the dominant reason for the destruction of the Temple, according to Mark 11:15–17, but idolatry may also be another reason. Idolatry as an issue in the cleansing of the Temple is an unusual interpretation, so before we come to its implications for the historical Jesus, this idea needs to be discussed.

There are examples of Jesus referring to idolatry being practiced by the Temple authorities. In Mark 14:58 the false witnesses claimed that Jesus had said he would destroy the present Temple "made with hands [τὸν χειροποίη-τον]" and replace it with one not made with hands. In the LXX, χειροποίητος is most frequently associated with idolatry. Jesus' turning over the money changers' tables may also be significant, as the coinage used was the Tyrian shekel, with the image of Melkart. There is also evidence of a degree of unease with the Herodian Temple and its links with idolatry. The golden eagle erected over the Temple gate in Herod the Great's rebuilding outraged the two Torah experts Judas and Matthias, enough for them to encourage their followers to tear it down (Josephus, *J.W.* 1.648–55; *Ant.* 17.149–68). More broadly, it might be worth noting that Pilate appears to have been allowed to bring standards into Jerusalem (Josephus, *Ant.* 18.55–59; *J.W.* 2.169–74; cf. Philo, *Legat.* 299–305) because, as we will see, destruction of the Temple was intimately linked with destruction of the city.

It is significant that the allegation of the Temple being "made with hands" is also attributed to Stephen, one of the earliest Christians, according to Acts 7:48. To what extent this is a tradition independent of Jesus' trial is difficult to assess, but the association with idolatry is presumably present. I have argued elsewhere that Stephen's speech accuses the Temple authorities of not observing the commandments as they should have done and so the Temple must be destroyed. As Peter Doble has shown, warnings of such things are clearly present in the scriptural background to Stephen's speech (e.g., Isa. 66; 1 Kgs. 8 par. 2 Chron. 6–7; Ps. 132[131]).[137] Indeed one of the crucial texts includes powerful warnings against idolatry in the context of Solomon's dedication of the Temple (e.g., 2 Chron. 7:19–22). This crucial role of the scriptural background can also be developed further in relation to present purposes. There are possible scriptural allusions to idolatry found in the Gospel accounts (Mark 11:17; Jer. 7:11). The famous Jeremiah 7 speech in the Temple does of course mention a multitude of sins before condemning the Temple as a robber's den: stealing, murder, adultery, swearing falsely, and of course offerings to Baal and going "after other gods that you have not known" (Jer. 7:9).

Indeed, Jesus' predictions of the destruction of Jerusalem and the Temple elsewhere in the Gospel tradition also suggest a concern for idolatry. In Luke 13:33–35, packed with biblical allusions, Jesus laments over the present and future of Jerusalem. Jerusalem, says the Lukan Jesus, is the city that kills the prophets and stones (λιθοβολοῦσα) those who are sent to it (Luke 13:34). Although the killing of the prophets and stoning those sent by God was not a major theme in the Jewish Scriptures, it is present. In 2 Chronicles 24:20–21 Zechariah son of the priest Jehoiada was stoned (ἐλιθοβόλησαν) to death "by the command of the king . . . in the house of the LORD." And why? Because Zechariah criticized the people for transgressing the commandments. More specifically, after the death of Jehoiada, people had abandoned "the house of the LORD," abandoned God, and starting worshiping idols, for which "wrath came upon Judah and Jerusalem for this guilt of theirs" (24:18). Prophets were sent; no one listened (24:19). Then came Zechariah. This death and general sinning was not to go unpunished. God sent the army of Aram against King Joash. They "destroyed all the officials of the people . . . and sent all the booty they took to the king of Damascus" (24:23). The message is clear: judgment and destruction occurred "because they had abandoned the LORD, the God of their ancestors" (24:24). And this abandonment includes killing a prophet and worshiping idols.

There are other possible allusions lurking in the background. According to Jeremiah 20:1–2 (cf. 38:6) Jeremiah was struck and put in stocks in the Temple by the priest Pashhur son of Immer, "the chief officer in the house of the LORD," because Jeremiah had been prophesying destruction on Judah and Jerusalem. The people "have stiffened their necks" refusing to hear God's words (Jer. 19:15). But just as the potter's earthenware jug is smashed, so too Judah and Jerusalem (Jer. 19). This disaster has to take place because the people abandoned the God of Israel. They made offerings to other gods, they have shed the blood of the innocent, and they have continued building the high places of Baal for child sacrifices (19:4–5). Again, the message is crystal clear.

Second Chronicles 36 catalogs what are regarded as evil kings reigning in Jerusalem before the destruction of city and Temple. They had their chances as 2 Chronicles 36:15–16, another possible allusion, makes perfectly clear. God persistently sent them his messengers "because he had compassion on his people and on his dwelling place." Yet, the chronicler continues, messengers and prophets were mocked and despised, "until the wrath of the LORD against his people became so great that there was no remedy." The acts of one of these kings, Zedekiah, the last in the list (2 Chron. 36:11–14), include general evil and not humbling himself before God's prophet Jeremiah. The leading priests and the people do not get off lightly either. They are guilty of "following all the abominations [βδελυγμάτων] of the nations; and they polluted the house of the LORD that he had consecrated in Jerusalem." These are among the specific reasons as to why Jerusalem and the Temple had to be destroyed and the people taken into exile (2 Chron. 36:17–21). Again, idolatry and related practices play a major role.

As is well known, gory traditions concerning the deaths of the prophets were elaborated and embellished (e.g., *Mart. Isa.*; *Liv. Proph.*). According to *Mart. Isa.* 5:1–14 Jeremiah was sawn in half for his opposition to Manasseh. Manasseh's sins included an increase in sorcery, augury, divination, fornication, and adultery, and we are told of his acts recorded in the book of the kings of Judah and Israel (*Mart. Isa.* 2:5–6; cf. 2 Kgs. 21:17 and 2 Chron. 33:18), which of course recalls a variety of almost comically bad idolatrous actions (2 Kgs. 21:1–16; 33:1–17). *The Lives of the Prophets* gives details of various prophets more often than not martyred at the hands of a wicked ruler. The example of Ezekiel is worth noting:

> This man from the land of Arira, of the priests, and he died in the land of the Chaldeans during the captivity, after having prophesied many things to those in Judah. The ruler of the people Israel killed him there as he was being reproved by him concerning the worship of idols. (*Liv. Proph.* 3:1–2)

These particular traditions are of some significance because they are postscriptural retellings. Clearly fear of idolatry, real or not, remained.

In Luke 13:34, Jesus longs for the well-being of the Jerusalemites, illustrated by the image of a hen gathering her brood under her wings (Luke 13:34b). There may well be an allusion to Deuteronomy 32:11–12, from the Song of Moses.[138] God guided Israel/Jacob and "no foreign god was with him," just like an eagle hovering over its young "as it spreads its wings, takes them up, and bears them aloft on its pinions." The song continues by recalling the blessings provided by God (32:13–14); yet, as ever, there is another more sinister side: "Jeshurun grew fat, and kicked. You grew fat, bloated, and gorged!" The story changes and speaks of abandoning God, worshiping strange gods, sacrificing to demons and unknown deities (32:15–18). This, predictably enough, displeased God (32:19ff.) who does not like to be provoked by idols (32:21). Thus disaster, devastation, and destruction will come upon Israel (32:22–27).

Disaster, devastation, and destruction become more explicit in Luke 13:35 (par. Matt. 23:38): "See, your house is left to you." It appears that there are allusions to Jeremiah 12:7 and 22:5.[139] Jeremiah 12:7 says, "I have forsaken my house" and the reasons are because of general wickedness and oppression (cf. 12:1–6, 8ff.). Jeremiah 22:5 says, "This house shall become a desolation [ἐρήμωσιν]"[140] if the people of Judah do not heed the words of God's messenger. This means acting with justice; dealing with the oppressor; protecting the oppressed; caring for the stranger, the orphan, and the widow; and not shedding innocent blood (22:1–4). Do this and live. Do not and destruction will come on Jerusalem. Nations will then pass by, asking, "Why?" The answer will be bluntly simple: "Because they abandoned the covenant of the LORD their God, and worshiped other gods and served them" (22:9). So idolatry is again immersed in the background, this time coupled with a heavy emphasis on social justice.

But it was widely believed that the first Temple was destroyed partly because of idolatry, so it could be coincidental that it occurs in the teachings of Jesus. Compare also the following from the Tosefta on the reasons for the fall of the Second Temple, which clearly puts idolatry aside in its scathing criticisms:

> Said R. Yohanan b. Torta, ". . . As to Jerusalem's first building, on what account was it destroyed? Because of idolatry and licentiousness and bloodshed which was in it. But [as to] the latter [building] we know that they devoted themselves to Torah and were meticulous about tithes. On what account did they go into exile? Because they love money and hate one another. This teaches you that hatred for one another is evil before the Omnipresent, and Scripture deems it equivalent to idolatry, licentiousness, and bloodshed. (t. Menaḥ. 13:22)

Note, however, the assumption of the magnitude of the sin of idolatry: it is something that is to be expected if the Temple is destroyed, and, according to this view, there is a degree of puzzlement as to why it was not involved. The early Christian tradition (Mark 14:58; Acts 7:48) does not appear so puzzled over the expectation of idolatry in the reasoning for the fall of the Temple, so the scriptural allusions to idolatry in the Gospel tradition take on greater force—not least when coupled with the unease concerning Herodian association with things idolatrous. There are of course historical problems with Mark 14:58: it is mentioned in the trial scene, which has not only historical difficulties of its own but also the problem of the allegations being placed on the lips of false witnesses. That said, as this allegation of a Temple made with hands is certainly present in earliest Christianity and placed on the lips of the Christian Stephen and as allegations of corrupt wealth are found in comments and actions concerning the destruction of the Temple (both from Jesus and other Jews), it is quite possible that the early Christian view might have arisen from the view that wealth leads to sins such as idolatry. Indeed, reference to idolatry in relation to hostility to wealth can occur outside the Temple passages. Compare Jesus' response to Pharisees over the issue of wealth in Luke 16:15, which uses βδέλυγμα, a word frequently associated with idolatry:[141] "For what is prized by human beings is an abomination [βδέλυγμα] in the sight of God."

Irrespective of whether the theme of wealth leading to idolatry was associated with the Temple by the historical Jesus, it remains that there is a strong argument of collective weight in favor of the themes of wealth leading to sin, hostility to wealth, and the reversal of rich and poor in association with the Torah and salvation going back to the historical Jesus. Individual passages bear strong traits of authenticity, and the theme is independently attested in different forms. Moreover, they are extremely plausible in a first-century Jewish context. Not only are all views advocated by Jesus reflected in Jewish literature, but they make excellent sense in the socioeconomic context of Galilee in the twenties. Some of the ideas I have attributed to Jesus may not all be so explicit in individual passages, but it is when they are discussed collectively that it may be seen how clearly present they actually are.

One final point: it seems that Jesus' sayings on the hostility to wealth are to be taken literally in the contexts in which they were delivered, and in some cases it appears that Jesus and/or his disciples have little if any money (e.g., Mark 2:23–28; Luke 14:33; Matt. 8:20 par. Luke 9:58); however, there are passages that refer to financial support of the Jesus movement (e.g., Mark 15:41; Luke 8:2–3) including, presumably, women who were not so poor (cf. Luke 8:3; Mark 14:3–9). Given that this tradition can stand alongside the tradition of hostility to wealth without any indication that they were contradictory, it is possible that they could both plausibly go back to the lifetime of the historical Jesus. Here are the seeds of the later watering down of Jesus' tricky sayings through emphasizing the correct use of wealth. This may have been one of the reasons why Christianity did not die out: if it did begin essentially as a movement of peasant resistance (whatever we make of Jesus' "class") then it would probably have needed the support of such outsiders. We might compare Kautsky once more on this point: "It appears that all peasant revolts that spread beyond local confines in societies undergoing commercialization or modernization from without did so under nonpeasant leadership or in alliance with nonpeasant movements."[142]

CONCLUSIONS

So, the socioeconomic conditions of first-century Palestine and Galilee in the 20s helped shape the content of Jesus' teaching on the law, particularly the aggressive attitude towards the rich. Given the general reaction to Roman and Roman-influenced Palestine in the form of bandits, prophets, messiahs, and so forth, and given that this shaped people's views of the Torah, we might expect some kind of reaction in the teaching of Jesus. Moreover, given the urbanization of Galilee at the time of Jesus, we must surely posit this as a key reason for the emergence of the Jesus movement and expect its impact to leave traces in his teaching. It certainly does this. For Jesus, following a long tradition, the law was to be interpreted in the light of the poor. But there was a darker side: the rich, openly Torah-observant or not, would suffer. And where bandits were partial to violent retribution on the rich, Jesus the eschatological prophet would leave that piece of dirty work to God. So much for the content of Jesus' teaching; to help explain the spread of earliest Christianity beyond Jews to Gentiles, we need to look at the crucial related issue of the people at whom Jesus aimed his teaching and how the approach to the law discussed here tied in with the needs of his audience: chapter 3, in other words.

3

Jesus and the Sinners

As we have just seen, Jesus' teaching on wealth was, naturally enough, aimed at people deemed rich, and there are significant hints that Jesus thought poor people would have fewer problems entering the kingdom and ultimately avoiding the vicious prodding of devilish pitchforks. If this is so, we might expect a significant concern for the repentance of the wealthy in Jesus' missionary practice. The most obvious place to look here, as countless scholars have indeed done, is Jesus' association with people labeled "the sinners," something that clearly riled his opponents, according to the Synoptic tradition.[1] E. P. Sanders, reacting vigorously against any suggestion that the sinners were something like (the) hoi polloi, polemically stressed that it is not just a question of "Jesus . . . the champion of plain folk against an intolerable bunch of bigots" and pointed out that "it trivializes Jesus, to understand the issue of 'Jesus and the sinners' as if it were 'Jesus and the common people versus the narrow, bigoted but dominant Pharisees.'"[2] Sanders added that while "the inclusion of the common people under the term 'sinners' is not correct" it "still seems that the erroneous view is popular enough, and is contained in sufficiently important books." Thus he felt obliged to provide another definition of "the sinners" that has since become controversial:

> There should be no confusion about the basic meaning of the term "sinners" in the Gospels. The word in English versions of the Bible translates the Greek word *hamartōloi*. Behind *hamartōloi* stands, almost beyond question, the Hebrew word *resha'im* (or the Aramaic equivalent). The Semitic languages have other words which are used in parallel with *resha'im*, but it is the dominant term. *Resha'im* is virtually a technical term. It is best translated "the wicked," and it refers to those who sinned wilfully and heinously and who did not repent . . . the term

75

would include professional sinners, such as usurers, who in their daily
business transgressed Lev. 25.36–38. . . . The clear implication of this
passage [Lev. 25:36–38] is that those who renounce the commandment
not to charge interest also renounce the Lord God, who brought them
out of the land of Egypt: they renounced the covenant. These are, in
later Jewish terminology, "the wicked." . . . There is every reason to
think that this understanding of the "wicked" prevailed also before 70.
How can one read the biblical passage and not see the point?[3]

This is an important definition in that it helps to show that it is extremely difficult to see the sinners as the common folk. It is, I think, along the right lines,
but it needs some significant qualification. Sanders provides only a small sample of texts to support his view and does not discuss Aramaic texts, something
we must do given that it was the language in which Jesus spoke. There are also
problems with Sanders's view of repentance and conflict in the Synoptic tradition. So to test Sanders's approach is absolutely necessary and requires a
more detailed analysis of the relevant words.

"SINNERS" FROM THE BIBLE
TO RABBINIC LITERATURE

As Sanders points out the LXX, ἁμαρτωλός usually translates some form of
רשע, and usually this is in the Psalms. It is very general in many instances, carrying the sense of "wicked," and it can of course be used for people who act as
if there is no God: "The wicked [רשע/ὁ ἁμαρτωλός] say, 'God will not seek it
out'; all their thoughts are, 'There is no God'" (Pss. 9:25 [10:4]; 57[58]:3–5).
The wicked are frequently said to be the opposite of "the righteous [צדיק/
ὁ δίκαιος]."[4] So, for example, "The wicked [רשע/ὁ ἁμαρτωλός] borrow and
do not pay back, but the righteous [צדיק/ὁ δίκαιος] are generous and keep giving' (Ps. 36[37]:21). It appears that sinners are effectively outside the covenant
and were no doubt understood, not least in the first century, as lawbreakers
(Ps. 49[50]:16–23; see also 93[94]:13; Ezek. 33:8, 19), which can also include
reference to purity and the cult (e.g., Prov. 15:8; Dan. 12:10). This tradition
of the wicked as lawbreakers reaches its nadir in Psalm 119:118 (119): "All the
wicked of the earth [בל־רשעי־ארץ/πάντας τοὺς ἁμαρτωλοὺς τῆς γῆς] you
count as dross; therefore I love your decrees" (see also Ps. 119:53, 61, 95, 110,
155). As part of their lawbreaking behavior they were violent, oppressive, and
exploitative rich people, a crucial usage that is important for understanding the
social status associated with the term "sinners":

> For I was envious of the arrogant;
>   I saw the prosperity of the wicked [רשעים/ἁμαρτωλῶν].

For they have no pain;
   their bodies are sound and sleek.
They are not in trouble as others are;
   they are not plagued like other people.
Therefore pride is their necklace;
   violence covers them like a garment.
Their eyes swell out with fatness;
   their hearts overflow with follies.
They scoff and speak with malice;
   loftily they threaten oppression.
They set their mouths against heaven,
   and their tongues range over the earth.
. . . .
Such are the wicked [רשעים/ἁμαρτωλοί];
   always at ease, they increase in riches. (Ps. 72[73]:3–9, 12; see also
   Pss. 9:24 [10:3]; 9:17–18; 36[37]:21; 72[73]:3–12; 81[82]:2, 4;
   93[94]:3–5; 111[112]:10).[5]

If the wicked were oppressive and prosperous lawbreakers who were effectively outside the covenant, then it naturally follows that these individuals were behaving like Gentiles or the nations, hence several passages similar to the following: "The wicked [רשעים/οἱ ἁμαρτωλοί] shall depart to Sheol, all the nations that forget God" (Ps. 9:17; see also Pss. 9:15–16; 9:36 [10:15]; 83[84]:10). Inevitably, the wicked will be punished, a refrain that pounds like a death knell throughout the Psalms and well beyond: "Wait for the LORD, and keep to his way, and he will exalt you to inherit the land, you will look on the destruction of the wicked [רשעים/ἁμαρτωλούς]" (Ps. 36[37]:34).[6]

Although Sanders downplays the evidence, it is worth noting that ἁμαρτωλός translates other words, namely, חנף, חרש, and רע and, most often after רשע, some form of חטא. There are clear similarities. Compare the following: "Let sinners [חטאים/ἁμαρτωλοί] be consumed from the earth, and let the wicked [רשעים/ἄνομοι] be no more" (Ps. 103[104]:35). As with ἁμαρτωλός for רשע, ἁμαρτωλός for חטא occurs in a general sense (e.g., Num. 32:14; 1 Kgs. 1:21; Isa. 1:4; Prov. 23:17) and in direct contrast with "the righteous" (e.g., Ps. 1:5; Prov. 13:31; cf. Prov. 11:9), to describe people who have behaved contrary to the covenant (e.g., Gen. 13:13; Num. 16:38), and in contrast with true law observance: "Happy are those who do not follow the advice of the wicked [רשעים/ἀσεβῶν], or take the path that sinners [חטאים/ἁμαρτωλῶν] tread . . . but their delight is in the law of the LORD, and on his law they meditate day and night" (Ps. 1:1–2; cf. Prov. 12:13). Naturally, these sorts of sinners will be punished too (e.g., Isa. 1:28; Amos 9:8, 10; cf. Gen. 13:13; Num. 16:38).

The use of ἁμαρτωλός in the Apocrypha and Pseudepigrapha is very similar to LXX usage, particularly in Sirach.[7] It is used in a general sense, sometimes reminiscent of Sanders's statement that the sinner acts as if there is no God.[8] As with the LXX, the sinner is to be contrasted with the good, the wise, and the righteous.[9] The sinner is often a person with some power. Sinners are frequently greedy, wealthy, and/or successful (e.g., Sir. 9:11; 11:21; 29:19; 39:26–27; *1 En.* 103:5; cf. Sir. 10:23; *1 En.* 97:7) and are potentially violent oppressors who sometimes revel in their ill-gotten gains (e.g., Sir. 27:30; 28:9; *1 En.* 100:2–3; 103:11, 15; 104:5–7; 106:18; *Ps. Sol.* 17:5).[10] Compare the following:

> Do not envy the success of sinners, for you do not know what their end will be like. (Sir. 9:11)

> Now I tell you, sinners, you have satiated yourselves with food and drink, robbing and sin, impoverishing people and gaining property, and seeing good days. Have you seen the righteous, how their end comes about, for no injustice is found upon them until their death? (*1 En.* 102:9–11)

They may judge a case (e.g., Sir. 11:9) and get whatever justice pleases them (e.g., Sir. 35[32]:17). They should be avoided as they have a bad influence on people (e.g., Sir. 12:14). Crucially, and presumably underlying everything else about the sinners, they are lawbreakers who effectively stand outside the covenant (see also, e.g., Sir. 15:7, 9; 1 Macc. 1:34; 2:44, 62; *1 En.* 104:10; *Ps. Sol.* 1:1; 2:1; 4:8; 14:6; 15:5, 8):

> And Matthias and his friends went around and tore down the altars; they forcibly circumcised all the uncircumcised boys that they found within the borders of Israel. They hunted down the arrogant and the work prospered in their hands. They rescued the law out of the hands of the gentiles and kings, and they never let the sinner [τῷ ἁμαρτωλῷ] gain the upper hand. (1 Macc. 2:45–48)

One notable use of ἁμαρτωλός in early Judaism, and stressed by James Dunn, is in the context of internal Jewish debate between rival Jewish groups.[11] So, for example,

> And the devout will prove their God's judgement to be right when sinners are driven out from the presence of the righteous [δικαίου], those who please men, who deceitfully quote the Law. (*Ps. Sol.* 4:8)

> And now I know this mystery: For they [the sinners] shall alter the just verdict [or: words of truth] and many sinners will take it to heart; they will speak evil words and lie, and they will invent fictitious stories and write out my scriptures on the basis of their own words. (*1 En.* 104:10; cf. 99:2)

And so the inevitable consequence of this is that, as with the Hebrew Bible/LXX, sinners are, or are like, Gentiles and idolaters (e.g., Tob. 13:6; Wis. 19:13; *1 En.* 99:6–7; 104:7–9). It should come as no surprise that Antiochus IV was the sinner par excellence:

And after Alexander had reigned twelve years, he died. Then his officers began to rule, each in his own place. They all put on crowns after his death, and so did their descendants after them for many years; and they caused many evils on the earth. From them came forth a sinful root [ῥίζα ἁμαρτωλός], Antiochus Epiphanes, son of King Antiochus. (1 Macc. 1:7–10)

And it should come as no surprise that the Romans, particularly in the context of the invasion of Jerusalem and the Temple in 63 BCE, were seen as especially unpleasant sinners, too (e.g., *Pss. Sol.* 1:1; 2:1; cf. *Sib. Or.* 3:304). Again, judgment on sinners is a deadly serious and an extremely repetitive theme.[12] So, for example:

The way of the sinners [ὁδὸς ἁμαρτωλῶν] is paved with smooth stones, but at its end is the pit of Hades. (Sir. 21:10)

The punishments did not come upon the sinners without prior signs in the violence of thunder, for they justly suffered because of their wicked acts. (Wis. 19:13)

Famine and sword and death shall be far from the righteous; for they will retreat from the devout like those pursued by famine. But they shall pursue sinners and overtake them, for those who act lawlessly shall not escape the Lord's judgment. (*Ps. Sol.* 15:7–8)

You, sinners, are accursed forever; there is no peace for you! (*1 En.* 102:5)

In the DSS the Hebrew and Aramaic use of רשע strongly echoes the Psalms, but predictably enough it, along with חטא, is often used in the light of the problems the community faced. All the usual themes associated with sinners are attested: general sinful behavior, sometimes describing people effectively acting as if there were no God;[13] the consistent contrast with the behavior of the righteous;[14] and people outside the law and covenant, often, but not always, outside the law and covenant as interpreted in the DSS.[15] Most commonly, and perhaps unsurprisingly, are the ferocious judgments awaiting sinners (e.g., 1Q28b V, 25: "May you kill the wicked [רשעים]") frequently tied up with covenant and correct law observance.[16] Naturally, then, sinners are either Gentiles or idolaters or tied up with such sinful behavior.[17] רשע can also be used to describe powerful evil spirits with the capacity to make great destruction and are tied in with the work of Belial (cf. 1QM IV, 1–4; 1QS II, 5; 11Q13 1 II, 11; 4Q511 I, 6). Once again whenever there is some indication of socioeconomic status the sinners are rich, more specifically oppressive rich, and/or generally powerful and/or violent and/or successful and wealthy.[18] Compare the following examples, one of which interprets the use in the Psalms with reference to one specific wealthy group, the house of Judah, and note too the general context of law observance:

"And the poor shall possess the land and enjoy peace in plenty [Ps. 37:11]." Its interpretation concerns the congregation of the poor who will tough out the period of distress and will be rescued from all the snares of Belial. Afterwards, all who shall po[sse]ss the land will enjoy and grow fat with everything enjoy[able to] the flesh. "The wicked [רשע] plots against the just person [לצדיק] . . . [Ps. 37:12–13]." Its interpretation alludes to the ruthless ones of the covenant who are in the House of Judah, who plot to destroy those who observe the law, who are in the Community Council. (4Q171 II, 9–16; cf. 4Q169 3–4 I, 11–12)

The princes of Judah are those upon whom the rage will be vented, for they hope to be healed but the defects stick (to them); all are rebels because they have not left the path of traitors and have defiled themselves in paths of licentiousness, and with wicked wealth [ובהון רשעה], avenging themselves, and each one bearing resentment against his brother, and each one hating his fellow. Each one became obscured by blood relatives, and approached for debauchery and bragged about wealth and gain. Each one did what was right in his eyes and each one has chosen the stubbornness of his heart. They did not keep apart from the people and have rebelled with insolence, walking on the path of the wicked ones [רשעים], about whom God says: "Their wine is serpents' venom and cruel poisons of asps." (CD VIII, 3–10)

There is a related use of the root רשע that is worth pointing out as it echoes virtually all the key themes. The infamous "Wicked Priest" is, in Hebrew, הכוהן הרשע. The Wicked Priest is said to have deserted the law, the law as interpreted by the writers of 1QpHab no doubt—for the sake of riches. He is said to rob and horde his wealth. He is said to be violent, including violence against the poor. He is also said to have defiled the sanctuary. Ultimately then the Wicked Priest will have to come under judgment (see, e.g., 1QpHab VIII, 8; IX, 9; XI, 4; XII, 2, 8–9).

The Hebrew רשע is relatively common in the earliest rabbinic literature, and there is no significant divergence from earlier Jewish literature except that on the whole it is probably less specific in its use. It occurs in a very general sense (e.g., m. Ned. 1:1; m. 'Abot 1:7–8; t. Soṭah 9:5; t. Sanh. 8:4; 13:1; 14:4). Some texts give a few more details. For example, the disciples of "Balaam the wicked [בלעם הרשע]" are noted for a grudging spirit, an evil eye, and a proud soul, and stand in direct contrast to the disciples of Abraham (m. 'Abot 5.19). Sinners can also be people associated with theft (e.g., m. Sanh. 10:6) and knife-wielding murderers (t. Sanh. 8:3; cf. Tg. [2 Sam. 16:7]). Interestingly, when רשע does occur in the sense of someone not conventionally of the oppressive rich, it is used of someone described as a bandit, and it is hardly a generally held view:

Abba Gurion of Sidon says in the name of Abba Gurya, "A man should not teach his son to be an ass driver, a camel driver, a barber, a sailor, a herdsman, or a shopkeeper. For their trade is the trade of thieves [לסטים]." R. Judah says in his name, "Most ass drivers are evil [רשעים], most camel drivers are decent, most sailors are saintly, the best among the physicians is going to Gehenna, and the best of butchers is a partner of Amalek." (*m. Qidd.* 4:14)

The common view that רשעים are of powerful standing with the resources to oppress is found in early rabbinic tradition (e.g., *m. Sanh.* 8:5; *m. 'Abot* 5:1) and in *m. Sanh.* 8:5 they are associated with two of life's great pleasures: sleep and, to a lesser extent, wine. In fact, one brutally honest opinion on the problem of suffering recorded in *m. 'Abot* 4:15, which sheds obvious light on why sinners were to be judged in the future, states, as if common fact, that sinners are unfairly successful, "R. Yannai says, 'We do not have in hand [an explanation] either for the prosperity of the wicked [הרשעים] or for the suffering of the righteous [צדיקים].'"

Perceptions of law observance also determine how sinners are to be defined. In general terms people beyond the law are deemed sinners (e.g., *t. Ned.* 1:1; *t. Soṭah* 7:4). More specifically, this "lawlessness" can include disagreement with legal authorities as the following saying indicates: "He who latches on to the lenient rulings of the House of Shammai and to the lenient rulings of the House of Hillel is an evil man [רשע]" (*t. Yeb.* 1:13 par. *t. 'Ed.* 2:3; cf. *m. 'Ed.* 5:6; *m. Neg.* 12:6; *t. 'Abod. Zar.* 6:18). It quite naturally follows that lawless Gentiles are deemed sinners, including the specific link of their being idolaters and beyond the law. Note that *m. Ned.* 3:11 has "sinners" or "evil ones" as a variant for "idolaters": "R. Eleazar b. Azariah says, 'The foreskin is disgusting, for idolaters [or: 'evil ones' (הרשעים)] are shamed by reference to it." However, it should be noted that although the association of Gentiles and sinners is present, this does not mean that there were no Gentiles who were righteous among the sinners, as R. Joshua stresses according to *t. Sanh.* 13:2.

As these texts already show, the classic sinner/righteous contrast is also well attested (e.g., *m. Sanh.* 6:5; 8:5; 10:5 [cf. *t. Sanh.* 14:4]; *m. 'Abot* 4:15; *t. Soṭah* 10:2–3; *t. Sanh.* 8:4; 13:2, 6; cf. *m. 'Abot* 5:19) and naturally it is the sinners who will eventually suffer punishment for their wrongdoing (e.g., *m. 'Ed.* 2:10; *m. Sanh.* 10:6; *m. 'Abot* 5:1, 19; *t. Soṭah* 10:2–3; *t. Sanh.* 13:1–2, 6). As a statement attributed to the house of Shammai resoundingly puts it,

There are three groups, one for eternal life, one *for shame and contempt* (Dan. 12:2)—these are those who are completely evil [אילו רשעים גמורים]. An intermediate group go down Gehenna and scream and come up again and are healed (Zech. 13:9). (*t. Sanh.* 13:3)

But this is only half the story, as the rabbinic portrayal also bears witness to the view that God cares for these unpleasant sinners, as in *m. Sanh.* 6:5: "Said

R. Meir, '. . . If thus is the Omnipresent distressed on account of the blood of the wicked [דמם של רשעים] when it is shed, how much the more so on account of the blood of the righteous [דמם של צדיקים]!'" (cf. *t. Qidd.* 1:16).

As with the MT, there is also close association between רשע, חטא, and רע, most notably in *m. Sanh.* 10:3, which brings several aspects of sinners' behavior together:

אנשי סדום אין להם חלק עולם הבא שנאמר ואנשי סדום רעים וחטאים
להיה מאד רעים בעולם הזה עולם הבא אבל עומדין בדין: רבי נחמיה
אומר אלו אין עומדין בדין שנאמר על־כן לא־יקומו רשעים במשפט
וחטאים בעדת צדיקים על כן לא־יקומו רשעים במשפט זה דור המבול
וחטאים בעדת צדיקים אלו אנשי סדום: אמרו לו אינם עומדים בעדת
צדיקים אבל עומדין בעדת רשעים:

> The men of Sodom have no portion in the world to come, since it is said, *Now the men of Sodom were wicked and sinners against the Lord exceedingly* (Gen. 13.13). *Wicked*—[means] in this world; And *sinners*—[means] in the world to come. But they will stand in judgment. R. Nehemiah says, "Both these and those will not stand in judgment, for it is said, *Therefore the wicked shall not stand in judgment, nor sinners in the congregation of the righteous* (Ps. 1.5). *Therefore the wicked shall not stand in judgment*—this refers to the generation of the flood. *Nor sinners in the congregation of the righteous*—this refers to the men of Sodom. They [the Sages] said to him, "They shall not stand in the congregation of the righteous, but they will stand in the congregation of the sinners."

The nature of the sins of Sodom has of course become an issue of some controversy due to the issue of homosexuality and Christian churches, but it is noticeable that their sins (Sodom's, that is) fit in with the ways in which "sinners" were defined in early Judaism. The sins of Sodom, usually adapted to a nation or city, led to their judgment (e.g., Deut. 29:23; Jer. 49:18; 50:40; Ezek. 16:50; Amos 4:11; Zeph. 2:9; cf. Ezek. 16:58). Even Babylon "the glory of kingdoms, the splendor and pride of the Chaldeans, will be like Sodom and Gomorrah when God overthrew them" (Isa. 13:19; cf. Jer. 50:40). Idolatry too plays its part in the judgment on the Sodomites, according to *Gen. Rab.* 50:12. As they worshiped the sun and the moon, they would have said that the moon would have protected them if God had destroyed them during the day, and the sun, if God had destroyed them at night. So what else could be done but have God destroying them on the sixteenth of Nisan when both the sun and the moon were simultaneously in the sky?

But it is the lack of social justice among the oppressive rich that is the most emphasized sin in early Judaism. As Ezekiel famously puts it, "This was the guilt of your sister Sodom: she and her daughters had pride, excess of food, and prosperous ease, but did not aid the poor and needy" (Ezek. 16:49). Sodom is effectively beyond the law as the inhabitants were "haughty, and did abominable things [תועבה]" (Ezek. 16:50). The remembrance of Sodom in the gemara (b. Sanh. 109a–b) is of most direct relevance, as it interprets m. Sanh. 10:3. And here there are some quite spectacular developments of the Sodom traditions with a major focus on the Sodomites as comically evil oppressors. Commenting on "The men of Sodom have no portion in the world to come" and the scriptural justification "*Now the men of Sodom were wicked and sinners* [רעים וחטאים] *against the Lord exceedingly*" (Gen. 13:13), Rab Judah is recorded as interpreting *wicked* with reference to their bodies and *sinners* with reference to their use of money. As for money, the scriptural justification is Deuteronomy 15:9, "and you would incur guilt [והיה בך חטא]." The context of Deuteronomy 15:9 makes it clear that we are dealing with oppression of the poor:

> Be careful that you do not entertain a mean thought, thinking, "The seventh year, the year of remission, is near," and therefore view your needy neighbor with hostility and give nothing; your neighbor might cry to the LORD against you, and you would incur guilt.

One Tanna gave the opposite interpretation to Rab Judah: *wicked* referred to money whereas *sinners* referred to bodies. The justification for *wicked* here is again Deuteronomy 15:9, "And therefore view your needy neighbor [brother] with hostility [ורעה עינך באחיך האביון]."

Despite the mention of bodies, the rest of the lengthy passage recorded in the Babylonian Talmud is concerned with the oppressive nature of Sodomite behavior. The Sodomites "waxed haughty" on account of the good things they had received, including ample bread and gold dust (with reference to Job 28:5–8). Like the Great British tabloid hack of the *you-couldn't-make-it-up* variety, they said, "Why should we suffer wayfarers, who come to us to deplete our wealth. Come let us abolish the practice of travelling in our land." The Sodomites also made some exceptionally harsh rulings, most of which directly affect the poor. Those with one ox must tend all the town's oxen for one day; but the one with none must tend them two days. But then what really is to be expected when the four judges in Sodom were called Shaqrai, Shaqurai, Zayyafi, and Mazle Dina—that is, "Liar," "Awful Liar," "Forger," and "Perverter of Justice"? Their rulings include a man assaulting his neighbor's wife and "bruising" her, which required the woman to be given to the assaulter so that he can impregnate her. If an ear was cut from a neighbor's ass, they would rule, "Give it to him until it grows again." If a neighbor was wounded, they would demand that the victim pay up for the pleasure of being made to bleed. Whoever wanted to use a ferry to cross water would have to pay four *zuzim*; whoever wanted to cross through the water had to pay eight. One person refused and was assaulted for his troubles and (wait for it . . .) had to pay a fee for his bleeding. Sodom also included interesting beds, and they are not criticized for any homoerotic connotations. No, if guests were too long for the bed, they physically shortened them; if guests were too short they physically stretched them out.

The poor were most cruelly insulted. If a poor person happened to pass by, all residents donated a *denar* each with their names written on them but donated no bread. When the poor person finally died, they came back and retrieved their *denars*. Once a young woman smuggled some bread out to a poor man, but when she was caught she was "daubed with honey and placed on the parapet of the wall, and the bees came and consumed her." According to Rab Judah in the name of Rab, it was on hearing the cries of the unfortunate lass that God had finally had enough. There is a slightly different tale in *Gen. Rab.* 49:6 where a hungry maiden acquires flour from another maiden. As charitable acts were out of the question, one of the unfortunate maidens was burned. It was on her cry that God acted, saying, "Even if I desired to be silent, justice for that maiden does not permit Me to keep silent."

Given a long tradition of associating the Sodomites with socioeconomic oppression, this extreme kind of behavior is an obvious development of *m. Sanh.* 10:3. This is also entirely in keeping with the way sinners were perceived from the Hebrew Scriptures through the Second Temple period. The late dating of the material recorded in the Babylonian Talmud is not important here because my present point is to show the stable use of the language of sinners over many hundreds of years. The traditions surrounding *m. Sanh.* 10:3 bring everything together: sinners are lawless, idolatrous, violent, oppressive, rich, and profoundly unpleasant towards the poor. It shows just how embedded the idea of the rich oppressive sinner had become over all those centuries up to the time of the Babylonian Talmud.

Probably the weakest aspect of Sanders's analysis of "the sinners" is the lack of discussion concerning potential Aramaic words underlying ἁμαρτωλός.[19] Importantly, Aramaic also uses רשע, as we saw in the DSS. Bruce Chilton has also pointed out various uses of the Aramaic root רשע in *Targum Isaiah*.[20] It should be added that a variety of uses of the root רשע are found elsewhere in the Targumim, translating a number of Hebrew words and consistent with the different themes outlined so far (e.g., 1 Sam. 30:22; 2 Sam. 7:10; 16:7; 20:1; 1 Kgs. 21:10, 13). For example, רשעא is used instead of ערלה ("foreskin") in *Tg.* (Jer. 4:4); רשיעא is used instead of the violent, oppressive פרצים ("robbers") in the famous Jeremiah 7:11 passage (*Tg.* [Jer. 7:11]; cf. Mark 11:17); רשיעיא in the sense of "the wicked one" or "evil" can be used alongside "the righteous one" or "righteous" (צדיקיא) instead of the biblical comparison of straw and wheat in *Tg.* (Jer. 23:28); the oppressively powerful Babylon is the "arrogant one" (זדון) in the MT but רשיעא in *Tg.* (Jer. 50:31–32). We also have a general echo of the legal disputes in the content of prophetic words and visions. Instead of false prophets speaking their own personal "visions" (חזון) to those who despise the words of the Lord, *Tg.* (Jer. 23:16) has them speaking evil (רשע); the "deceit" (תרמית) of false prophets is also something rendered with רשעא (e.g., *Tg.* [Jer. 14:14; 23:26]); opponents of Jeremiah and the word of God are "all the arrogant men" (כל־האנשים הזדים) in the MT but "all the wicked men" (כל גבריא רשיעיא) in *Tg.* (Jer. 43:2). רשעא can of course be added with no Hebrew equivalent, so it is used in the typical contexts of judgment (e.g., *Tg.* [Jer. 4:18]). Interestingly the root רשע is often used to translate בליעל ("Belial," "worth-lessness," "base wickedness," "ruin") in the Targumim (e.g., *Tg.* [1 Sam. 2:12; 25:25; 30.22]; *Tg.* [1 Kgs. 21:10, 13]). This may be significant as Belial was not only understood by certain Jews of Jesus' time to be a powerful "demonic" force who would lead Israel astray, away from the law and towards sins such as wealth, sexual immorality, and temple defilement (e.g., CD IV, 15–19) but was also tied in with the language of sinners in the DSS (cf. 1QM IV, 1–4; 1QS II, 5; 11Q13 1 II, 11; 4Q511 I, 6). The Aramaic/Syriac root רשע can, predictably enough, directly translate the Hebrew רשע, and so it is found in the sense of judgment (e.g., *Tg.* [1 Sam. 2:9]; *Tg.* [Jer. 23:19; 25.31; 30.23]), in terms of violence (e.g., *Tg.* [1 Sam. 24:14 (13)]), in wonderment at why the wicked prosper (e.g., *Tg.* [Jer. 12:1]) in parallel with "righteous" (e.g., *Tg.* [2 Sam. 4:11] [Heb. צדיק/Aram. זכי]), a parallelism, of course, repeated in the Aramaic and Syriac translations of the Psalms. Indeed, and most signifi-cantly, רשיעא/ܪܫܝܥܐ is also frequently found in the Peshitta Psalms where ἁμαρτωλός is used in LXX and רשע is used in Hebrew.[21]

Yet there are also other words in Pesh. Psalms where ἁμαρτωλός is used in LXX and רשע is used in Hebrew: עולא/ܥܘܠܐ[22] and חטיא/ܚܛܝܐ.[23] Unfortu-nately it adds even more uncertainty as to what Aramaic word underlies the Synoptic tradition. The interchangeableness of these words is illustrated by Psalm 1.1, 5:

> Happy are those
>   who do not follow the advice of the wicked [MT: רשעים; LXX: ἀσεβῶν; Pesh.: עולא/ܥܘܠܐ],
>   or take the path the sinners [MT: חטאים; LXX: ἁμαρτωλῶν; Pesh.: חטיא/ܚܛܝܐ]
>   tread,
>   or sit at the seat of the scoffers;
> . . . .
> Therefore the wicked [MT: רשעים; LXX: οἱ ἀσεβεῖς; Pesh.: רשיעא/ܪܫܝܥܐ]
>   will not stand in the judgment,
>   nor sinners [MT: וחטאים; LXX: ἁμαρτωλοί; Pesh.: חטיא/ܚܛܝܐ] in the
>   congregation of the righteous.

However, it is not all bad news, as these semantically overlapping words func-tion in similar ways to רשע. The use of חטיא/ܚܛܝܐ should come as no surprise given the use of חטא in Hebrew, as noted above, which it naturally translates on several occasions (e.g., Pss. 1:1, 5; 103[104]:35; Prov. 23:17; Amos 9:8; Isa. 1:4, 28; 1 Kgs. 1:21). In Pesh. (Gen. 13:13), חטיא/ܚܛܝܐ is used with reference to those arch sinners, the people of Sodom, and is also used for the MT חטא. חטיא/ܚܛܝܐ is also used of the Sodomites in Pesh. (Gen. 18:23), but this time for the other favored word for these people, רשע, and in parallelism with "the righteous [צדיקא/ܙܕܝܩܐ]." In Pesh. (Num. 16:26), חטיא/ܚܛܝܐ is used in the context of warnings to avoid the dwellings of Dathan and Abiram and is used for the MT רשע, although חטיא/ܚܛܝܐ is used where the MT has חטא in Pesh. (Num. 16:38[17:3]). In Pesh. (Num. 32:14), חטיא/ܚܛܝܐ is used of behavior not befitting God's covenant where the MT has חטא. In Pesh. (Dan. 12:10) חטיא/ܚܛܝܐ is used in opposition to the wise where the MT has רשע.

עולא/ܥܘܠܐ is quite common in the Peshitta and is used for a number of semantically overlapping Hebrew words in addition to רשע, most notably עון ("iniquity"), a word to which we will shortly return. עולא/ܥܘܠܐ can be used for the Hebrew חמס ("violence, wrong") in the context of the violent sinfulness of the earth in the time of Noah (Gen. 6:11, 13), for עון in the sense of "punishment for iniquity" (e.g., Lev. 20:17, 19) and elsewhere in the context of punishment for עון (e.g., Lev. 26:39, 41; Num. 14:18–19, 34) and for רשע (e.g., Ezek. 33:8; Prov. 24:19–20). It is also used of transgressions against the law where the MT has מעל ("unfaithful, treacherous act," e.g., Lev. 5:15; 26:40, 43; Num. 5:6), פשע ("transgression," e.g., Lev. 16:16, 21), רשע (e.g., Deut. 9:27; Ezek. 33:19), or עון (e.g., Lev. 16:22; 18:25; 26:40, 41; Num. 18:23), including specific sins, such as incest, where the Hebrew has זמה ("wickedness," e.g., Lev. 18:17) or נדה ("impurity," e.g., Lev. 20:21) whereas not acting in accordance with proper cultic regulations where the Hebrew has עון (e.g., Lev. 22:16; Num. 18:1), unacceptable sacrifice where the Hebrew has רשע (e.g., Prov. 15:8), marital unfaithfulness where the Hebrew has מעל (Num. 5:12), intentional "highhanded" sins where the Hebrew has עון (Num. 15:31), and, significantly, social injustice (cf. Deut. 19:16) where the Hebrew has מעל ("injustice, unrighteousness," e.g., Lev. 19:15, 35; Deut. 25:16). Interestingly, עולא/ܥܘܠܐ is also used for בליעל ("worthlessness," "Belial," etc., e.g., Deut. 15:9).

Chilton also notes another important Aramaic word commonly used in *Targum Isaiah* to cover "a variety of defects in the Masoretic text": חובא, "debtor" or "sinner." In *Targum Isaiah* "debtors" can refer to people punished by the Messiah (11:4), destroyed by the Lord (14:4–5), wicked Gentiles (34:2), or an enemy of Jerusalem (54:17).[24] This is of course completely in line with the themes associated with sinners discussed above. In addition to Chilton's use of *Targum Isaiah*, it should be noted that חובא is used in relation to "sin" throughout the Peshitta. In Pesh. Pentateuch, חובא/ܚܘܒܐ most commonly translates עון ("iniquity"), consistent with the other descriptions of sinners throughout the literature so far surveyed. In this sense it is used to describe the following: Amorites (Pesh. [Gen. 15:16]), the sin of idolatry in the Decalogue (Pesh. [Exod. 20:5]; Pesh. [Deut. 5:9]), general deviancy in the context of God's commandments and the new tablets made by Moses (Pesh. [Exod. 34:7, 9]), and, of course, punishment (Pesh. [Num. 14:18]; cf. Pesh. [Exod. 20:5]; Pesh. [Deut. 5:9]; Pesh. [Exod. 34:7, 9]). The importance for the Aramaic use of "debtor" in the Gospel traditions (e.g., Matt. 6:12 par. Luke 11:4; Matt. 18:23–25; Luke 7:36–50; 16:1–9) has long been recognized.[25] Moreover, the Aramaic root חוב is attested by the time of Jesus (e.g., 11Q10 XXI, 5; XXXIV, 4) and the language of debtor/sinner is obviously echoed in Gospel traditions (Matt. 6:12 par. Luke 11:4; cf. Matt. 18:23–35; Luke 7:36–50; 16:1–9). The use of חוב must therefore be taken as another serious contender for a potential Aramaic root underlying the Synoptic ἁμαρτωλός.

We can therefore conclude that the linguistic evidence is consistent and stable over a one-thousand-year period in terms of the issues raised for this book. Some generalizations can be made. Sinners tend to act outside law and covenant—or someone's definition of law and covenant—and they will ultimately be punished. It also follows quite naturally that Gentiles can be called sinners. But, perhaps most crucially for the moment, whenever the socioeconomic status of the different words for "sinner" is discussed, it is always the oppressive rich who are unfairly successful. So what relevance does all this have for the identification of the Gospel sinners? And can any more order be drawn from this slightly chaotic set of results?

SINNERS AND THE GOSPEL TRADITION

The diversity of similar overlapping Aramaic words also makes it difficult to assess whether there was one single term used by Jesus and his opponents.[26] That said, the very fact that the different Semitic words have a significant degree of overlap means it does not affect the issue of Jesus' precise phrasing in any dramatic way. While we must live with the possibility that more than one Aramaic word may potentially underlie the Synoptic tradition, the translators themselves give us a clue of its general frame of reference by constantly using ἁμαρτωλός, a word that also overlaps considerably with the Semitic words. Furthermore, given the concentration of this term in the Psalms and the subsequent influence on Jewish literature, this would strongly suggest that they believed the tradition to be referring to something like the types of behavior outlined above.

In the Synoptic tradition, there are some general uses, such as when Jesus refers to this adulterous and sinful generation in Mark 8:38. Although quite general, there is a fairly clear implication of violent and wealthy sinners in

Mark 14:41 (par. Matt. 26:45; cf. Luke 24:7) when Jesus is betrayed into the hands of the authorities, and there is perhaps even a reference to Gentiles here. In Mark 2:15–17 and parallels (Matt. 9:10–13; Luke 5:29–32) Jesus reclines with Levi, tax collectors, and sinners, and here we also have the conventional contrast between righteous and sinner. It is also possible that there is some intra-Jewish legal debate here. Handwashing before ordinary meals was practiced by some Pharisees so as to avoid the transmission of any impurities from hands to food to eater, a concern that may lie behind the criticism of Jesus and the disciples reclining with these figures.[27] Presumably the association with tax collectors could imply that these sinners were rich and, if so, oppressively so.[28] We see such views of tax collectors reflected in Luke 19:1–9. Josephus mentions John the tax collector, who appears to be filthy rich (*J.W.* 2:287, 292). That tax collectors were rich, and not always justly so, persisted in later Judaism. In the Mishnah tax collectors are placed alongside robbers and murderers (*m. Ned.* 3:4). In the Babylonian Talmud tax collectors were recorded as being known for overcharging (*b. Sanh.* 25b). Outside Judaism Cicero famously regarded the jobs of tax collector and usurer as taboo; they resulted only in making the collectors and usurers hated (Cicero, *De Officiis* 1.150). In the Q tradition of Matthew 11:19 and Luke 7:34, Jesus is accused of being a glutton and drunkard who associates with tax collectors and sinners. Not only is the link with the tax collectors present but also the kind of eating and drinking more associated with the rich and not the poor (e.g., *1 En.* 97:8–10; 98:2; Matt. 6:25–34 par. Luke 12:22–32).[29]

Luke has the most references to sinners, and they usually complement the other Synoptic uses. Luke 13:2 talks of Galilean sinners killed by Pilate, but it is quite general. Given the context is repentance, it may involve Torah observance, and given that Pilate killed them, it may imply that they were violent in some way. In fairness, however, this can only be regarded as speculative. Luke 7:36–50 has a story of a woman identified as a sinner. Quite what her sinning involved is not immediately clear. The evidence for her being a prostitute is an old assumption for which there is little evidence (cf. *m. Ket.* 7:6). The fact that she is criticized in the context of Jesus' eating in a Pharisee's house may perhaps imply that table purity is an issue. This story may well be inspired by other Gospel traditions and may not be a wholly reliable guide to the historical Jesus, but note also that she brings an alabaster jar of ointment (Luke 7:37), which is probably an indication of some wealth (cf. Mark 14:3).

In Luke 15 the parables are framed by a reference to Pharisees and scribes grumbling about Jesus eating with sinners, and the parables of the Lost Coin and Lost Sheep mention sinners repenting. Note again the mention of tax collectors and eating. The discussion of repentance may well assume a context of returning to observe the commandments. The parable of the Prodigal Son, which in the Lukan context at least must be tied in with the reaction of scribes and Pharisees to Jesus' association with people deemed sinners, may well be a parabolic explanation of repentance, possibly of Jews who had not only neglected Pharisaic halakah but even a major commandment of the law itself: after all the Jewish boy goes off to work with pigs, exactly what a good Jewish boy should not be doing, before returning home for a big kosher feast. In Luke 18:13 the tax collector in the parable of the Pharisee calls himself a sinner. In Luke 19:7 Zacchaeus, a rich chief tax collector with a past of defrauding people, which is clearly contrary to the Torah, is a sinner.

The only possibility of the poor being sinners is Luke 5:8, where in the calling of the disciples Peter says, "I am a sinful man [ἀνὴρ ἁμαρτωλός]." But it is only in Luke and could well be an example of Luke's using a favorite word. Consequently it can hardly carry much weight for the study of the historical Jesus. There is no indication as to what kind of sinner Peter was, but presumably he was not a prostitute.

Even if certain individual passages are creations of the early church, the fact that this conflict over the sinners is multiply attested and consistent with early Judaism should mean we are close to the historical Jesus on this issue. In this case it is clear that the sinners are not the ordinary masses but rather the rich and presumably the oppressive rich. They were presumably not particularly observant of Pharisaic law, and given that the Gospel narrators can label these people sinners (Mark 2:15–16; Luke 7:37; 15:1), that Jesus can label these people sinners (Mark 2:17; Matt. 11:19 par. Luke 7:34; Luke 13:2; 15:7, 10), that people like Zacchaeus presumably did not observe commandments concerning social justice, and that the Prodigal Son associates with pigs, there is a good chance that some sinners were not observing major biblical commandments. As there is a huge Jewish background of unrepentant sinners ultimately being punished and no contradiction of this in the Gospel tradition, we may also assume that the idea that the sinners will be damned if they do not repent is present for Jesus, his opponents, and the Gospel writers.

SINNERS AND REPENTANCE

From what we have seen, it appears that Jesus was going out to these sorts of Jews in order to bring them back to the fold, as the parables of Luke 15 perfectly illustrate. As has long been recognized, this message of repentance was not simply change of mind, as the Greek μετανοέω/μετάνοια might suggest, but a total reorientation of behavior, a return to God associated with the Semitic *teshubah* concept (Aramaic root: תוב/תיב). As I have argued elsewhere, this sort of language was also associated particularly with the return of Jews to the fold.[30.] Furthermore, the idea of giving sinners time to repent is found in the Jewish Scriptures, and presumably this would have provided some inspiration for Jews such as Jesus:

> So you, mortal, I have made a sentinel for the house of Israel; whenever you hear a word from my mouth, you shall give them warning from me. If I say to the wicked [לרשע/τῷ ἁμαρτωλῷ], "O wicked ones [רשע], you shall surely die," and you do not speak to warn the wicked [רשע/τὸν ἀσεβῆ] to turn from their ways, the wicked [הוא רשע/αὐτὸς ὁ ἄνομος] shall die in their iniquity, but their blood I will require at your hand. But if you warn the wicked [רשע/τῷ ἀσεβεῖ] to turn [לשוב/ἀποστρέψαι] from their ways, and they do not turn [ולא־שב/μὴ ἀποστρέψῃ] from their ways, the wicked shall die in their iniquity, but you will have saved your life. . . .
>
> Say to them, As I live, says the Lord GOD, I have no pleasure in the death of the wicked [הרשע/τοῦ ἀσεβοῦς], but that the wicked turn [רשע בשוב/τὸ ἀποστρέψαι τὸν ἀσεβῆ] from their ways and live; turn back, turn back [שובו שובו/ἀποστροφῇ ἀποστρέψατε] from your evil ways; for why will you die, O house of Israel?
>
> . . . And when the wicked turn [ובשוב רשע/ἐν τῷ ἀποστρέψαι τὸν ἁμαρτωλὸν] from their wickedness, and do what is lawful and right, they shall live by it. (Ezek. 33:7–9, 11, 19)

The idea of sinners repenting is also found in later Jewish literature:

> And immediately a voice came down from heaven to the Commander-in-chief, speaking thus, "O Michael, Commander-in-chief . . . Abraham has not sinned and he has no mercy on sinners [τοὺς ἁμαρτωλούς]. But I made the world, and I do not want to destroy any one of them; but I delay the death of the sinner [τοῦ ἁμαρτωλοῦ] until he should convert [ἐπιστρέψαι] and live." (T. Ab. [A] 10:13–15; cf. Tob. 13:6; Wis. 19:13; T. Benj. 4:2; Pr. Man. 5–8).[31]

Notably, it is also possible for the Aramaic "debtors" to repent:[32]

> Continually do the prophets prophesy to instruct, if by chance the ears of the guilty/debtors [חייביא] may be opened and they receive instruction. If the house of Israel would but set their faces to observe the law, would he not gather them again from among the nations? (T. Isa. 28:24–25)

In fact it would be quite plausible for certain Pharisees to have had some agreement with Jesus on the point of trying to make sinners repent. Ezekiel 33 was a sacred text, and crucially its influence on this issue is found in rabbinic literature—for example, in the following case of death-bed repentance:

> [If] a man was evil [רשע] his entire life but at the end he repented [תשובה], the Omnipresent accepts him, as it is said, *And as for the wicked-*

ness of the wicked [ורשעת רשע], *he shall not fall by it when he turns from his wickedness* [שובו מרשעו]. (Ezek. 33:12) . . . (*t. Qidd.* 1:16)

What is also notable about the biblical call to repentance, in keeping with the nature of sinners, is to bring people back to observing the commandments, although this has not always been fully appreciated in scholarship.[33] The idea of turning to the law runs throughout the theme of repentance in subsequent Jewish literature. In the Apocrypha and Pseudepigrapha, as with the biblical literature, returning to the law and the commandments is central, or at the very least assumed, and judgment is usually looming somewhere close by (e.g., *T. Iss.* 6:3; *T. Dan* 5:1–13; *T. Ab.* [B] 12:13; *Ps. Sol.* 9:10; Tob. 13:1–6; 14:5–11; Wis. 16:5–13; Sir. 5:4–8; 17:25; 18:13–14, 19–23; 21:1–14; 49:1–3; 4 Macc. 13:1–18). So, for example, the statement by Achior, leader of the Ammonites, in the book of Judith in language obviously reflecting the law and covenant:

"As long as they did not sin [ἕως οὐχ ἥμαρτον] against their God they prospered, for the God who hates iniquity [ἀδικίαν] is with them. But when they departed from the way [ἀπέστρησαν ἀπὸ τῆς ὁδοῦ] he had prescribed for them, they were utterly defeated in many battles and were led away captive in a foreign land. . . . But now they have returned [ἐπισρέψαντες] to their God . . . and have occupied Jerusalem, where their sanctuary is. . . .

"So now . . . if there is any oversight in this people and they sin [ἁμαρτάνουσιν] against their God and we find out their offense, then we can go up and defeat them. But if they are not a guilty nation [εἰ δ' οὐκ ἔστιν ἀνομία ἐν τῷ ἔθνει αὐτῶν], then let my lord pass them by; for their Lord and God will defend them." (Jdt. 5:17–21)

In the DSS when שוב/תוב is used in the sense of repentance, it is explicitly the Torah as interpreted by the Qumran community that is the primary focus (e.g. 1QS III, 1; X, 20; 4Q171 XI, 1; 4Q256 IX, 7; 4Q266 V, i.15; CD VI, 5; X, 3; XI, 5; XV, 12; XVI, 1–5; 4Q375 I, 1–4; 4Q378 XI–XIII; XIV–XVII; 4Q504 I–II, ii.13).[34] The interpretation of Psalm 37:8–9 in the DSS is a standard view in this respect:

Its interpretation concerns all who converted to the law [כול השבים לתורה], who do not refuse to convert from their wickedness [לשוב מרעתם], for all those who resist to convert from their sin [לשוב מלונם] will be cut off. (4Q171 II, 2–4).

As ever there is a clear eschatological emphasis that is of some relevance to understanding repentance according to John the Baptist and Jesus:

And we are aware that part of the blessings and curses have occurred that are written in the b[ook of Mos]es. And this is the end of

days, when they will return in Israel to the L[aw] and not turn bac[k]
[(ר)אחו ישובו ולוא . . . (ורה לת בישראל [שישובו]. (4Q398 XI–XIII, 3–5)

While repentance can be discussed in general terms in early rabbinic literature, it is usually assumed or stated explicitly that it involves turning to the commandments and good deeds (e.g., *m. Giṭ.* 5:5; *m. 'Abot* 4:11, 17; *m. Ned.* 9:3; *m. B. Meṣi'a* 4:10; *y. Mak.* 2:6, 31d; *b. Yoma* 86a–b; *b. Yeb.* 105a).[35] The following is a classic example:

> Sin offering and the unconditional guilt-offering effect atonement; death and the Day of Atonement effect atonement if there is repentance [התשובה]. Repentance [תשובה] effects atonement for lesser transgressions against both positive and negative commands in the law; while for graver transgressions it suspends punishment until the Day of Atonement comes and effects atonement. If a man said, "I will sin and repent [ואשוב], and sin again and repent [ואשוב]," he will be given no chance to repent [תשובה לעשות]. (*m. Yoma* 8:8–9)

There is, then, a consistent use of repentance in Jewish literature: turning to God involved keeping the law. But is this pattern repeated in the Synoptic tradition? There is good reason to think it is. First, as I keep stressing, the teaching of the historical Jesus is Torah based and never contradicts any biblical commandment.[36] Second, the theme of repentance is independently attested in the gospel tradition (e.g., Mark 1:14–15, 40–45; 6:12; Matt. 11:20; Matt. 11:21 par. Luke 10:13; Matt. 12:41 par. Luke 11:32; Matt. 18:12–14 par. Luke 15:3–7;[37] Matt. 5:23; Luke 13:1–5; 15; 19:1–9). Sanders's view that repentance was not a significant theme in the historical Jesus' teaching because of the relatively few occurrences of μετανοέω and μετάνοια in Mark and Matthew compared with their frequency in Luke misses the point here.[38] It is the *theme* of repentance that is crucial and should not be ignored by overemphasizing the (lack of) occurrences of the *words* for repentance.[39] Moreover, the theme of repentance independently occurs in passages that assume the validity of Jewish institutions and practices in an uncontroversial and non-polemical way (e.g., Mark 1:40–45; Matt. 5:23; Luke 19:1–9) and at least reflect what would appear to be a very early tradition. Given these two points it should be obvious that repentance ideally involved observance of the commandments, no doubt the fruits of repentance (cf. Matt. 3:8–10 par. Luke 3:8–9 [with Sir. 5:5–8]; Luke 13:1–9; Matt. 7:15–20). Perhaps the most memorable example of return-repentance is the parable of the Prodigal Son (Luke 15:11–32), and it can only be plausibly read as a return to kosher conditions. Here the rebellious Jewish boy goes off to work with pigs and returns for a good kosher meal, thereby not only locating the passage in a Jewish context but also firmly within the tradition of Jewish repentance.[40] Compare for example the following rab-

binic parallel that is surely part of the general tradition in which Luke
15:11–32 stands:

> Another explanation: You will return to the Lord your God (Deut.
> 4:30). R. Samuel Pargrita said in the name of R. Meir: this can be com-
> pared to the son of a king who took to evil ways. The king sent a tutor
> to him who appealed to him saying, "Repent, my son." The son, how-
> ever, sent him back to his father [with the message], "How can I have
> the effrontery to return? I am ashamed to come before you." There-
> upon his father sent back word, "My son, is a son ever ashamed to
> return to his father? And is it not to your father that you will be return-
> ing?" Similarly the Holy One, blessed be He, sent Jeremiah to Israel
> when they sinned, and said to him: "Go and proclaim these words, etc."
> (Jer. 3:12). Israel asked Jeremiah: "How can we have the effrontery to
> return to God?" . . . But God sent back word to them: "My children, if
> you return, will you not be returning to your father?" (*Deut. Rab.* 2:24)

So even if the parable of the Prodigal Son has been worked over by Luke it
can still tell us something significant about Jesus and repentance, not least as
it is entirely consistent with independent Gospel traditions.

This is not to say, of course, that Jesus' teaching on association with and
repentance of sinners was uncontroversial. Clearly some Jews were not comfortable with this aspect of Jesus' teaching. A part of Sanders's reasoning that
Jesus downplayed repentance is that "no one would have objected if Jesus persuaded tax collectors to leave the ranks of the wicked: everybody else would
have benefited. If he were a successful reformer of dishonest tax collectors,
Jesus would not have drawn criticism."[41] This is difficult to accept. Would the
people who wrote the Dead Sea Scrolls be elated if a group of tax collectors
and sinners might potentially repent and follow Pharisaic Law? Would Pharisees be over-the-moon if a group of sinners might potentially repent and join
the Sadducees? Or the Jesus movement? Probably not, for there is plenty of
evidence that Jewish groups in the Second Temple period engaged in some
pretty nasty disputes (e.g., Josephus, *Ant.* 13.296–98, 408–11; *J.W.* 1.650–63;
1QpHab XI, 2–8; 4Q171 IV, 8–9; Gal. 1:14).[42] As noted above, it is possible
that Jesus' lack of concern with handwashing and table purity could underlie
these disputes (cf. Mark. 2:15–17; Matt. 11:19 par. Luke 7:34) and if so would
be a visible rejection of expanded purity laws. With potentially increasing
numbers in the Jesus movement supporting Jesus' take on the law, it is understandable that the Pharisees would be worried at a potential opposition group.
This comes across strongly in the parable of the Prodigal Son, at least in its
Lukan context (15:1–2, 25–32). As this is an intra-Jewish dispute with little
concern for Gentiles, and as it is the kind of dispute with Pharisees and others echoed independently across the Synoptic tradition (e.g., Mark 2:15–17,

23–28; 3:1–6; 7:1–23; Matt. 23:23 par. Luke 11:42; Matt. 23:25–26 par. Luke 11:39–41; Matt. 23:1–22, 24; Luke 13:10–17; 14:1–6), the bitterness present in the Parable of the Prodigal Son and its context in Luke 15 may well reflect problems from the ministry of the historical Jesus.

Another cause of offense would be the mere fact of *associating* with a group deemed as dangerous outsiders, as has been argued from approaches inspired by social-scientific and cross-cultural analyses of table fellowship.[43] Jesus' opponents were not necessarily mean spirited in contrast to kind and loving Jesus. No, associating with sinners was, in light of the Jewish heritage, deemed to be a genuine threat because they could have a profoundly threatening influence (e.g., Sir. 28:9; 41:5). Jesus' opponents had just as much traditional authority for their actions: "Who pities a snake charmer when he is bitten, or all those who go near wild animals? So no one pities a person who associates with a sinner [ἀνδρὶ ἁμαρτωλῷ] and becomes involved in the other's sins" (Sir. 12:13–14). Moreover, given that the sinners are frequently cited as unpleasant rich folk, Jesus' opponents had a point. In fact this may provide another reason for the controversy: namely, a lack of justice, ill-gotten gains, and violence—all associated with the term "sinner"—were, as we saw in the previous chapter, traits associated with the very people whom many Jews like Jesus were reacting against. To make things worse it seems that most of the Gospel sinners had not yet necessarily converted in the Gospel stories, and, with exceptions such as the Lukan story of Zacchaeus, we have no idea how successful Jesus was at making them repent.[44] Indeed it is quite possible that Luke invented the Zacchaeus story precisely because Jesus and/or the early church were *not* successful in reforming Jewish sinners and tax collectors. Surely, then, Jesus was sleeping with the enemy?

There have been other explanations. One which has received a lot of support in recent years is the idea that Jesus bypassed the Temple system. Even Sanders proposes that Jesus may not have imposed certain requirements on sinners:

> He may have offered them inclusion in the kingdom not only while they were still sinners but also without requiring repentance as normally understood, and therefore he could have been accused of being a friend of people who indefinitely remained sinners. Here at last we see the full implication of the repeated observation that Jesus did not issue a call for repentance and that it was Luke who emphasized the reform of the wicked who accepted him.[45]

As we have already seen, Sanders is almost certainly wrong to suggest that Jesus did not make a call to repentance. Also there is absolutely no evidence that Jesus advocated a bypassing of the Temple system,[46] although an alien observer of modern Gospel studies might be forgiven for thinking that he did, given that it is a view constantly repeated in scholarship. Again, no such sentiments are advocated in the Synoptic tradition and nowhere is Jesus ever criticized for saying such a thing, something for which we would surely have some evidence if it were the case. Moreover, the criticism is for associating with such people. So Mark 2:16: "Why does he eat with tax collectors and sinners?"[47] As Jesus is said to have upheld the Temple system and restitution in the Synoptic tradition (Mark 1:40–45; Matt. 5:23; Luke 19:1–9), and is never criticized for the opposite, we must assume that Jesus acted in a thoroughly Jewish way with regard to sinners in this instance and that the proposals of Sanders and countless others are not to be followed.

CONCLUSIONS

Whenever the socioeconomic status of sinners is mentioned in Jewish sources it is perfectly clear who they were and who they were not: they were not to be associated primarily with the poor, the exploited, the uneducated, or the ordinary folk but rather the better off, the exploiters, and the lawless rich—people, in other words, who might as well have been Gentile oppressors. These people were going to be punished sooner or later even if they seemed to be enjoying the good life in the present. There was also a Jewish tradition that looked to the possibility of sinners repenting and turning to the law. This is all consistent with the portrayal of the sinners in the Synoptic tradition. However, Jesus' association proved to be controversial for a number of reasons. Those who were *potentially* going to repent provided potential followers for Jesus and support for his view of the law, something that would not go down particularly well with those who advocated a different interpretation. Table fellowship with these people would have contradicted the purity laws of many, such as those who wash hands before eating ordinary food. Still more controversial perhaps is that those with whom Jesus was associating were people deemed to be exploitative, rich, unjust, and possibly in cahoots with the Romans and/or Antipas. Many might not have shown any signs of reforming. It is not without reason, therefore, that certain aspects of Jewish tradition warned that the sinners were people who have a negative influence, not least on a respectable teacher like Jesus of Nazareth.

So how does all this fit in with the picture of Jesus portrayed in this book so far? Quite well, I think (naturally enough). The idea of sinners as oppressive rich is entirely consistent with the emergence of Jesus' specific view of the law, explained in the previous chapter, where Jesus aimed his teaching on law and wealth at rich people to provoke them into repentance and law observance oriented to the poor before it was too late. As for the rest of this book we now need to work out how law observance spread among Gentiles. As it turns out, the analysis of sinners will prove crucial in the link between a Jewish mission and Gentile inclusion because the term "sinner" also denotes someone who is behaving beyond law and covenant, and it is no coincidence that Gentiles are sinners by default. Jesus' mission to Jewish sinners can therefore provide the crucial link to the inclusion of Gentiles in earliest Christianity. More on this, next.

4

From Jewish Sinners to Gentile Sinners

The Beginnings of the Spread of Earliest Christianity

As we have just seen, the behavior attributed to Jewish sinners was very similar to the behavior attributed to Gentile sinners (cf. 1QM I, 2; CD VIII, 8–12). The significant stress on Jesus' mission to Jewish sinners could potentially provide a strong ideological impetus for increased association with Gentiles in earliest Christianity. This association with Gentiles was also early, although it is very unlikely that the historical Jesus had too much concern for Gentiles (cf. Matt. 10:5–6).[1] Some kind of interaction with Gentiles is attested very early according to Acts (Acts 2:10–13; 6:5; 8; 9:15), and Paul also claims to have been interested in a mission to the Gentiles when he recalls his conversion (Gal. 1:15–17; cf. Acts 9:1–19; 26:12–18). It is also significant that it is in Christianity that Paul could undertake a large-scale Gentile mission. We will see in the next chapter what kinds of social contact there were between earliest Jewish Christians and Gentiles. But, like the mission of the historical Jesus, there was also a concern for law observance among the very first Christians. As I have shown elsewhere, it is only when we get to the 40s that we start to get evidence for certain people not observing major parts of the law.[2] This means that in the 30s law observance was still a feature of Christianity even though there were Gentiles among the ranks. This aspect of earliest Christianity was a logical and expected development of the historical Jesus' mission to sinners.

THE SOCIOECONOMIC ORIGINS OF A UNIVERSAL MONOTHEISM

In addition to these ideological factors there were further socioeconomic influences on increased contact with Gentiles. On a macrosociological level

97

the comments of Patrick Nolan and Gerhard Lenski are so important they deserve extensive quoting:

> During the era in which advanced agrarian societies were dominant, there were a number of important developments in the religious sphere. The most important by far was the emergence and spread of three new religions, Buddhism, Christianity, and Islam. Each proclaimed a *universal faith*, and each succeeded in creating a community of believers that transcended societal boundaries. In contrast, in older religions, people's beliefs and loyalties were thought of as local affairs. Where one lived determined the god or gods one worshiped, for the prevailing view was that there were many gods and that, like kings, each had his or her own people and territory. . . . The ancient Israelites were some of the first to reject this view and move toward a more universalistic outlook. Centuries before the birth of Christ, the prophets proclaimed that there was only one God and that He ruled over the entire world. For a time, Judaism was a missionary religion and won converts in many parts of the Roman world. This ended, however, when early Christian missionaries won most of these Gentile converts to the new faith. From then on, implementation of the universalistic vision became the mission of Christians and Muslims, who eventually converted, at least nominally, most of the population of Europe, North Africa, and the Middle East, and some of the people of India, Central Asia, China, and South East Asia. . . . The emergence and spread of universal faiths reflected the broader social and intellectual horizons that resulted from advances in transportation technology and the spreading web of trade relations. Empire building, by bringing diverse populations under a single government, also helped to weaken parochial or "tribal" views. As people's knowledge of other societies increased, and with it their awareness of the essential unity of all humanity, the basic postulate of the older ethnic faiths (i.e., the belief in tribal deities) was gradually undermined.[3]

The details of the rise of monotheism, the missionary nature of early Judaism, and Christians' winning over Jewish converts are of course much more thorny issues than this quotation suggests, but the overall point of the rise of monotheistic faiths in advanced agrarian societies (see chap. 2) cannot be ignored. By the time of the first century many key developments were in place, "ready," as someone like Rodney Stark would argue (see also the next chapter), for a monotheistic movement like Christianity to cover a whole range of peoples. Extensive road, transport, and communication systems provided the connections for more universalistic tendencies,[4] not to mention massive, ranging preexisting social networks (see the next chapter). There was a well-established common language—*koine* Greek—across much of the urbanized empire, and it is no coincidence that the NT writers of the emerging missionary religion of Christianity use this language. There was also an interest in Jewish monotheism in the pagan world. There were Gentiles noted for taking an interest in Judaism, including the worship of one god. Compare the following from Juvenal:

> Some who have had a father who reveres the Sabbath, worship nothing but the clouds, and the divinity of the heavens . . . and in time they take to circumcision. Having been wont to flout the laws of Rome, they learn and practise and revere the Jewish law, and all that Moses handed down in his secret tome. (Juvenal, *Sat.* 14.96–103)

There is even acknowledgment of cross-cultural similarities addressed in theological terms. *Aristeas* 16 (cf. 140) attributes a grand, inclusive claim to the Gentile Aristeas that Jews worship the God who is the creator and overseer of all while Gentiles such as he refer to this as Zeus or Dis. Of course this is a Jewish text attributing such claims to Gentiles, but it does show that such universalism was at least a broader potential option. Indeed there are some useful Gentile comments from the ancient world that acknowledge cross-cultural similarities. There is the famous, not irrelevant, and multiply attested comment attributed to Numenius the Pythagorean philosopher: "For what is Plato, but Moses speaking in Attic?"[5]

So were all the pagans simply polytheists of some stripe or other? In fact there has been a challenge to the view that the Greco-Roman world was all *Jason and the Argonauts*. Effectively covering the period from around 125 BCE to the rise of Islam (though with most focus on the first four centuries CE), papers from an ancient history seminar on "Pagan Forms of Monotheism in Late Antiquity" held at Oxford in 1996 were collected and published in 1999 by Polymnia Athanassiadi and Michael Frede. The seminar and book arose out of a "dissatisfaction with . . . a misconception found not only among laymen but even among scholars: that in the Greco-Roman world . . . Christianity, in the tradition of Jewish monotheism, succeeded in replacing invariably polytheistic systems of religious belief with a monotheistic creed" and that the participants' view was that "monotheism, for the most part quite independently of Judaism and Christianity, was increasingly widespread by the time of late antiquity, certainly among the educated and in particular in the Greek east." Indeed the participants were "inclined to attribute much of the success of Christianity in that world to its advocacy of a way of seeing things, of thinking and acting, which it shared with a growing number of pagans." Of course much depends on definition here but, they point out, belief in and possibly worship of a number of divine beings was seen as entirely compatible with one God who was the source of all.[6] Views such as these are reflected in discussions of Jewish monotheism with the various companies of angels, archangels, and whatnot.[7] It is, unsurprisingly, all very monarchical; or, put another way, like heaven as it is on earth.

But it is not merely some scholarly opinion. All the contributors give plenty of evidence to back up their case, evidence that stretches back to the early Greek philosophers. So, for instance, Athanassiadi and Frede point to numerous examples of sentences that proclaim one God who has many names. Indeed Celsus tried to explain this to Christians when he claimed it made no real difference whether Zeus is called the Most High, Zeus, Adonai, Sabaoth, and so on (Origen, *Cel.* 5.41). Stephen Mitchell collected literary, epigraphic, and archaeological evidence of a more popular form of pagan monotheism present particularly in the second and third centuries CE (although certainly attested in the first century) and ranging widely in the eastern Mediterranean: the famous "cult" of what may be generally called Theos Hypsistos, the highest and frequently abstract god, and a belief something akin to that held by the groups commonly referred to as "god-fearers."[8] All this evidence too would suggest that there was a broad, perhaps slow-moving trend in at least some sections of Greco-Roman society of a notably universalistic monotheism, with obvious echoes in and confusion with the ever-permeable boundaries of Jewish and early Christian theology (cf., e.g., Mark 5:7; Luke 1:32, 35, 76; 6:35; 8:28; Acts 7:48; 16:17; Heb. 7:1). As Stephen Mitchell concludes with his eye on the bigger picture,

> The cult of Theos Hypsistos and the monotheistic conceptions of a wide-spread and popular religious culture were the seed-bed into which Jewish and Christian theology could readily be planted. Without them, the transformation of ancient patterns of belief from pagan polytheism to the predominantly monotheistic systems of Judaism, Christianity, and Islam would not only have been far less tidy and unidirectional than it was, it might not have occurred at all.[9]

And there is more to add to this general context. By the first century, Judaism also had a relatively long and increasingly stable tradition of monotheistic belief already in place, with broader, more universalistic tendencies, dating back at least to the Persian period, where its own particular brand of monotheism may have developed in tandem with the suppression of "magic" in biblical texts.[10] Yet, although some have detected missionary tendencies in early Judaism, it was hardly a distinguishing feature of the religion.[11] Additionally, one stumbling block to Gentile conversion may have been circumcision for males (see next chapter): it is presumably no coincidence that there are a striking amount of women with close connections to Judaism (cf. Josephus, *J.W.* 2.560; *Ant.* 18.81–84; 20.35). A key Jewish boundary marker (to use an ever-popular phrase) that would have hindered extensive missionary activity, and not unrelated to circumcision, was kinship and ethnicity. Crucially, however, there were Jews who developed ideas of fictive kinship alongside actual kinship (e.g., Josephus, *Ant.* 3.87; *J.W.* 2.119 par. *Ant.* 18.18–22).[12] This was also developed in the Gospel tradition (e.g., Mark 3:31–35 pars.; Mark 10:29–30 pars.; Matt. 8:22 par. Luke 9:60; Matt. 10:37 par. Luke 14:26) and something found useful by the early church.[13] So here we have a good parallel to the restricting (in terms of conversion) function of culturally internalizing views implied by Nolan and Lenski combined with a stress on those conventionally outside constructed social boundaries and the deep-rooted monotheistic beliefs. We might add to this that Jewish communities had spread far and wide throughout the Roman Empire and thus already provided widespread monotheistic networks and influence (see next chapter). To generalize: there were cultural conditions that provided the potential for a "worldwide" monotheistic religion to spread, and the new Jewish sect associated with Jesus had everything necessary to actualize this potential.

So why did Christianity spread among Gentiles and eventually become a Gentile religion as opposed to some other Jewish group of the time? This in itself is a topic for another book, but some points should be made. It is the emergence of Jesus' mission to the sinners that becomes crucially important. Compare, for example, the Dead Sea Scrolls (DSS). They too developed the idea of fictive kinship but remained and would no doubt have always remained a Jewish sect because they had a hostile view of sinners and particularly bad lawbreakers who were deemed outsiders and effectively like Gentiles. Even the Pharisees were not particularly interested in a mission to "the sinners" if the early rabbinic literature is anything to go by. Of course, both groups were perfectly capable of accepting people who repented and no doubt encouraged people to do just that. Thus it is more a question of emphasis. It should also be stated that this argument is not a rehashing of the dubious view that Christianity was superior to the rest of Judaism and that Christianity was more loving towards the downtrodden outsider. Hostile Jewish views towards sinners were, as shown in the previous chapter, aimed at some particularly violent and rich oppressors, sometimes associated with tyrannical Gentile powers. Indeed a case could be made for Jesus and the Christians flattering some particularly unpleasant human beings: these sinners were not poor outcasts of society who had been dealt a cruel hand in life.

With these arguments in mind we can now turn to how the earliest Christian traditions dealt with the problem of associating with people deemed immoral, from Jewish sinners to Gentile sinners. To do this we must analyze some of the earliest handling of legal material in the Gospel tradition. This is because in the earliest Gospel traditions we get the combination of concern for Jewish sinners and law observance, yet while these traditions were being transmitted, Gentiles were becoming associated with Christianity. We may begin with the source(s) conventionally labeled Q.

Q AND THE LAW

Despite recent criticisms of the very existence of something called Q, in very general terms it is something I still accept, albeit in a very qualified or vague form.[14] Whether Q was a gospel or sayings collection, as is often thought, or a more chaotic and dispersed set of traditions, as Maurice Casey has recently argued, or indeed oral material, as Richard Horsley and Jonathan Draper suggest, I will leave open and comment in passing where such issues might affect my arguments.[15] For now I will work with the assumption that material particular to Matthew and Luke but not in Mark is from an independent source or independent sources. Quite what this source or these sources looked like is not, thankfully, a pressing issue for my present concerns.

So why bother with Q at all? Q is particularly important for my present concerns because it contains material earlier than Matthew and Luke, with the former and perhaps the latter datable to around 70 CE,[16] and more particularly legal material that looks very early in many cases. This material, I have argued and will further argue, accepts the validity of biblical law. Yet if it does contain such early material this means it was transmitted when the Christian movement was still largely law observant while simultaneously including some Gentiles (c. 30 CE–c. 40 CE). Q potentially could prove to be a key witness in this early aspect of the Christian movement. If it were a lost Gospel or sayings source then it would provide an insight to pre-70 Christians, retaining some very early traditions. If the chaotic or oral model is taken then we would have insight into pre-70 Christians, transmitters of some very early traditions that were deemed worthy of retaining.

A steady stream of scholarship acknowledges that the Q traditions show no indication of rejecting the law and the observance of major commandments was accepted or assumed, at least in reconstructions of the earliest layers of Q.[17] Some brief generalizing comments on a law-observant Q need to be made. As I have argued elsewhere, there is not a single tradition in Matthew or Luke that contradicts biblical law.[18] It should come as no surprise to find the same in pre-Matthean and pre-Lukan Q material. Despite Gospel redaction, it is not difficult to see that the following Q passage makes this absolutely clear:

> "But it is easier for heaven and earth to pass away, than for one stroke of a letter in the law to be dropped." (Luke 16:17)

> "For truly I tell you, until heaven and earth pass away, not one letter, not one stroke of a letter, will pass from the law until all is accomplished." (Matt. 5:18)[19]

The phrase "all is accomplished" is often held to be Matthean redaction, but even if it were original, it is of some importance that in Matthew at least it cannot be seen as a claim for the law being no longer valid, at least at the time he was writing, as Matthew 5:19 strongly suggests. Indeed, it is surely significant that the following "antitheses" are entirely consistent with the range of contemporaneous Jewish legal debates on these issues.[20] To confirm that Q accepted the general validity of the law, we need to complement Luke 16:17 and Matt. 5:18 with specific instances of legal practice.

The attitude towards the law in Q traditions is, unsurprisingly perhaps, reflective of the attitude of the historical Jesus. They both downplay the significance of the expansion of biblical purity laws,[21] and by implication allow social interaction with Jews not dedicated to the certain expansions of biblical law. The following, which looks like an independent saying attributed to Jesus, is a good example of this approach to the law:

> Then he said to them, "If one of you has a child [var. donkey] or an ox that has fallen into a well, will you not immediately pull it out on a sabbath day?" (Luke 14:5)

> He said to them, "Suppose one of you has only one sheep and it falls into a pit on the sabbath; will you not lay hold of it and lift it out?" (Matt. 12:11)

This view would have been rejected by the writers of the DSS: "No one should help an animal give birth on a Sabbath day. And if it falls into a well or a pit, he should not take it out on the Sabbath" (CD XI, 13–14). Yet this is a question of the *interpretation* of biblical law and no rejection of biblical law itself, not least because the situation envisaged is not dealt with in biblical law. Moreover, the Q saying assumes that its original opponents would have agreed with aiding an animal on the Sabbath (cf. *m. Betzah* 3:4).

A similar debate over legal interpretation underlies the following much misunderstood passage:

> "You have heard that it was said, 'An eye for an eye and a tooth for a tooth.' But I say to you, Do not resist an evildoer. But if anyone strikes you on the right cheek, turn the other also." (Matt. 5:38–39)

> "If anyone strikes you on the cheek, offer the other also." (Luke 6:29)

While Luke's version is almost certainly the more original, lacking as it does the typical Matthean formula, let us assume for the moment that the seemingly stronger contrast with the law found in Matthew is more like Q. Even here the supposed contrast with Exodus 21:24 does not have to be absolute. The phrase ἠκούσατε ὅτι ἐρρέθη ... ἐγὼ δὲ λέγω ὑμῖν does not necessarily denote a strong contrast, and the second half could equally be translated ". . . and I say to you" or simply ". . . I say to you."[22] That a weaker conjunction should be used is confirmed by the view that virtually all of the earliest rabbis were said to accept a nonviolent interpretation of Exodus 21:24 involving financial/material compensation, a view that became dominant in rabbinic literature (e.g., *m. B. Qam.* 8:1; *b. B. Qam.* 83b–84a; *Tg. Ps.-J* and *Tg. Neof.* [Exod. 21:24]; *Mek.* [Exod. 3:67]), as explicitly opposed to a literal, violent interpretation involving physical compensation. Yet there was a minority view (at least in terms of evidence that has survived) that adhered to the violent view (e.g., *Jub.* 4:31; Ps.-Philo, *Bib. Ant.* 44.10; *m. Mak.* 1:6; cf. *Ant.* 4.280).[23] As I argued elsewhere, this suggests that "the Matthean Jesus is claiming how Exod. 21.24 should *not* be interpreted, that is do *not* interpret it in terms of violent retribution. . . . Matthew would have to be much more explicit given the differing interpretations and condemn both totally not just criticise a literal interpretation."[24] If we take Luke's version, then there are some close parallels in Jewish texts that themselves are hardly controversial innovations (cf., e.g., Lam. 3:30; *T. Benj.* 4:2; 1QS X, 17–18). Thus if Luke's version is in conflict with interpretations of Exodus 21:24, it can only be the violent interpretation and nothing more.[25]

While not denying the possibility of different stages in the development or transmission of Q, the view of the law is very consistent throughout all the Q texts. John Kloppenborg argues that issues of law observance are a feature of a late redaction of Q.[26] Against this I think it can be shown that the importance of law observance was assumed from the very beginning of the transmission of the Q material and that it is consistent with the entire Synoptic tradition. This is further shown when we look at the traditions relevant for the emergence of earliest Christianity in more detail.

We may begin with the following tradition, which will prove to be of central importance for my analysis of Q:

"Woe to you, scribes and Pharisees, hypocrites! For you clean the outside of the cup and of the plate, but inside they are full of greed and self-indulgence. You blind Pharisee! First clean the inside of the cup [and of the plate], so that the outside also may become clean."	οὐαὶ ὑμῖν, γραμματεῖς καὶ φαρισαῖοι ὑποκριταί, ὅτι καθαρίζετε τὸ ἔξωθεν τοῦ ποτηρίου καὶ τῆς παροψίδος, ἔσωθεν δὲ γέμουσιν ἐξ ἁρπαγῆς καὶ ἀκρασίας. φαρισαῖε τυφλέ, καθάρισον πρῶτον τὸ ἐντὸς τοῦ ποτηρίου, ἵνα γένηται καὶ τὸ ἐκτὸς αὐτοῦ καθαρόν. (Matt. 23:25–26)

Then the Lord said to him, "Now you Pharisees clean the outside of the cup and of the dish, but inside you are full of greed and wickedness. You fools! Did not the one who made the outside make the inside also? So give for alms those things that are within; and see, everything will be clean for you."

εἶπεν δὲ ὁ κύριος πρὸς αὐτόν· νῦν ὑμεῖς οἱ φαρισαῖοι τὸ ἔξωθεν τοῦ ποτηρίου καὶ τοῦ πίνακος καθαρίζετε, τὸ δὲ ἔσωθεν ὑμῶν γέμει ἁρπαγῆς καὶ πονηρίας. ἄφρονες, οὐχ ὁ ποιήσας τὸ ἔξωθεν καὶ τὸ ἔσωθεν ἐποίησεν; πλὴν τὰ ἐνόντα δότε ἐλεημοσύνην, καὶ ἰδοὺ πάντα καθαρὰ ὑμῖν ἐστιν. (Luke 11:39–41)

Despite the differences there are some important, general similarities.[27] Although there are linguistic differences between Matthew and Luke, the view that Pharisees cleanse the outside of vessels and the allegation that they are full of bad things is obviously original to Q. Luke's inclusion of "Did not the one who made the outside make the inside also?" may also be from Q. Luke does have tendencies to simplify the more complex aspects of Jewish law for Gentiles in his audience, making it is less likely that he would ordinarily include such a sentence. Admittedly it is not as easy to see why Matthew might have removed it. One possible reason is that Matthew agreed that there was some importance in distinguishing between insides and outsides of vessels.[28] Matthew's cleansing of the inside of the cup is to be preferred to Luke's giving alms. There is, of course, the famous argument put forward by Wellhausen that Q goes back to an Aramaic source reading דכו, "purify": Matthew, it is argued, read it correctly with the sense of cleansing (23:26) whereas Luke misread דכו for זכו in the sense of "give alms" (11:41).[29] There is something in this. Whether there would have been confusion between ד and ז is not clear,[30] but the possibility of deliberate misreading should be at least entertained because of the striking similarities of meaning between Matthew's version and Luke's version and the respective Aramaic words. It seems more likely that Luke would be mistaken here, as he is on the tithing saying (Luke 11:42; cf. *m. Seb.* 9:1), probably because washing insides of cups is another piece of Jewish culture that was not easily understood, at least by Gentiles among his audience, and all things being clean now refers more obviously to the morality of humans alone, thereby shifting well away from the purity of vessels. This interpretation does of course also tie in with Lukan theological motivations. Matthew, on the other hand, clearly has fewer problems with complex pieces of Jewish culture, and it is not easy to see why he would feel the need to drop almsgiving here (cf. Matt. 6:2–4). So, I would suggest that the following points are original to Q:

Pharisees cleansing outsides of vessels
The allegation that Pharisees are full of some kind of unpleasantness
The one who made the outside made the inside
First clean the inside then the outside will also become clean

Despite there being no obvious attack on purity laws in Matt. 23:25–26/
Luke 11:39–41 as such,[31] this has not stopped scholars from attempting to find
such a rejection. Kloppenborg, for example, argues,

> The Q woe betrays knowledge of the Shammaite distinctions, but no
> sympathy with them. By subverting the boundaries between inside and
> outside and by diverting attention to ethical issues, Q is actually
> undermining the entire system of purity that depends for its existence
> on a well defined taxonomy of the cosmos.[32]

There is a serious problem with this idea. Q's Jesus does not attack any biblical law whatsoever, the very foundation of the entire system of purity. If Q
wanted to make such a spectacular attack on purity then why not fire at a biblical law? Instead we have polemic aimed at Pharisees and aimed at one particular aspect of their *interpretation* of biblical law. Indeed the stress on morality
over purity and/or cult is famously found in Jewish texts. *Aristeas* 234 can say
"honour God, and that not by offerings and sacrifices but by purity of heart
and of the devout conviction that all things are fashioned and administered by
God according to his will." This did not mean a rejection of sacrifices, hence
Aristeas can praise them elsewhere too (170–71). This sort of idea is of course
deeply rooted in the prophetic tradition (e.g., Isa. 1:10–17; Jer. 6:20; 7:21–28;
Hos. 6:6; Amos 5:21–27; Ps. 51:15–19). What is particularly interesting about
such examples is that the contrast is much sharper and it is with biblical purity
law itself whereas the contrast in Matt. 23:25–26/Luke 11:39–41 is with an
interpretation of biblical law. Consequently Kloppenborg's argument is difficult to accept.

All this is entirely consistent with what we have already seen in Q and the
Synoptic tradition as a whole. But this leads to an obvious question for my study:
If Q is attacking Pharisaic interpretations, then how does this relate to the spread
of earliest Christianity? To answer this we must turn to the details of this Q dispute and later see how it relates to the transmission of such traditions. The transmission of impurity is crucial to understanding this passage and, as we will see,
crucial to understanding Jesus' audience and followers. The role of impurity
underlying the assumptions of this passage is also complicated, leading to some
confusion in scholarship, and so needs to be discussed in some depth.[33]

Common to both Matthew and Luke and thus original to Q is that the outside of vessels can become unclean. The distinction between insides and outsides of cups is a view reflected in rabbinic literature. Mishnah tractate *Kelim*

25 is the most relevant halakic discussion for Matt. 23:25–26/Luke 11:39–41.[34]
It is clear, for example, that some Jews did distinguish between the inside and
outside of utensils:

כל־הכלים יש להם אחוריים ותוך

All utensils have outsides and an inside (*m. Kelim* 25:1)

This would seem to settle the issue but for some there are more than two parts
of a utensil:

כל־הכלים יש להן אחוריים ותוך ויש להם בית צביעה

All utensils have outer parts and an inner part, and they [further] have
a part by which they are held. (*m. Kelim* 25:7a)

However, there is some debate over the issue, first between R. Tarfon and
R. Aqiba, and then between R. Meir and R. Yose:

רבי טרפון אומר לעריבה גדולה של עץ: רבי עקיבא אומר לכוסות:
רבי מאיר אומר לידים הטמאות והטהורות: אמר רבי יוסי לא אמרו
אלא לידים הטהורות בלבד:
כיצד היו ידיו טהורות ואחורי הכוס טמאים אחזו בבית צביעתו אינו
חושש שמא נטמאו ידיו באחורי הכוס: היה שותה בכוס שאחוריו טמאים
אינו חושש שמא נטמא המשקה שבפיו באחורי הכוס וחזר וטימא הכוס:
קומקום שהוא מרתיח אינו חושש שמא יצאו משקין מתוכו ונגעו באחוריו
וחזרו לתוכו:

R. Tarfon says, [This distinction in the outer parts applies only] to a
large wooden trough. Aqiba says, To cups. R. Meir says, To the unclean
and the clean hands. Said R. Yose, They have spoken only concerning
clean hands alone. How so? [If] one's hands were clean, and the outer
parts of the cup were unclean, [and] one took [the cup] with its holding part, he need not worry lest his hands be made unclean on the
outer parts of the cup. [If] one was drinking from a cup, the outer parts
of which are unclean, one does not worry lest the liquid which is in his
mouth be made unclean on the outer parts of the cup and go and render the [whole] cup unclean. A kettle [unclean on the outside] which
is boiling—one does not worry lest the liquids go forth from it and
touch its outer parts and go back to the inside [and make it unclean].
(*m. Kelim* 25:7–8)

There is also an independent rabbinic tradition that discusses the impurity of
cups and in a way consistent with the general views of *m. Kelim* 25. The earliest attestation of the tradition is a famous passage from *m. Ber.* 8:2: 'The House
of Shammai say, 'They wash the hands and then mix the cup [of wine]. But the
House of Hillel say, 'They mix the cup and then wash the hands.'' The Tosefta
makes explicit what the Mishnah can assume:

The House of Shammai say, They wash the hands then mix the cup—
lest liquids on the outer surface of the cup become impure through
contact with hands and in turn render the cup impure. The House of
Hillel say, The outer surface of the cup is always deemed impure. (*t.
Ber.* 5:26)

What is particularly notable about these two positions is that there is connection with the two different positions of R. Meir and R. Yose in *m. Kelim*
25:7–8, as R. Biban in the Palestinian Talmud makes unambiguously clear:
"R. Biban in the name of R. Yohanan, The opinion of the House of Shammai
accords with the view of R. Yose, and the opinion of the House of Hillel
accords with the view of R. Meir" (*y. Ber.* 8:2). Recalling the details of Yose's
argument above, this means that for the Yose/Shammai position, in Yose's
words: "[If] one's hands were clean, and the outer parts of the cup were
unclean, [and] one took [the cup] with its holding part, he need not worry lest
his hands be made unclean on the outer parts of the cup" (*m. Kelim* 25:8). But
this cannot apply to unclean hands "lest," in the words of the House of Shammai, "liquids on the outer surface of the cup become impure through contact
with hands and in turn render the cup impure" (*t. Ber.* 5:26).

The Meir/Hillelite position rejects this. In the case of clean hands, Yose's
view effectively applies to Meir with respect to the distinction between handles and outsides: "[If] one's hands were clean, and the outer parts of the cup
were unclean, [and] one took [the cup] with its holding part, he need not worry
lest his hands be made unclean on the outer parts of the cup" (*m. Kelim* 25:8).
But whereas Yose/Shammaites first washed the hands "lest liquids on the outer
surface of the cup become impure through contact with hands and in turn render the cup impure," Meir/Hillelites do not think this point is relevant, so even
unclean hands could not make the whole cup impure through contact with the
liquid on the outside of the cup. For Meir, another possibility is presumably
introduced in the case of the outside being clean:[35] unclean hands can hold the
handle of the cup and, contrary to Yose and the House of Shammai, there need
not be worry "lest liquids on the outer surface of the cup become impure
through contact with hands and in turn render the cup impure."

At first sight it may seem that Matt. 23:25–26/Luke 11:38–41 is firing at a
view related with R. Tarfon because Tarfon was not associated with the distinction between outsides and handles of cups (*m. Kelim* 25:7). Would Tarfon
not then just distinguish between insides and outsides of cups, a general situation which *m. Kelim* 25 takes for granted, and thus simply wash the outside
of the cup? This is difficult to maintain because in this case an objection to
reading Matt. 23:25–26/Luke 11:38–41 as an attack on a specific purity practice carries some force:

It is unquestionable that there was only one way of washing ritually-unclean vessels, whether wholly or partly unclean: to immerse them totally in a *Miqveh* (ritual immersion pool) . . . there was no custom of washing cups on the outside only.[36]

It is therefore difficult to see how Matt. 23:25–26/Luke 11:38–41 works if unclean cups had to be immersed (cf. *m. Miqw.* 5:6; 6:2, 5–6). But this is not the whole story. There is some reason to believe that Matt. 23:25–26/Luke 11:38–41 is critical of a line of thought connected with Aqiba as *Kelim* mentions the cleansing of, among other things, the handle:

כני כלים והוגניהם ואוזניהם וידות הכלים המקבלים שנפלו עליהן משקין
מנגבן והם טהורים . . . כל' שנטמא אחוריו במשקין אחוריו טמאים תוכו
ואוגנו ואזנו וידיו טהורין: נטמא תוכו כולו טמא:

Bases of utensils, and their rims, and their hangers, and the handles of utensils which hold [something = which have a receptacle], on which fell [unclean] liquids—*one dries them, and they are clean.* . . . A utensil, the outer parts of which have been made unclean with liquids—the outer parts are unclean. Its inside, its rims, hangers, and handles are clean. [If] its inside is made unclean, the whole is unclean. (*m. Kelim* 25:6, my italics)

But the handle is not technically the outside, so it would seem that Matt. 23:25–26/Luke 11:38–41 is not precisely correct. However, while acknowledging the imprecision, it is reasonable to think that Matt. 23:25/Luke 11:39 uses the language of outside (ἔξωθεν) to refer to the cleansing of parts such as the rim, hangers, and handles as distinct from the insides. The reason for this may be a precise lack of knowledge or, more likely given some very detailed knowledge of Jewish law in the Synoptic tradition and Matthew, a deliberate manipulation of the tradition to fit the polemical imagery of insides and outsides of human beings. Using the wiping of handles and rims would not make a particularly useful comparison for human beings. More precisely, it does not fit easily with the imagery of inner and outer moral purity, imagery used or implied elsewhere in the Synoptic tradition (e.g., Mark 7:15–23; Matt. 5:27–28; 6:16–18; 23:27–28).

In fact there is some linguistic support for the Q tradition's referring to something other than the rabbinic outside of a cup. As noted, both Matthew and Luke have ἔξωθεν as the word used for the outside of cups and plates. In the LXX this almost always translates some form of חוץ.[37] The Hebrew חוץ is well attested in rabbinic literature and has an Aramaic equivalent ברי (e.g., *Tg. Ps.-J.* [Exod. 25:10; 26:35; 27:21; 37:2; 40:22]; Lev. 24:3; Deut. 32:25; Judg. 12:9; 1 Kgs. 6:6; 7:9; 2 Kgs. 4:3; 23:6; Jer. 21:4; Ezek. 7:15; 40:5; 41:9, 17, 25; 42:7; 43:21; 46:2; 47:2) along with שוק in the sense of "streets" (*Tg.* [Jer. 6:11;

9:20; 33:10; 44:6, 9, 17, 21; 51:4]).[38] On the other hand, *m. Kelim* 25 always uses some form of אחור (lit. "back," "behind") for the outside of vessels, including the outside of cups in *m. Kelim* 25:7–8. אחור is also found in biblical Hebrew, and several Greek words are used to translate it, such as ὀπίσθιος (1 Kgs. 7:25; 2 Chron. 4:4), ὀπίσω (Isa. 59:14; Jer. 15:6), ἐξόπισθεν (1 Chron. 19:10), and τὸ/τὰ ὄπισθε(ν) (2 Sam. 10:9; Jer. 7:24; Ezek. 2:10).[39] But, significantly, ἔξωθεν is never used. Note also that אחור is also found in Aramaic (אחורא) and appears to be the preferred word in such instances (e.g., *Tg.* [1 Kgs. 7:25]; 2 Chron. 4:4; Isa. 59:14; Jer. 15:6; 2 Sam. 10:9; Ezek. 2:10). As there are two different uses of *outside* in both Q and the rabbinic tradition, it can be suggested that Q has deliberately used a different term. Given that the relevant rabbinic text only discusses the wiping of handles and so on and not the outside of the cup as such, and given that Q uses a different word from the rabbinic *outside*, then it presumably indicates precise knowledge in this specific Q tradition. It might also be added that the Syriac versions (Pesh., Sin., Hark, Cur.) of Matt. 23:25/Luke 11:39 also use ברה/בםיה, the Aramaic equivalent of the Greek ἔξωθεν and the Hebrew חיץ, thus providing further support from a Semitic context.

Although Jesus is opposing another expansion of biblical law, notice again that he tacitly endorses the validity of cleansing cups by claiming "first cleanse the inside." This should not come as a surprise as biblical law says so for certain circumstances:

> And anything upon which any of them [swarming things] falls when they are dead shall be unclean, whether an article of wood or cloth or skin or sacking, any article that is used for any purpose; it shall be dipped into water, and it shall be unclean until the evening, and then it shall be clean. (Lev. 11:31–32)

> Any earthen vessel that one with the discharge touches shall be broken; and every vessel of wood shall be rinsed in water. (Lev. 15:12)

Jesus' tacit endorsement of biblical law and criticism of a detail of expanded purity law is significant in this case as in others. And it again concerns purity and boundaries. The washing of cups was important for groups such as the Pharisees because it was part of the means of keeping the insides clean, particularly through handwashing and bodily immersion (see below for more details).

The downplaying of expanded table purity laws in favor of moral purity is found in Luke's use of the Q tradition. Luke 11:39–41 is a reaction to a Pharisee wondering why Jesus does not immerse himself before a meal (Luke 11:37–38). Bodily immersion is also part of the tradition of expanded table purity. This is where the issue of *tebul yom* (one who has immersed that day and is waiting until sunset to become clean—Lev. 15) is important. A *tebul yom* is second-degree impure, which should mean the contamination of ordinary nonpriestly food upon touch when a liquid is present, as happens with second-degree unclean hands (e.g., *m. Hul.* 2:5; *m. Zabim* 5:12; *m. Parah* 8:7). However, a *tebul yom*, according to rabbinic tradition, does *not* contaminate ordinary nonpriestly food (e.g., *m. Zabim* 5:2; *m. T. Yom* 2:2). This explains why the Pharisee is shocked in Luke 11: Jesus, who has just been teaching crowds, could easily have contracted impurity and by failing to immerse opens himself up to the probability of making his insides unclean. While Luke 11:37–38 may not have been part of Q, and most probably a rewriting of Mark 7:1–23 that he omitted in case it gave the impression Jesus overrode food laws,[40] his interpretation is consistent with the transmission of impurity associated with immersion, handwashing, and the washing of cups. This general sort of interpretation is almost certainly assumed in Matt. 23:23, even if the Lukan setting is fictitious. Note in Matt. 15:20 that the purity dispute is unambiguously a rejection of a handwashing tradition, a central means of keeping the insides pure for expanded table purity, as we will see below in the discussion of Mark 7:1–23. Given the fact that all the key rabbinic debates on washing cups are set in the context of laws of handwashing, and therefore ultimately concern the purity of the inside of the body (just as we also find in Mark 7:4), the metaphorical use of cleansing the inside of the cup would therefore have obvious force.

There have been objections to reading Matt. 23:25–26/Luke 11:38–41 in terms of Jewish purity halakah, particularly by Hyam Maccoby, who thought everyday hygiene was the real issue. Maccoby pointed out that καθαρίζω, used in both Matthew and Luke, "can be used of literal, spiritual or ritual cleansing. For the literal use, see, for example, Septuagint Proverbs 25:4, καθαρισθήσε-ται, referring to the purification of silver from dross."[41] This is very misleading. What Maccoby did not mention is that Proverbs 25:4 appears to be the only occurrence found of καθαρίζω in the "literal" sense in LXX from over one hundred occurrences. Besides, Proverbs 25:4 and the removal of dross from silver is not a very close parallel to a supposed use concerning the common dirt Maccoby saw in Matt. 23:25–26/Luke 11:38–41. Moreover, the general NT use of καθαρίζω is not the so-called "literal" sense. This evidence—only one very weak parallel in LXX—actually weakens Maccoby's argument. Furthermore, in the LXX, καθαρίζω almost always translates some form of טהר ("clean," "pure"), which is the most common root used for issues surrounding levitical purity in rabbinic texts and, as might be expected, found throughout *m. Kelim* 25 and the traditions surrounding *m. Ber.* 8:2, the key texts concerning purity of the inside and outside of cups.

These points make Maccoby's reading highly improbable but Maccoby had a further argument:

> All Jews were familiar with the difference between a clean and a dirty
> cup, and the image of a vessel that was clean on the outside but dirty
> on the inside as a metaphor of hypocrisy was perfectly intelligible to
> them, as was the similar figure of the whitewashed tomb which is "full
> of dead men's bones and all kinds of filth."[42]

But again this in fact weakens his argument. Corpse impurity was the strongest
form of "ritual" impurity, and again we see the image of something unclean on
the inside being used to refer to the supposed moral impurity of Jesus' opponents. The Greek word for "filth" in Matt. 23:7 is ἀκαθαρσίας. In the NT,
ἀκαθαρσία is used of moral uncleanness, not unrelated to "ritual" uncleanness
of course. The LXX ἀκαθαρσία usually translates some form of טמא, a very
common word for levitical uncleanness, both in the MT and the rabbinic literature. This adds even more weight to the rejection of Maccoby's view that
we are dealing with common dirt as opposed to impurity.

There should now be no doubt that Matt. 23:25–26/Luke 11:38–41 is an
attack on a Pharisaic emphasis on purity laws and in no way can it be the case
that it rejects the purity system as a whole. This is quite clear from the Jewish
legal background, and it is quite clear from textual analysis. What is particularly interesting is where the emphasis is placed, namely, keeping moral purity.
In this case the attack on Pharisaic interpretation of purity law coupled with
the stress on moral purity closely parallels the interpretation of Mark 7:1–23
that will be given below. This happens to be a common theme in Q. An obvious parallel in Q, presumably transmitted in the same literary or oral context
as Matt. 23:25–26/Luke 11:38–41, is the following:

> "But woe to you Pharisees! For you tithe mint and rue and herbs of all
> kinds, and neglect justice and the love of God; it is these you ought to
> have practiced, without neglecting the others." (Luke 11:42)

> "Woe to you, scribes and Pharisees, hypocrites! For you tithe mint,
> dill, and cummin, and have neglected the weightier matters of the law:
> justice, mercy and faith. It is these you ought to have practiced with-
> out neglecting the others." (Matt. 23:23)

Matthew most accurately reflects Jewish practice whereas Luke gets it wrong.
Rue is explicitly said not to be tithed along with certain other herbs (*m. Sheb.*
9:1), so, if taken literally, the generic "all kinds of herbs [πᾶν λάχανον]" may
also be said to contradict the Mishnah on this point. In contrast to Luke,
Matthew's dill and cummin are tithed by some according to the Mishnah (*m.
Ma'as.* 4:5; *m. Demai* 2:1). Yet the validity of this observation has been challenged by Kloppenborg: "That it accurately reflects current tithing practice is
most unlikely. Even a cursory glance at the Mishnaic discussions of tithing is

sufficient to indicate that there was no unanimity in regard to the liability of any of the items of [Q] 11:42a."[43] So what are Kloppenborg's precise reasons?

Kloppenborg notes that the tithing of dill is attributed to Eliezer b. Hyrcanus (*m. Ma'as.* 4:5) and his view was based on an underlying disputed principle (cf. *m. Ma'as.* 4:6). Kloppenborg further argues that it is difficult to imagine that Eliezer's view was "universally adopted."[44] These arguments are not strong enough to support Kloppenborg's view that the herbs listed in the Matthean version of Q are an inaccuracy. Eliezer, from the Mishnaic perspective, provides questionable *reasons* for the tithing of certain crops, but there is no challenge as to whether dill itself should be tithed. It is the underlying principle that is at stake:

> R. Eliezer says, Dill is subject to the law of tithes [in regard to its] seeds, leaves and pods. But the Sages say, Nothing is subject to the law of tithes [in regard to both its] seeds and leaves save cress and field rocket alone. . . . R. Eliezer says, The caper bush is subject to the law of tithes [in regard to its] stalks, berries and blossoms. R. Aqiba says, No [part of the caper bush] is subject to the law of tithes except the berries, for they are the fruit. (*m. Ma'as.* 4:5–6)

Furthermore, it would surely be an interesting coincidence if Q invented the tithing of dill only for it to be attributed to rabbis active just a few decades later. And it is not wholly relevant whether or not a view was "universally adopted." All that is required is for some Pharisees to be tithing such produce to get a polemical reaction. Kloppenborg also notes that cummin is to be tithed (*m. Demai* 2:1), but he points out that "this ruling is unattributed and therefore its date is uncertain."[45] But again, if this is the case, then we are left with the problem of Matthew falsely attributing such a ruling to Pharisees only for it to emerge later as a rabbinic view. Combined with the same unlikely thing happening with dill, it is very difficult to accept Kloppenborg's argument here.

There is more support for Kloppenborg's view on the issue of tithing mint. Mint, certainly present in the original Q passage, is not mentioned in the Mishnah in regard to tithing. As there are suggestions that wild herbs are exempt from tithing (*m. Sheb.* 9:1) this could be seen to add weight to Kloppenborg's argument. Yet it is possible that mint is effectively covered in some general statements on tithing:

> All tithes from the land, whether the seed from the ground or the fruit from the tree, are the LORD's. (Lev. 27:30)

> A general principle they stated concerning tithes: anything which is food, cultivated, and which grows from the earth is subject to [the law of] tithes. (*m. Ma'as.* 1:1)

Furthermore, if mint was used for oil then it would be covered by further general biblical statements on the tithing of oil (Num. 18:12; Deut. 14:23), which are of course taken up in the Mishnah (e.g., *m. Ma'as.* 1:5–7; cf. *m. Ma'as. S.* 2:1–2).[46] Another reason for the confusion about mint is that mint grows wild, which, as just noted, may seem to contradict the ruling in *m. Ma'as.* 1:1. But that mint was used more domestically may be implied in a discussion about the role of a "nipple end," "handle," or "hand" (יד) in transmitting impurity:

> The roots of garlic, onions, and leeks, when they are wet, and the nipple end thereof, whether wet or dry, and the scape that is close to the bulb, "the roots of lettuce, the long radish, and round radish," the words of R. Meir—R. Judah says, "The large root of the long radish joins together, but its fibrelike roots do not join together"—the roots of the mint [המיתנא, read: מינתא, מינתה] and of the rue, and wild herbs which one uprooted to transplant, and the spine of an ear [of corn] and its husk, R. Eleazar says, "Also the downy growth"—lo, these contract uncleanness and impart uncleanness and join together. (*m. 'Uq.* 1:2)

However, here there is further chaos, as mint here is grouped together with "rue" and "wild herbs," both of which are not cultivated because they are wild, as stated (rue) and obviously implied (wild herbs) in *m. Sheb.* 9:1. This led Kloppenborg to suggest that the exemption of other wild crops "suggests that wild mint is exempt from tithes."[47] But notice that in *m. Shebiit* 9:1 "mint" is conspicuously absent, despite being mentioned alongside "rue" and a generalizing "wild herbs" in *m. 'Uq.* 1:2, and that *m. Sheb.* 9:1 actually specifies which wild herbs are in mind:

> Rue, goosefoot, wild coriander, water parsley, and eruca of the field are exempt from [separation of] tithes and may be bought from anyone during the Sabbatical year, because produce of their type is not cultivated [but grows wild]. (*m. Seb.* 9:1)

One obvious reason for the exclusion of mint here is that it was an accompaniment for meals. In *m. Sheb.* 7:1, דנדנה, a Hebrew word commonly translated "mint,"[48] is obviously eaten:

> They stated an important general rule concerning [the laws of] the Sabbatical year: All produce which is fit for human consumption, animal consumption, or is a species [of plant used for] dying, and which does not continue to grow in the ground is subject to [the laws of] the Sabbatical year. . . . Now what is [considered for human consumption]? The leaf of wild arum, the leaf of [הדנדנה; Danby: "miltwaste"; Blackman: "mint"; Jastrow: "mint"; Neusner: "miltwaste"; Soncino: "miltwaste"], chicory, leeks, purslane, and ornithogalum.

No matter how דנדנה is translated, it remains that mint as we know it could easily be regarded as fit for human consumption. Elsewhere, נינא, which could be thought of as mint,[49] and found in medicinal contexts (e.g., *b. 'Abod. Zar.* 29a; *b. Giṭ.* 69b), was apparently a palatable flavoring for cress:

> Mar Zutra said. . . . If cress was chopped up on the eve of the Sabbath, on the morrow one may put oil and vinegar into it and add *ammitha* [אמיתא] thereto; and he must not beat them up but may mix them. If garlic was crushed on the eve of the Sabbath, on the morrow one may put beans and grits therein, yet he must not pound them, but may mix them, and one may add *ammitha* [אמיתא] to it. What is *ammitha* [אמיתא]? *Ninya* [נינייא] [Jastrow: "Bishop's Weed"]. Abaye observed: This proves that *ninya* [נינייא] is good for [seasoning] cress [לתחלי]. (*b. Šabb.* 140a)

Although there is some confusion over the precise nature of "mint," it should be clear that as there is no evidence for it being exempt from tithing despite being wild and as it is certainly edible, its inclusion by Matthew can hardly be taken as a misrepresentation of Judaism. In fact the reason it grew wild may well be the reason it is not mentioned in the Mishnah.[50]

Matthew is often taken to be the more original because of its accuracy, and I would cautiously accept this reason. If Luke was more reflective of the original, it might be expected that Matthew would happily keep an attack on the Pharisees, which makes them out to be tithing herbs they never would. Moreover, it is possible that Luke does not have the inclination or possibly the detailed knowledge to include various aspects of Jewish law as found in Matthew, as appears to have been the case in Luke 11:38–41/Matt. 23:25–26. Additionally, as Kloppenborg points out, the herbs listed by Luke betray some signs of secondary formation: "herbs of all kinds" can be seen as a typical Lukan generalization; dill is not an herb usually associated with Europe whereas mint is well known (Theophrastus, *His. plan.* 9.7.3; cf. 1.3.4; Nicander, *Alex.* 49), and this may account for Luke's exclusion of dill and inclusion of mint.[51] This may also have influenced a (deliberate?) misreading of a possible underlying Aramaic שבתא ("dill") for שברא ("rue").[52] There is a less weighty argument in favor of Luke's reflecting Q more accurately, namely, that it may be that Matthew felt the need to correct an earlier, inaccurate Q tradition.

But whichever version is more original, it should be absolutely clear that tithing remained important for the transmitters of Luke 11:42/Matt. 23:23, because common to both Matthew and Luke, and thus presumably Q, is the idea that tithing ought to be practiced without abandoning other key areas of morality. It has often been suggested that the concern for tithing is a gloss added somewhere in the tradition, designed perhaps to make sure tithing is not rejected. Although something along these lines is certainly possible, it is extremely difficult to prove when and where such a thing happened. Besides, even if this were a late gloss, perhaps not long before Matthew and Luke employed the tradition, based on everything else we know about Jesus, Q, and the Synoptic tradition, it would have been previously assumed that tithing was acceptable because it is biblical and the tithing of herbs mentioned by Matthew was still covered in general biblical statements on tithing.[53] But crucially for present purposes, we now have another Q legal text that stresses the importance of morality and how one aspect of the law associated with the Pharisaic movement should not be ignored at morality's expense.[54]

Q, THE LAW, AND SOCIAL INTERACTION

We now need to assess the relevance of such legal material for the spread of earliest Christianity. As we have seen in the previous two chapters, Jesus' audience and potential recruits consisted of people who may be described generally as both "poor" and "rich." This is highly significant, as we know of the existence of people both rich and poor who could be lumped together as people who for whatever reason did not observe expanded non-Temple purity laws associated with groups like the Pharisees. The population of Tiberias according to Josephus is a good example:

> Tiberias. . . . The new settlers were a promiscuous rabble, no small contingent being Galilean, with such as were drafted from territory subject to him [Herod Antipas] and brought forcibly to the new foundation. Some of these were magistrates. Herod accepted as participants even poor men who were brought in to join the others from any and all places of origin. It was a question of whether some were even free beyond cavil. These latter he often and in large bodies liberated and benefited imposing the condition that they should not quit the city, by equipping houses at his own expense and adding new gifts of land. For he knew that this settlement was contrary to the law and tradition of the Jews because Tiberias was built on the site of tombs that had been obliterated, of which there were many there. And our law declares that such settlers are unclean for seven days. (*Ant.* 18.36–38)

A relevant example from rabbinic literature of people not observing expanded non-Temple purity laws concerns the famous "people of the land." It may well be the case that the majority of "the people of the land" ('*am ha-aretz*) were of the poorest and lowest classes, or at the very least there were some, hence many traditions are found in contexts of agricultural workers. However, the people of the land also included the more wealthy and aristocratic members of society,[55] just as the impure Tiberians included wealthy as well as poor Jews. So we get examples such as the following where we see that the fact that at least some people of the land came from a higher social class can simply be assumed in rabbinic literature:

> A *haber* who leased from an *'am ha-aretz* fig-trees and vine branches
> . . . (*t. Demai* 3:5)

> They purchase from an *'am ha-aretz* slave boys and slave-girls whether
> adults or minors. They sell to an *'am ha-aretz* slave-boys and slave
> girls, whether adults or minors. (*t. 'Abod. Zar.* 3:9)

It is notable that tax collectors too can be described in similar ways to the people of the land in terms of purity (*m. Tohor.* 7:6). Indeed, the people of the land as a group are defined in relation to their observance or nonobservance of rabbinic purity and tithing laws (*t. 'Abod. Zar.* 3:10; *b. Ber.* 43b; *b. Git.* 61a; *b. Ned.* 90b; *Abot R. Nat.* [A] 41), which of course had its roots in Pharisaic law (cf. *m. Hag.* 2:7 below). For example,

> It has been taught, "Who is an *'am ha-aretz*? Anyone who does not eat
> his secular food in ritual purity." This is the opinion of R. Meir. The
> Sages however said, "Anyone who does not tithe his produce properly." (*b. Ber.* 47b)

Therefore the people of the land as has long been observed, and long abused,[56] provide a very important analogy to the audience of Jesus and the Q traditions.

As this all implies there are general passages speaking of the people of the land being suspect in the transmission of impurity. So, for example:

> He who gives over his key to an *'am ha-aretz*—the house is clean, for
> he gave him only [the charge of] guarding the key. (*m. Tohor.* 7:1)

> He who leaves an *'am ha-aretz* inside his house awake and found him
> awake, asleep and found him asleep, awake and found him asleep—the
> house is clean. [If he left him] sleeping and found him awake—"the
> house is unclean," the words of R. Meir. And the sages say, "Unclean
> is only [the space] up to the place to which he stretch out and touch
> his hand and touch." (*m. Tohor.* 7:2)

> R. Simeon says, "He who gave a key to an *'am ha-aretz*—the house is
> unclean" (*t. Tohor.* 8:1).

What is significant here is that for all the differences over specifics there remains the common assumption that the people of the land transmit impurity. One central passage is *m. Hag.* 2:7, where we not only get the frequently cited contrast between the Pharisees and the people of the land, along with other parallel relationships, but also one that appears to be defined in terms of defilement of food:

> The clothing of *'am ha-aretz* is in the status of *midras* uncleanness for
> Pharisees [who eat ordinary food in a state of uncleanness], the cloth-
> ing of Pharisees is in the status of *midras* uncleanness for those who

eat *terumah* [priests]. The clothing of those who eat heave offering is
in the status of *midras* uncleanness for those who eat Holy Things
[officiating priests] etc. . . . (*m. Ḥag.* 2:7)

Thus the Mishnah compares the impurity of clothes of the people of the land
to that which has contracted impurity from one with a discharge (and consequently a father of impurity) in relationship to a Pharisee who is assumed,
especially given the subsequent relationships of impurity of eating priestly and
Temple food, to eat ordinary food in a state of purity. Such impurity is found
in other rabbinic comments on the people of the land but also, crucially, comments concerning articles (כלים), perhaps because a menstruating wife has
come into contact with them: "He who deposits utensils [כלים] with an *'am-
ha-aretz*—they are unclean with corpse uncleanness and unclean with *midras*
uncleanness" (*m. Tohor.* 8:2). It is worth noting the following examples in addition to this because it shows the people of the land, while clearly not deemed
liars, are not likely to take proper care with liquids, which have the potential
to intensify the transmission of impurity:

> An *'am-ha-aretz* is believed to testify, "These pickled vegetables did I
> pickle in a state of uncleanness, and I did not sprinkle liquids [capable
> of imparting susceptibility to uncleanness] upon them." But he is not
> believed to testify, "These fish I caught in a state of cleanness, and I
> did not shake the net over them." (*t. 'Abod. Zar.* 4:11)

> The water which comes up (1) on the snares, (2) on the gins, and (3)
> on the nets is not under the law, *If water be put.* And if he shook [them
> to remove the water], it [the water which is detached] is under the law,
> *If water be put.* (*m. Makš.* 5:7)

> He who undertakes to be a *haber* . . . does not purchase from him wet
> [produce, produce which has been rendered susceptible to unclean-
> ness] . . . (*m. Demai* 2:3)

> . . . this implies that it is permitted [for the *haber* to purchase from the
> *'am-ha-aretz*] dry [produce], since *'ammei ha-aretz* are deemed trust-
> worthy with respect to rendering produce susceptible to impurity. (*y.
> Demai* 2, 22d)

This is all based on the laws of liquids and their particular role in defiling,
based on Lev. 11:34. As we saw above and as we will see in more detail below,
this is crucial in understanding the transmission of impurity: unclean hands
cannot defile ordinary food unless a liquid comes between them. This is precisely the concern underlying the washing of cups.

In fact, table purity, the purity of vessels, and the defiling significance of liquids are all crucial for the halakic background to the washing cups debate in
the Mishnah. Moreover, we can now see more precisely the function of a pas-

sage such as Luke 11:37–41/Matt. 23:25–26. As we have seen, washing cups involves debates about preventing the transmission of impurity. The implied criticism of this in Luke 11:37–41/Matt. 23:25–26 would tie in with the even stronger criticisms of non-Temple table purity and hand washing in Mark 7:1–23/Matt. 15:1–20, which will be discussed below. From this perspective it would not be so relevant that people like the rabbinic people of the land were not particularly observant of non-Temple purity law yet still be within the boundaries of law observance. In other words the critique of this non-Temple table purity law by Jesus in Q justifies the interaction with a broad range of people who could not or would not observe expanded purity. In general we can say, then, that there would have been people among Jesus' followers or associated with the transmitters of the Q traditions who would not have been known for keeping themselves in a state of purity very often at all. This fits in too with other aspects of the Q tradition and the Synoptic tradition as a whole, such as the problems of Jesus associating with tax collectors and sinners (Matt. 11:19/Luke 7:34). It is also important to notice the context of both the Q traditions on purity and tithing discussed above (Matt. 23:23–28/Luke 11:37–44). In both Matthew and Luke the passage occurs in the same literary context as warnings against laying burdens on others without being prepared to help (Luke 11:46; Matt. 23:4). Presumably then, as is often observed, this concern was in the Q setting or transmitted alongside the tithing and purity texts. This is no doubt partly how the concerns for ethics and justice are to be interpreted in the two Q traditions.

If this approach to purity and tithing laws allows greater interaction with people suspect in their attitude towards Pharisaic/rabbinic approaches to purity, if it covers a broad range of socioeconomic backgrounds, and if it is consistent with the teaching of the historical Jesus, then it follows quite naturally that it was important for association with those sinners described in the previous chapter (i.e., the rich, the oppressive, the violent, lawbreakers, etc.). In this respect, it is crucial where Jesus places the emphasis in his fierce disputes with the Pharisees in Q: on morality or on moral purity. It is significant, and surely no coincidence, that the behavior Jesus attributes to the Pharisees and the kind of behavior Jesus proposes in these Q traditions echo the kinds of practices either performed by sinners or neglected by sinners. Sinners do the exact opposite of upholding justice, mercy, and faith (τὴν κρίσιν καὶ τὸ ἔλεος καὶ τὴν πίστιν, so Matt. 23:23) or justice and the love of God (τὴν κρίσιν καὶ τὴν ἀγάπην τοῦ θεοῦ, so Luke 11:42). The one obvious candidate for inclusion in the Q source here is of course "justice" (ἡ κρίσις), the exact opposite of what is to be expected of sinners (e.g., Sir. 11:9; 35[32]:17; 4Q511 63–64 III, 1–5; *Gen. Rab.* 49:6; *b. Sanh.* 109a–b). Or take "greed/plunder" and "self indulgence" (ἁρπαγῆς καὶ ἀκρασίας, so Matt. 23:25) or "greed/plunder" and "wickedness" (ἁρπαγῆς καὶ πονηρίας, so Luke 11:39). Common to both is of course "greed/plunder" (ἁρπαγή), something notoriously associated with practices of the stereotypical sinner (e.g., *1 En.* 102:5–10; 103:11–15; 104:2–7; *Ps. Sol.* 17:5; *m. Qidd.* 4:14; *b. Sanh.* 109a–b). As mentioned in the previous chapter, it is no coincidence that sinners are associated with tax collectors, people deemed no better than jumped-up thieves (cf. Luke 18:11; 19:1–10).

Matt. 23:28 ("So you also on the outside look righteous to others, but inside you are full of hypocrisy and lawlessness") may well be a Matthean addition to the Q tradition, but if Matthew is at least largely reflective of Q here, then it hardly contradicts the meaning of Matt. 23:27 ("For you are like whitewashed tombs, which on the outside look beautiful, but inside they are full of the bones of the dead and of all kinds of filth"). Moreover, it is still worth looking at Matt. 23:28, because it counts as a very early interpretation of the Q tradition. It too contains fairly typical language we saw associated with sinners in the previous chapter. There is of course the contrast with righteousness (οὕτως καὶ ὑμεῖς ἔξωθεν μὲν φαίνεσθε τοῖς ἀνθρώποις δίκαιοι) so common in the language of sinners and also found in the context of a dispute with the Pharisees in the Synoptic tradition (Mark 2:15–17). We might also compare the common thread in Jewish literature on sinners or bad people appearing blessed when in fact the opposite is the case. The reference to "hypocrisy and lawlessness" (ὑποκρίσεως καὶ ἀνομίας) could of course come straight from a description of sinners in a whole host of Jewish texts analyzed in the previous chapter (e.g., Pss. 49[50]:16–23; 93[94]:13; 119; Ezek. 33:8, 19; Sir. 15:7, 9; 1 Macc. 1:34; 2:45–48, 62; *1 En.* 104:10; *Ps. Sol.* 1:1; 2:1; 4:8; 14:6; 15:5, 8).

Crucially and predictably, this also echoes the behavior of Gentile sinners, which may partially explain why these texts were transmitted (anti-Pharisaic polemic being another reason, of course). The behavior that the Pharisees should be practicing is fairly obviously covenantal behavior. It follows that not behaving in a covenantal manner is effectively lawless Gentile behavior (cf. *T. Reub.* 3:1–8; *T. Levi* 17:11). So, for instance, "justice" (ἡ κρίσις) in Matt. 23:23/Luke 11:42 is not to be expected of sinful Gentiles (cf. Ps. 9:15–16; 1QM XI, 12–14; *Gen. Rab.* 49:6; *b. Sanh.* 109a–b).[57] "Greed/plunder" (ἁρπαγή) in Matt. 23:25/Luke 11:39 would be at home on lists that no doubt refer to stereotypical Gentile behavior (e.g., 1 Cor. 6:9–11; Mark 7:21–23; Wis. 14:25), as indeed would the extras recorded in the Matthean (καὶ ἀκρασίας) and Lukan (καὶ πονηρίας) versions. If we take Matt. 23:28–29 as having some value, then again we see important parallels with behavior attributed to Gentiles. The attack on Pharisaic morality with the mention of insides being "full of the bones of the dead and of all kinds of filth" again would have some relevance for how Gentile behavior was understood. According to *Jubilees*, for example, the polluted ways of the nations, explicitly contrasted with the commandments, involve offering sacrifices to the dead and eating among graves (*Jub.* 22:16–17).

Furthermore the Matthean charge of "lawlessness" (ἀνομίας) in Matt. 23:28, which from certain perspectives was effectively what Gentiles were deemed to be, and Torah righteousness (Matt. 23:28) were the kinds of practice that marked Jew from Gentile. Similar points can also be made concerning the other material particular to either Luke or Matthew in these sources. For example, Matt. 23:23 mentions "faith" (τὴν πίστιν) among the weightier parts of the law, which is precisely what idolaters do not practice, according to Wis. 14:25 ("faithlessness"—ἀπιστία). The Matthean mention of "mercy" (τὸ ἔλεος) in Matt. 23:23 refers to a covenant-defining behavior or a sign of divine favor (cf. Hos. 6:6; Wis. 3:9; 15:1; 1 Macc. 2:57; 13:46; 2 Macc. 6:16; 7:23; 3 Macc. 6:4), even in contrast to the nations (e.g., Wis. 4:15). Human mercy in many ways echoes divine mercy, and in this tradition God acts as a kind of role model for human behavior (cf. Matt. 5:48/Luke 6:36). It is interesting in this respect that Sir. 18:13 can say, "The compassion [ἔλεος] of human beings is for their neighbors, but the compassion [ἔλεος] of the Lord is for every living thing/all flesh" (cf. Sir. 28:4; 29:1), which would show that the potential for a broadening out of this principle of imitation was present. Furthermore it was recognized that righteous Gentiles were also capable of showing mercy (e.g., 2 Macc. 4:37). Luke 11:42 mentions "the love of God [τὴν ἀγάπην τοῦ θεοῦ]" among neglected things, again something commonly associated with the kinds of practice sinful Gentiles obviously do not do (cf. Ps. 9:17), yet something like the love of God was also attributed to righteous Gentiles (see next chapter). More examples could be given, and indeed will be when we discuss Mark 7:21–23, but it should be a fairly uncontroversial point that the behavior attributed to the Pharisees is behavior that would mark a Jew to be outside the covenant and consequently behaving no better than a Gentile, even if those boundaries were inevitably blurred.

The transmitters of the Q traditions, along with Paul, were quite happy to acknowledge that Gentiles were expected to behave lawlessly. An excellent example is that Gentiles are simply assumed to be bad types in Matt. 5:46–47, which ends "And if you greet only your brothers, what more are you doing than others? Do not even the Gentiles do the same?" The version found in Luke 6:32–33 is a bit different. One notable difference is that instead of Gentiles (and tax collectors) Luke has "sinners." Perhaps Luke made the change here to fit his theological concerns, but it is hardly too far removed from the Matthean version in this respect. We might also recall the rabbinic variant of "sinners" for "idolaters" in *m. Ned.* 3:11. That Gentiles are the kinds of people interested in what they wear, what they eat, what they drink in Q (Matt. 6:32/Luke 12:30) is also of some relevance because of the close Gentile link with sinners. Matthew 6:32/Luke 12:30 mentions the kinds of things that concern the rich. More significantly these are the things that concern the rich, oppressive sinners in *1 En*. 97–98, verses that have some very close thematic parallels with the Q passage.[58] So once again we find, as should be expected by now, very close behavioral similarities between Gentile sinners and Jewish sinners.

GENTILES AND Q

Although many of the Q texts may well have emerged in the context of the historical Jesus' preaching to Jewish sinners and developed by later followers with similar and continuing concerns, these traditions were clearly of ongoing relevance for the new movement, which contained a number of Gentiles. This would surely not be lost on the earliest Christians transmitting the Q traditions. But is there a Gentile mission or an overt concern for Gentiles? Views range from a fully blown Gentile mission to great disdain for Gentiles that tend to be based on either Luke 10:8 or Matt. 10:5–6, respectively. As these are singularly attested texts, to use them in reconstructing Q is, however, perhaps too speculative. Even if we assume Luke 10:8 ("eat what is set before you") was in Q, its use would not support a Gentile mission.[59] It would be difficult to see Luke using such a tradition without any qualification if it so radically contradicted his view that food laws were overridden through a divine vision well after the resurrection (Acts 10–11:18). Indeed Luke 10:8 does not contradict food laws in any way. Whichever way we look at it, it can only be seen as part of Jesus' ministry in Palestine. Given that there is no explicit indication of a Gentile mission elsewhere, it would surely be assumed that the disciples would be going to Jewish people, and it would simply be assumed also that no one would offer pork, shellfish, or any other prohibited food. If Q wanted Jesus to be seen overriding food laws then Q would have to say so. Matthew 10:5–6 supports the view that Q had no Gentile mission, assuming for the moment that Matt. 10:5–6 can be classed as a Q tradition.[60]

But the extent of the negative attitude is difficult to measure. It may accurately reflect an attitude from the historical Jesus' ministry that was transmitted "faithfully." But then it is probably fair to say that Jesus never did have a Gentile mission or all that much to say on the issue of Gentile salvation, so such a passage would hardly be surprising. Moreover, note how Matthew can accept these sentiments without too much difficulty but still recognize the importance of the Gentile mission (esp. Matt. 28:18–20). It is quite possible that the transmitters of Q could acknowledge the intra-Jewish mission of Jesus while still holding a positive role of Gentiles after his death. As these two texts are of limited use, we need to look at some of the material that might imply a positive view of Gentiles. An obvious starting text would be the following:

> I tell you, many will come from east and west and will eat with Abraham and Isaac and Jacob in the kingdom of heaven, while the heirs of the kingdom will be thrown into the outer darkness, where there will be weeping and gnashing of teeth. (Matt. 8:11–12)

> There will be weeping and gnashing of teeth when you see Abraham and Isaac and Jacob and all the prophets in the kingdom of God, and you yourselves will be thrown out. Then people will come from east and west, from north and south, and will eat in the kingdom of God. (Luke 13:28–29)

At first sight, despite the minor differences, these passages might seem to point to a promise of salvation to the nations.[61] However, as Dale Allison has shown in some detail, it is at least possible to read this Q tradition as a judgment on unfaithful Jews in the land of Israel and a promise of the ingathering of Diaspora Jews (cf. Jer. 24; Ezek. 11).[62] Another obvious Q text that seems to point in favor of a concern for Gentiles is the healing of the centurion's slave/son (Matt. 8:5–10, 13 par. Luke 7:2–10). But even here it is far from certain, as David Catchpole has shown.[63] It is not clear that the centurion is necessarily a Gentile (cf. 1 Macc. 3:55; Josephus, *Ant.* 6.4; 7.233, 368; 9.143, 148, 151, 156, 188; *J.W.* 2.578). Nor is it clear that the Matthean Jesus' phrase "in no one in Israel have I found such faith" (Matt. 8:10) refers to Gentile status. It can equally be interpreted to mean that this centurion is the most righteous Jew Jesus has found in Israel (cf. Matt. 9:33). It is of course possible that some Gentile and some Jewish Christians read these texts (Matt. 8:5–10, 13 par. Luke 7:2–10; Matt. 8:11–12 par. Luke 13:28–29) differently, but it is important to acknowledge that we cannot use them with any great certainty to support an overt concern for a Gentile mission or Gentile salvation in Q. Even if such passages did have Gentiles in mind, at best they show isolated examples of a positive attitude towards Gentiles in the future when judgment comes.

There are some Q traditions where there is a view of Gentiles that would not seem to exclude them from eschatological salvation. Compare the following:

> "Woe to you, Chorazin! Woe to you, Bethsaida! For if the deeds of power done in you had been done in Tyre and Sidon, they would have repented long ago, sitting in sackcloth and ashes. But at the judgment it will be more tolerable for Tyre and Sidon than for you." (Luke 10:13–14 par. Matt. 11:20–22)

Christopher Tuckett claims that in Q 10:13–15 "it is predicted that Gentiles will fare better than . . . Jews in the eschatological kingdom."[64] This may be pushing the evidence too far. It is clear that Chorazin and Bethsaida are being rhetorically compared with a notoriously anti-Jewish town like Tyre (Josephus, *Ag. Ap.* 1.70; *Ant.* 14.313–21; cf. *J.W.* 2.478; Isa. 23; Jer. 25:17–22; 47:4; Ezek. 26–28; Joel 3:4–8; Amos 1:9–10; Zech. 9:2–4; Acts 21:3–4), and there are also echoes of the saying on the legendary sinful place of Sodom (Luke 10:12 par. Matt. 11:24; 10:15).[65] The saying is focused on the judgment of Chorazin and Bethsaida and has little if anything to do with the salvation of Gentiles. Put another way, Chorazin and Bethsaida are so wicked that they have less chance of surviving judgment than a legendary, sinful biblical town and a notoriously anti-Jewish town—that is, no chance at all (cf. *Mek. Exod.* on 15.5–6). A better and probably the clearest example of a positive attitude towards Gentiles is Luke 11:31–32/Matt. 12:41–42, along with positive mention of the Queen of the South and the people of Nineveh, but it only represents one positive example recorded in Israel's sacred history and how they will act in future judgment. In this instance there is still a major stress on judging unbelieving Jews and little to say on Gentiles in the present.

We might also point to Luke 16:17/Matt. 5:18 as evidence for a Q passage functioning at a time when there were challenges to the validity of the law, and it would most likely have to be in the context of the Gentile mission. If this is the case it is notable that the Q version shows no signs at all of polemic aimed at Gentiles being punished for being Gentile lawbreakers. Instead it would be a saying designed to defend the validity of the law against Christian lawbreakers in general, and this may have included Jews too (cf. Gal. 2:11–14). That said, the Q saying alone cannot be pushed this far. There is no definitely known context, and it might simply be a very general proverbial-style saying. Taken alone, the Q saying could easily be seen as a general Jewish comment that would have little difficulty being read as a fairly uncontroversial rabbinic saying. Without a context, this saying offers little in the way of firm evidence for an attitude towards Gentiles by transmitters of the Q traditions.[66]

Is there any evidence that Q simply excluded Gentiles? Siegfried Schultz has suggested that the "Q-community" would not have a Gentile mission before end times because, in principle at least, there is nowhere in Q that the Torah is consciously abrogated.[67] But inclusion of Gentiles does not automatically mean that the law must be rejected in any significant way. As we will see in the next chapter, the acknowledgment and even acceptance of Gentiles attracted to Judaism is not quite the same as the Gentile mission, but it shows that Gentiles could be present at a gathering of law-observant Jews or Jewish Christians and, naturally, keep the law at least whilst present. Moreover, there is well-known evidence from the NT showing that the Gentile mission could entail law observance for some. According to Acts 15:1–5, certain individuals and Pharisees believed that it was necessary for Gentiles to be circumcised and keep the law of Moses. Paul's letter to the Galatians polemically deals with the issue of Gentiles being convinced that full law observance was necessary.[68] Clearly, then, at least some thought Gentile Christians ought to keep the law. Law observance did not necessarily equal Jewish exclusivity, and a law-observant Q does not necessarily equal a lack of Gentile mission or nonacceptance of Gentiles.

Is Q a bit more extreme and advocate hostility towards Gentiles? The following is a Q text that may imply a negative attitude towards Gentiles:

> And if you greet only your brothers and sisters, what more are you doing than others? Do not even the Gentiles do the same? (Matt. 5:47 par. Luke 6:32–33)[69]

And this Q text is not alone:

> For it is the nations of the world that strive after all these things. . . . (Luke 12:30)

> For it is the Gentiles who strive for all these things. . . . (Matt. 6:32)

Tuckett notes that the "tone in both cases is not overtly polemical" and is not "a piece of violent invective against Gentiles themselves." Yet he also points out that "the very fact that the sayings are so *un*polemical" may point to a mentality of Gentiles as outsiders "almost without thinking."[70] From this, Tuckett claims that "it is very hard to conceive of Gentiles forming anything more than a tiny minority in the group of Christians responsible for Q" and it is "correspondingly hard to believe that Q Christians were actively engaged in any positive mission to Gentiles." At most, Q is "aware of a Gentile Mission, but not actively engaged in it."[71]

Tuckett's view that Gentiles are effectively outsiders does not automatically follow from these Q traditions. Even the famous apostle to the Gentiles could make comments like this to a fellow Jew and record it in a letter to Gentiles: "We ourselves are Jews by birth and not Gentile sinners" (Gal. 2:15). This shows how traditions such as Matt. 5:47 and Luke 12:30/Matt. 6:32 could potentially be transmitted alongside traditions that have a very positive attitude to Gentiles or communities that included Gentiles. Tuckett may well be correct when he says the people who transmitted these traditions were Jewish and had little concern with the Gentile mission and that Gentiles formed only a tiny minority of the Q Christians, but it is not proven by the existence of Matt. 5:47 and Luke 12:30/Matt. 6:32. The key points for present purposes are that these traditions in no way contradict openness to sympathetic Gentiles or a Gentile mission, nor do they contradict the usefulness of the Q legal material in the spread of earliest Christianity.

However, Tuckett's view that Q is aware of a Gentile mission but not actively engaged in it is a generally convincing approach, or at least the best we can do with the evidence available. The Gentile mission, or at least a concern for and association with Gentiles, would have begun when the Q material was being transmitted. This, combined with a lack of general Gentile punishment traditions in Q or hostility towards a Gentile mission, suggests that concern for Gentiles in earliest Christianity was not something the people who transmitted the Q traditions would oppose and that it was something they would have simply accepted as valid. Paul D. Meyer's view that the transmitters of Q ("the Q-community" for Meyer) accepted the validity of the Gentile mission and used this assumed success as a warning against unrepentant Jews is difficult to prove on the basis of the textual evidence alone, but it would be an intriguing possibility given that there was a significant number of Gentiles attached to Christianity as the Q traditions were being transmitted (cf. Luke 11:31–32 par. Matt. 12:41–42).[72]

So although Gentiles may not be a major concern for Q, it is significant that the transmission of the material on issues of purity and tithing stress the importance of ethics without having too much concern for the specifics of expanded purity laws. They in no way, however, reject the biblical purity system, probably because the kinds of moral practices these traditions attack are also stereotypically associated with Gentile sinners in Jewish thought. It is surely significant that not only Matthew but even the arguably more Gentile-oriented Luke also had access to and happily used these traditions. Much of the Q legal material is probably very early, much of it probably going back to the 30s; for the evidence of any worries that nonobservance of biblical law was a problem is minimal, perhaps nonexistent. This approach to the law in Q would allow greater social interaction not only among Jews not dedicated to the expansion of the law but also among Gentiles sympathetic towards Judaism and Jewish law. It may be that these traditions fairly accurately reflect the words of the historical Jesus, but they were no doubt transmitted because they were deemed continually useful. Or at least Jesus' attitude reflected the attitude of the transmitters of Q, and continuing disputes with Pharisaic opponents presumably continued. But it was probably also because of a concern for Gentiles in the Q tradition.

The Q material is compatible with the spread of law-observant Jewish-Gentile communities. While this general point is undoubtedly accurate it remains that by itself it does not provide hard proof of Christian effort to make law observance among Gentiles explicit. This means we must look elsewhere to provide an independent early witness to add collective weight to the argument. We must now turn to Mark 6–8 because here we have what I would regard as decisive and explicit evidence of such concerns.

MARK 6–8 AND THE JUSTIFICATION
FOR THE SPREAD OF EARLIEST CHRISTIANITY

In *The Date of Mark's Gospel* I argued at some length that Mark 7:1–23, and indeed the Gospel as a whole, must be dated before the early 40s and more particularly at a time when Christianity was largely law observant. If this is the case then Mark 7:1–23 has to be read against the scholarly consensus as a passage that adheres to biblical law. If this is true then the narrative location of Mark 7:1–23 becomes particularly interesting: it is sandwiched between two major feeding miracles, one Jewish and one Gentile. It would therefore provide some explicit evidence of law observance in a Gentile context in narrative form. As I gave a relatively radical rereading of Mark 7:1–23, which has also led to criticisms, this argument ought to be summarized in some detail then defended.

In Mark 7:1–13, "human tradition" or "tradition of the elders" occurs six times. There are discussions about what Mark regards as "tradition": handwashing; meal-time immersing of cups, pitchers, bronze kettles, and beds/dining couches (καὶ κλινῶν);[73] qorban; and general practice of "tradition."[74] These practices, from Mark's perspective, are not biblical law; in fact Mark explicitly sets "tradition" over against "the commandment of God [τὴν ἐντολὴν τοῦ θεοῦ]" and "the word of God [τὸν λόγον τοῦ θεοῦ]" (Mark 7:8, 9, 13). It would be at least a little odd if Mark were then to go and nullify the word of God in 7:15, 19. On the contrary, Mark has carefully established the context in which to interpret verses 15 and 19. If Mark wanted us to believe that Jesus was rejecting biblical laws, would he not have criticized them specifically instead of praising them in contrast to "tradition"? Moreover, this approach would be in line with what I would regard as a tendency in Mark and the Synoptics as a whole: to portray Jesus as a law-observant Jew.[75]

Of some importance is that this interpretation fits in with the highly relevant Jewish discussions of handwashing and the transmission of impurity, the very frame of reference given in Mark, not to mention the parallel Matt. 15:1–20. Mark 7:1–5 is crucial here.[76] The first practice we get is handwashing before ordinary food, something well-documented in rabbinic literature (e.g., *m. Ḥag.* 2:5; *m. Ḥul.* 2:5; *m. Yad.* 3:2; *t. Ber.* 4:8; 5:6; *t. Demai* 2:11–12; *b. 'Erub.* 21b). This should be regarded as a first-century practice, for it would be incredible if Mark had invented it only for rabbis to later independently develop it and attribute something very similar to first-century sources. Moreover, it is also exceptionally unlikely that Matthew would have made a further attack on handwashing (Matt. 15:20) if it did not exist as a practice. For Mark it is a "tradition" placed alongside related "traditions," all concerning table purity. Mark 7:4 speaks of Pharisees' immersing themselves on return from the market, the most historically plausible understanding of what must be the correct translation of Mark 7:4a, ἀπ' ἀγορᾶς ἐὰν μὴ βαπτίσωνται οὐκ ἐσθίουσιν. As we will see, bodily immersion is important for purity at the meal table for certain Jews. Mark 7:4 also mentions traditions of immersing cups, pitchers, and bronze kettles. These are grounded in the specific laws of Lev. 11:32–33 and interpreted more generally in rabbinic literature (e.g. *m. Miqw.* 3:10; *m. Kelim* 5:11; 11:1; 14:1). Leviticus also gives some precise rulings for wooden objects to be immersed if impure (Lev. 11:32; 15:12) and these were interpreted more generally in the Mishnah (e.g. *m. Ḥul.* 1:6; *m. Kelim* 2:1; 13:6; 15:1; 16:1–2; 17:1; 20:2; 22:1–2; 27:1). Mark 7:4 also has a textual variant: καὶ κλινῶν. Such "beds" were associated with the meal table and had to be immersed if they became impure (*m. Miqw.* 7:7; *m. Kelim* 19:1). These too were based on the laws of Lev. 11:32 and 15:11.[77]

Mark 7:1–5 is therefore a very precise and accurate representation of Pharisaic laws concerning food purity, and Mark must have included these detailed verses for a reason. The most obvious reason for their inclusion is to form part of the polemic against "tradition" that is placed over against Scripture. As noted above, the context was to interpret what follows, particularly Mark 7:15, 19. This is doubly so in the case of Mark 7:1–5, as these verses directly relate to issues of the transmission of impurity from unwashed hands to ordinary (as opposed to priestly or Temple) food to the eater, an issue that needs to be discussed further in order to see its precise relevance for interpreting Mark 7:15, 19.

Ordinary food is at most susceptible to second-degree impurity, at a second remove from the scriptural source (e.g., *m. Ṭ. Yom* 4:1, 3; *m. Soṭah* 5:2). The conventional rabbinic view holds that unclean hands, deemed second-degree impure, could not render ordinary food impure because something deemed second-degree impure could not defile something else susceptible at most to second-degree impurity (e.g., *m. Yad.* 3:1). In other words, unclean hands could not make ordinary food unclean and so would make little sense for interpreting Mark 7. This has led some to think that the rabbinic system of impurity was not in place in the first century.[78] However, the role of liquids changes things significantly.[79] The strong defiling function of liquid in the transmission of impurity is very specific in Lev. 11:29–38 but was expanded more generally in rabbinic literature and elsewhere (e.g., 4Q284a; 4Q274 III; 4Q394 VIII, 4, 5–7; CD XII, 15–17)—so that something of second-degree impurity, such as unclean hands, could pass on impurity to ordinary food (e.g., *m. Parah* 8:7; *m. Zabim* 5:12; *m. Ḥul.* 2:5; *b. Ḥul.* 33a).[80]

It is also worth noting that the liquids which defile—namely, dew, water, wine, oil, blood, milk, and honey (*m. Makš.* 6:4; cf. CD XII, 15–17)—have obvious relevance for the meal table. So why wash hands? There are different reasons but an important and highly relevant argument has been made by John Poirier, who points out that a passage such as *b. Ber.* 28a suggests that the idea of a person whose "insides are not as their outsides" would have taken on reference to those outside the pre-70 Pharisaic movement who did not keep their insides pure through the washing of hands.[81] Given that Mark 7:4 mentions bodily immersion, we should note once again that particularity of the transmission of impurity, namely, the issue of the *tebul yom*: someone who has immersed that day and is waiting for sunset to be deemed pure again (Lev. 15). A *tebul yom* is deemed second-degree impure (e.g., *m. Zabim* 5:3). However, a *tebul yom* cannot render liquid impure in contrast to unclean hands even though both are second-degree impure. Yet at the same time it was possible for a *tebul yom* to have the hands second-degree impure apart from the rest of the body, and these defiled hands are able to defile apart from the rest of the body (e.g., *m. Ṭ. Yom* 2:2). Hands were, quite obviously, always liable to contract impurity apart from the body because they are "fidgety [עסקניות]" (e.g., *b. Šabb.* 14a; *b. Sukkah* 26b).

With this background to Jewish purity law, we are now in a better position to understand Mark 7:1–23. In fact, the Pharisaic/rabbinic logic of the transmission of impurity fits Mark 7:1–23 very precisely. Mark 7:1–5 is once again crucial here. Impurity could be contracted, for example, at the marketplace, so bodily immersion was required to remove potential impurity and halt the transmission. Yet while the post-immersed body could not defile ordinary food, hands could. Handwashing prevents the transmission of impurity from hands to food (via a liquid) to the insides. Given the attention to this detail in Mark, including a crucial editorial aside (Mark 7:3–4), we can see more clearly what the Markan Jesus meant by saying, "There is nothing outside a person that by going in can defile, but the things that come out are what defile" (Mark 7:15) and "He declared all foods clean" (Mark 7:19): the Markan Jesus is rejecting the transmission of impurity, through a lack of handwashing, to the insides; thus all foods (permitted in the Torah) must be clean from this perspective. By using this frame of reference—which is the most-obvious frame of reference given the detailed content of Mark 7:1–23—we can see that Mark 7:1–23 fits more neatly into a Jewish context that does not assume that biblical food and purity law has been overridden. Because of a tendency in the Synoptic tradition as a whole and an analysis of the law in the first twenty years of Christianity, we must assume a date before the mid-40s CE when we start to get the first indication of notable nonobservance in earliest Christianity.

This view on the transmission of impurity almost certainly reflects the position of the historical Jesus. If we remove the editorial Mark 7:3–4, we potentially have a source that assumes the complex transmission of impurity and would fit into an early Jewish context with little or no Gentile influence. This

view on impurity coheres with Jesus' general teaching on the law, and, significantly, the assumptions made in this passage are also made in the independent
tradition of Luke 11:37–41/Matt. 23:25–26. This rejection of handwashing
would also permit contact with a wide range of people who would have been
deemed impure by at least some Pharisees, something of obvious relevance to
Jesus' mission, and echoed, as we saw, in the Q traditions on purity.

SOME ALTERNATIVE VIEWS

One publication not available to me when I wrote *The Date of Mark's Gospel*
takes a very different approach. It is a 2004 article by Christian Stettler on Mark
7:14–23, an analysis more concerned with the historical Jesus. That by itself
would still be relevant, for it would affect my interpretation of Mark 7:1–23,
and it is made even more so by Stettler's conservative attitude to the Gospel tradition. Stettler uses Mark 7:14–23 and Matt. 15:10–20 to argue for a modified
version of the traditional view that the historical Jesus and his Gospel interpreters in principle overrode the biblical food and purity laws.[82] Stettler takes
the key saying in Mark 7:15 as absolute ("There is *nothing* outside a man that
can defile him by going into him . . ."), so, against several recent exegetes, it
cannot be understood in the sense of a "Semiticizing relative negation." The
Matthean form ("not so much . . . as . . .") is deemed to be more ambiguous but,
it is argued, essentially makes the same point. According to Stettler's exegesis
it is only impurity of the heart that now defiles. Stettler argues that this view
does not automatically imply that the disciples are expected to abandon food
and other laws in practice but rather that they are no longer required of the
people of God.[83]

Stettler notes that Mark 7:14–23 (par. Matt. 15:10–20) is a new scene, hence
a new introduction, where Jesus calls people to him (Mark 7:14; Matt. 15:10)
and thus bases his argument on these verses.[84] Yet it is the omission of the pre-
ceding verses that leads to a major problem with Stettler's analysis. These
verses, as I noted above, set the scene for Mark 7:15, 19. If Jesus is talking about
food and purity in 7:15, 19 it is absolutely crucial that Mark 7:1–5, with all its
details on table purity, is at the very least discussed in the light of 7:14–23, not
to mention the contrast between tradition and commandment set up by Mark.
Assisted by the omission of such key verses, it is only natural that Stettler has
no proper discussion of Jewish purity law. Not only was this available to Stettler in the rabbinic primary sources and the DSS, but also a detailed discussion of the transmission of impurity was provided by Roger Booth in an
extremely important book on Mark 7:1–23 which Stettler notes on several
occasions. Given the nature of the Mark 7:15 saying and given that Mark has

at least provided a narrative frame in the context of purity details, then the legal background surely cannot be ignored! Consequently, it is difficult to accept an analysis which states that Jesus was in some sense indifferent about Jewish purity and food laws in Mark 7 but which does not discuss the passage in the light of Jewish purity and food laws.

There have also been some criticisms of my approach to Mark 7:1–23, such as that by Lois Fuller. She argues that just because Mark may have portrayed Jesus as a law-observant Jew elsewhere, it does not follow that he does so in Mark 7:1–23. Furthermore, if Mark had to explain certain purity laws then would he not have to explain issues of defiled food in Mark 7:19? Alternatively, Fuller argues, in declaring all foods clean "surely Jesus is following his usual strategy of pursuing the spirit rather than the letter of the law."[85] Against Fuller, I would counter that while it is certainly true that we should not assume that Mark 7 must portray Jesus as a law-observant Jew just because of portrayals elsewhere, I would point out that this is not quite what I argued. I argued that in *every* instance in the Synoptic Gospels Jesus is portrayed as a law-observant Jew and that *additionally* this had to be supplemented by a close textual analysis of Mark 7:1–23 which is precisely what I gave, irrespective of whether I was right or wrong. Furthermore, it is not necessarily the case that Mark would feel obliged to write an explanation concerning food defilement: indeed, it is not always easy to predict what someone should have written if x, y, or z had been the case.

That Mark has provided numerous details of an intra-Jewish dispute and mentioned the nondefilement of food should not be ignored. If this was set in the context of law-observant Christianity, then there would simply be no need to qualify a statement if everyone was kosher. The weakest part of Fuller's critique is Jesus' supposedly stressing the spirit over the letter of the law as his usual practice. This is hardly obvious, as Fuller implies. In fact, there is simply no evidence for this approach in the Synoptic tradition. For what it is worth, there have been several prominent, detailed, and well-argued attempts to show that Jesus was acting within the boundaries of Jewish legal debate by scholars such as Geza Vermes, E. P. Sanders, Markus Bockmuehl, and Maurice Casey, to name but a few. To put it mildly, Fuller has referenced a very outdated and long-debunked view on Jesus and "the spirit of the law."

A predictable opinion on the matter has been dictated by Elliott Maloney.[86] Unfortunately, most of Maloney's comments are unsubstantiated opinion, so it is consequently difficult to respond to points raised where no noticeable reasoning is present. He accuses me of a "very tenuous and convoluted" examination of "talmudic texts" on purity and contamination of food in relation to Mark 7:1–23.[87] That is not really much of a counter case, and it certainly should not be believed simply because some scholar says so. I just do not understand why such a connection is supposed to be tenuous and convoluted. Mark gives a detailed aside on purity laws associated with table purity in Mark 7:3–4—a Markan *editorial* aside—which also happens to be accurate when compared with the earliest rabbinic purity material recorded in the Mishnah. And there are similar issues in Mark 7:1–23 which would suggest that looking at contemporary purity laws might just be worthwhile: the Pharisees also ask a question about handwashing; there is a contrast between the biblical commandments and "tradition" (such as handwashing); Jesus talks about the defilement of insides; and there is mention of food being defiled. Moreover, it is the earliest rabbinic material on handwashing—which is as close as we can possibly get to Pharisaic views on handwashing, the very topic which opens Mark 7—where we in fact get lots of extremely similar details on the transmission of impurity and the contamination of ordinary food (not to mention material from the DSS). This is hardly coincidental.

Moreover, and for what it is worth, those who have studied the purity background to Mark 7 have utilized the same rabbinic background as I did, sometimes in great detail.[88] This does not necessarily mean we were right to do so, but such important argumentation will hardly be undermined by condescending remarks. The following must now be asked of Maloney: given all the above, is it not right to see if we can find how purity laws functioned in the contemporary culture and how the Markan text interacted with such views? This is no radical methodological idea; I am only using a standard historical practice. Maloney must have misunderstood my argument, because if he did not, the logical implications of his opinion would be that historical analysis of a given practice has to ignore external evidence that discusses the details of the exact same practice! Consequently, Maloney's frustrating evidence-free attack on the use of the legal background to Mark 7 and his dismissive general opinion should not be taken seriously until he produces at least *some* reasoning.[89] Thankfully there has been an academic reaction against the kinds of approaches that are intimately associated with Maloney's approach—a reaction that such-minded scholars really ought to take note of.[90]

MARK 7:1–23 IN THE CONTEXT OF MARK 6–8

With that depressing episode behind us, Mark 7:1–23, within the broader narrative context of Mark 6–8, can now prove to be of some importance for the concerns of this book. It is widely observed that Mark 6–8 has a clash over purity strategically placed between two feeding miracles, with one eye on the Gentile mission. The first feeding miracle is for Jews, but after the supposed rejection of food laws (Mark 7:15, 19), so the argument goes, Jesus can then move into Gentile territory to provide various healings and another feeding miracle for Gentiles. We might describe this argument as something like the principle of "to the Jew first and also to the Greek" (Rom. 1:16) in story form (cf. Mark 7:27–28). The general outline of a development of the Jewish message to eventually include Gentiles is difficult to deny, as is the strategic placing of Mark 7:1–23. However, where I differ is of course in the function of Mark 7:1–23, which I argue is an attack on the transmission of impurity though handwashing and biblically permitted food deemed impure.

So, if Mark 7:1–23 is upholding the food laws, what relevance does it have for the emergence of an early law-observant Jewish-Christian movement that included Gentiles? To begin we should turn to the narrative context that many scholars have seen in terms of a concern for Gentiles in addition to a concern for Jews. I will provide what I think are the strongest points in favor of this view and try to avoid some of the sometimes necessarily speculative aspects of the general argument (e.g., the symbolic value of the numbers in the second miracle).[91]

The first feeding, of the five thousand who appear to be Jews (Mark 6:30–44), and the second feeding, of the four thousand who appear to be Gentiles (Mark 8:1–21), provide an obvious framework for this section of Mark. There are plenty of other narrative interconnections. Purity language provides a connection between Mark 7:1–23 and the rest of Mark 7. The daughter of the Syro-Phoenician woman has an unclean spirit (7:25). As Gentiles, the Syro-Phoenician woman and her daughter are regarded as dogs (7:27–28). Dogs could also be regarded as unclean animals: "All that walk on their paws, among the animals that walk on all fours, are unclean for you" (e.g., Lev. 11:27; cf. Exod. 22:31; 1 Kgs. 4:11; Matt. 7:6; b. BQ 83a). We may also add the continual criss-crossing over and about Lake Galilee in Mark 6:30–8:21 as another narrative interconnection.[92]

But the most common narrative link is the recurrence of "bread" (ἄρτος) and bread-related things throughout Mark 6:30–8:21. Obviously bread and related imagery are mentioned in the two feeding miracles (6:38, 41, 43, 44; 8:4–6, 8). But this also occurs in between. In Mark 7:2 the disciples are eating bread when they are criticized for eating with unclean hands; in Mark 7:27 Jesus talks of the bread of the children; and in 7:28 the woman speaks of the crumbs (τῶν ψιχίων). After the second feeding miracle the disciples forget to bring bread and had only one loaf of bread in the boat (Mark 8:14). It is surely not for unrelated reasons that Jesus warns of the yeast of Pharisees and of Herod in the next verse, followed by verses on the clueless disciples' wondering about the significance of bread and Jesus' questioning them on the issue of bread (Mark 8:16–21). This sustained and dense use of bread and bread-related language in Mark 6:30–8:21 is hardly likely to be coincidental.

But it is not simply the narrative consistency of Mark 6:30–8:21 that concerns us here: the spread of the message to include Gentiles is of utmost importance in this section of Mark. It is of some significance that Jesus' movements after Mark 7:1–23 place him in what may be called Gentile territory. In the first instance—the trip to the region of Tyre (Mark 7:24)—he is placed in an area infamously poles apart from Jewish territory in popular imagination.[93] As Josephus says, "The Egyptians, the whole race without exception, and among the Phoenicians the Tyrians, are notoriously our bitterest enemies" (*Ag. Ap.* 1.70; cf. *J.W.* 2.478; 4.105; Acts 21:3–4). Moreover, Tyre's Galilean hinterland also meant the usual exploitation of the peasantry, largely Jewish peasantry to be more precise (e.g., *Ant.* 14.313–21; Acts 12:20). We may add to this a list of biblical hostilities aimed at a wealthy, oppressive Tyre, usually alongside Sidon, where Jesus travels next (e.g., Isa. 23; Jer. 25:17–22; 47:4; Ezek. 26–28; Joel 3:4–8; Amos 1:9–10; Zech. 9:2–4).

After leaving the region of Tyre, Jesus is then said to have returned "by way of Sidon towards the Sea of Galilee, in the region of the Decapolis" (Mark 7:31). It is possible Mark meant that Jesus toured these places, but it is also possible that we have an extremely odd diversionary journey towards the Decapolis, as a glance at any map of the area would show. Whatever we make of this, it is again placing Jesus in territory associated with Gentiles, possibly connecting Jesus with the location of Christians at the time Mark wrote—a "shout out" or "big up," to use the language of youth for the first and mercifully last time in this book—or *perhaps* even connecting Jesus with the place where Mark's Gospel was written.[94] There is also a hint of what may be termed "theological geography." As is often noted, the language of people coming from far away in Mark 8:3 may reflect the idea of Gentiles being far from God whereas Jews are close, language that was also employed to describe Gentile converts to Judaism and Christianity (cf. Deut. 28:49; 29:22; Josh. 9:6, 9; 1 Kgs. 8:42; Ps. 148:14; Isa. 5:26; 39:3; Tob. 13:11; *Mek.* [Exod. 18:15]; Acts 2:39; 22:21; Eph. 2:13).[95] It is also important that it is only *after* Jesus performs the second feeding miracle that he returns to distinctively Jewish territory: "And immediately he got into the boat with his disciples and went to the district of Dalmanutha" (8:10). There are some historical, geographical, and textual problems with the location of Dalmanutha: it is not otherwise known and manuscripts feel the need to alter the wording. But what is crucial for present purposes is that this is a return to *distinctively* Jewish territory, hence the reappearance of Pharisees in the narrative in the immediately following verse (8:11). There should be little doubt that the emphatic and at times forced use of geography in Mark 6:30–8:21 is strong indication of a resounding nod in the direction of Gentile Christians.

Linked closely to the geography are the issues of ethnicity and custom. The first individual named after Jesus moves into Gentile territory is of course the

Syro-Phoenician woman (Mark 7:24–30), and it is surely no coincidence that she is very definitely Gentile ('Ελληνίς—Mark 7:26; cf. Rom. 1:16; 2:9–10; 1 Cor. 1:22–24). It is also significant that this woman as a Gentile is also to be classed as a dog, an animal sometimes associated with Gentiles (e.g., *1 En.* 89:42–49; *Pirqe R. El.* 29), and very much secondary to the children, that is, Jews (Mark 7:27–28). This further reinforces the argument that Gentiles are a serious narrative issue.[96] It may well be significant that the Syro-Phoenician woman is the only woman who speaks aloud in the whole of Mark's Gospel, for it may imply more typically Gentile behavior (i.e., she does not keep quiet like good Jewish women). Such concerns can be found in the following passage:

> And those women go forth without the payment of the marriage contract at all: She who transgresses against the law of Moses and Jewish law. . . . And what is Jewish law? If she goes out with her hair flowing loose or she spins in the marketplace or she talks with just anybody. . . . R. Tarfon says, "Also: if she is a loudmouth." What is a loudmouth? When she talks in her own house, her neighbors can hear her own voice. (*m. Ketub* 7.6)

Given that Mark is now locating Jesus in Gentile territory and has set the scene by explicitly noting Jesus' dealing with a Gentile, it is presumably the case that the man with a hearing and speech impediment on the journey from Tyre to Decapolis (Mark 7:31–37) is also a Gentile in Mark's eyes. Finally, we should add Joel Marcus's contrast between the different baskets used in the two feeding miracles. In the feeding of the five thousand Jews, the twelve baskets are κοφίνων (Mark 6:43). Like many commentators Marcus notes that Juvenal twice characterizes Jewish travelers with their κόφινοι (Juvenal, *Sat.* 3.14; 6.542).[97] But Marcus goes further and observes that, in contrast, the baskets in the feeding of the four thousand Gentiles are σπυρίδας (Mark 8:8). Marcus adds that the "word does not have the special association with Jews that its counterpart in 6:43, *kophinos*, does."[98]

There is much more that has been said and no doubt will be said about Mark 6:30–Mark 8:21, but the above comments should show the general validity of what many scholars argue, namely, that in this section we have an explicit concern for not only Jews but Gentiles too. If, therefore, the concern for Gentiles is a legitimate reading of Mark 6–8, then what does this tell us about 7:1–23? Well, first—especially given the clear narrative links—it would obviously imply that the Christian movement requires Gentiles to be law observant. It could also be argued that the lack of concern for the transmission of impurity from hands to food to eater would mean that there were no purity worries for Jewish Christians eating permitted food with unclean Gentiles, just as it had meant such concerns did not bother Jesus when associating with Jewish sinners. But while it would be an attractive line of thought for my reading of Mark

6–8, there are serious reasons to reject it. The view vigorously argued by Gedaliah Alon that Gentiles had a special kind of impurity has been seriously challenged.[99] Jonathan Klawans has shown that biblical and Second Temple sources push the line that Gentiles tend to be idolaters and were consequently regarded as morally impure and intermarriage could lead the righteous astray (e.g., Lev. 18:26; Deut. 7:1–4; 1 Kgs. 11:1–2; Ezra 9:1–3, 10–12; Neh. 13:26; 4Q381 69 I–II; *Jub.* 22:16–20). Early rabbinic texts discuss social interaction with Gentiles without mentioning any concerns about becoming impure (e.g., *m. Ber.* 7:1; *m. ʿAbod. Zar.* 5:5). The idea that Gentiles had some kind of impurity was a later rabbinic novelty.[100] Christine E. Hayes develops this idea but takes it one step further, arguing that not only is the idea of an inherent Gentile impurity absent in biblical and Second Temple sources but that none of Alon's evidence, especially the key text *m. Pesaḥ.* 8:8, bears the interpretative weight he placed on it. Most important perhaps are passages where Gentiles are allowed to handle *terumah*—priestly food—(*m. Ter.* 3:9) and offer sacrifices (e.g., *m. Šeqal.* 7:6; *m. Zebaḥ.* 4:5; *m. Menaḥ.* 5:3; 5:6; 6:1; 9:8), both of which would be impossible if they had intrinsic impurity.[101]

As both Klawans and Hayes point out, one of the real problems with Gentiles was their tendency towards bad behavior, although this is not inherent like Alon's Gentile impurity. Or, if you like, the fundamental issue is the defiling impact of "moral purity" rather than "ritual purity," to use a not always helpful distinction. Such depraved Gentile acts—depraved being in the eye of the beholder in many cases—can include murder, idolatry, and sexual immorality. This is grounded in biblical literature (e.g., Exod. 34:15-16; Lev. 18:24–30; Deut. 7:2–4, 16; 20:18) and continued in early Judaism (e.g., *Jub.* 9:15; *Aristeas* 152; Philo, *Spec. Laws* 1.51; *Sib. Or.* 3:492, 496–500; 5:168; Tob. 14:6).[102] In this context it is hugely significant that we have what is at the very least repetition and most probably also a piece of interpretation of an earlier tradition in Mark 7:14–23 where we get details of what comes out from a person to defile.[103] Look at the details given:

> For it is from within, from the human heart, that evil intentions come: fornication, theft, murder, adultery, avarice, wickedness, deceit, licentiousness, envy/evil eye, slander, pride, folly [πορνεῖαι, κλοπαί, φόνοι, μοιχεῖαι, πλεονεξίαι, πονηρίαι, δόλος, ἀσέλγεια, ὀφθαλμὸς πονηρός, βλασφημία, ὑπερηφανία, ἀφροσύνη]. All these things come from within, and they defile a person. (Mark 7:21-23)

There are plenty of parallels to Mark 7:21-23 given in the secondary literature, whether this is reference to Jew castigating Jew, "pagan" castigating "pagan," or whatever. They are perfectly legitimate parallels but, given the narrative context of Mark 6–8, the fact that such a list represents, from certain Jewish perspectives, the kinds of mischievous things Gentiles do is of prime importance for my present concerns. Given that immediately following Mark 7:1–23 Jesus moves into Gentile territory, it is surely no coincidence that Mark is concerned with certain types of supposedly typical Gentile behavior. Considering the discussion of the previous chapter, finding texts that are fiercely critical of Gentiles doing the kinds of things Mark 7:21–23 thinks defile should come as no surprise. The following is a good example from the Wisdom of Solomon of the mischief idolaters are likely to get into:

> . . . and all is a raging riot of blood and murder, theft and deceit, corruption, faithlessness, tumult, perjury, confusion over what is good, forgetfulness of favors, defiling of souls, sexual perversion, disorder in marriages, adultery, and debauchery [αἷμα καὶ φόνος, κλοπὴ καὶ δόλος, φθορά, ἀπιστία, τάραχος, ἐπιορκία, θόρυβος ἀγαθῶν, χάριτος ἀμνηστία, ψυχῶν μιασμός, γενέσεως, ἐναλλαγή, γάμων ἀταξία, μοιχεία καὶ ἀσέλγεια]. (Wis. 14:25–26)

It is unsurprising therefore that some texts can simply refer to all the evil and abominable things that Gentiles do (e.g., *T. Dan* 5:5). These behavioral lists and stereotyping of Gentile behavior found their way into early Christianity and are used in a striking way. Paul is an excellent example. When dealing with the Corinthian Christians Paul said the following, with some obvious parallels with the Markan text,

> Do you not know that wrongdoers will not inherit the kingdom of God? Do not be deceived! Fornicators, idolaters, adulterers, male prostitutes, sodomites, thieves, the greedy, drunkards, revilers, robbers [οὔτε πόρνοι οὔτε εἰδωλολάτραι οὔτε μοιχοὶ οὔτε μαλακοὶ οὔτε ἀρσενοκοῖται οὔτε κλέπται οὔτε πλεονέκται οὐ μέθυσοι οὐ λοίδοροι οὐχ ἅρπαγες]—none of these will inherit the kingdom of God. And this is what you used to be. But you were washed, you were sanctified, you were justified in the name of the Lord Jesus Christ and in the Spirit of our God. (1 Cor. 6:9–11; cf. 2 Cor. 12:20–21)

In general terms it may be said that 1 Cor. 6:9–11 is a similar argument to Mark 7–8. The bad kinds of supposedly typical Gentile behavior have to be left behind, and moral purity has to be the fruits of being a Christian. Similar things can be said about Paul's argument to the Gentile Galatian Christians:

> Now the works of the flesh are obvious: fornication, impurity, licentiousness, idolatry, sorcery, enmities, strife, jealousy, anger, quarrels, dissensions, factions, envy, drunkenness, carousing, and things like these [πορνεία, ἀκαθαρσία, ἀσέλγεια, εἰδωλολατρία, φαρμακεία, ἔχθραι, ἔρις, ζῆλος, θυμοί, ἐριθεῖαι, διχαστασίαι, αἱρέσεις, φθόνοι, μέθαι, κῶμοι, καὶ τὰ ὅμοια τούτοις]. I am warning you, as I warned you before: those who do such things will not inherit the kingdom of God. (Gal. 5:19–21)

Such lists concerning Gentile behavior and what needs to be done about it were not restricted to Paul. First Peter is quite explicit in stereotyping Gentile behavior:

> You have already spent enough time in doing what the Gentiles like to do, living in licentiousness, passions, drunkenness, revels, carousing, and lawless idolatry [πεπορευμένους ἐν ἀσελγείαις, ἐπιθυμίαις, οἰνοφλυγίαις, κώμοις, πότοις, καὶ ἀθεμίτοις εἰδωλολατρίαις]. They are surprised that you no longer join them in the same excesses of dissipation, and so they blaspheme [βλασφημοῦντες]. But they will have to give an accounting to him who stands ready to judge the living and the dead. For this is the reason the gospel was proclaimed even to the dead. . . . (1 Pet. 4:3–6)

Revelation is even more damning of Gentiles:

> The rest of humankind, who were not killed by these plagues, did not repent of the works of their hands or give up worshiping demons and idols of gold and silver and bronze and stone and wood, which cannot see or hear or walk [τῶν ἔργων τῶν χειρῶν αὐτῶν, ἵνα μὴ προσκυνήσουσιν τὰ δαιμόνια καὶ τὰ εἴδωλα τὰ χρυσᾶ καὶ τὰ ἀργυρᾶ καὶ τὰ χαλκᾶ καὶ τὰ λίθινα καὶ τὰ ξύλινα, ἃ οὔτε βλέπειν δύνανται οὔτε ἀκούειν οὔτε περιπατεῖν]. And they did not repent of their murders or their sorceries or their fornication or their thefts [τῶν φόνων αὐτῶν οὔτε ἐκ τῶν φαρμάκων αὐτῶν οὔτε πορνείας αὐτῶν οὔτε ἐκ τῶν κλεμμάτων αὐτῶν]. (Rev. 9:20–21; cf. 21:8)

Collectively, then, this is all very strong evidence that vice lists aimed at Gentiles were of some importance in earliest Christianity. Given that the journey into Gentile territory and the concerns for Gentiles immediately follow the reemphasized theme of Mark 7:21–23, it may be argued that Mark 7, and more broadly Mark 6:30–8:21, puts this early Christian concern for Gentile behavior into an overall story form.

Now we can see the link with the previous chapter on "the sinners" and the above argument on the transmission of Q material. The pre-Markan origins of Mark 7:1–23 no doubt lie in a criticism of expanded purity law that allowed greater social interaction with a broad range of people, including sinners. It is notable that Jesus places an emphasis on moral purity in Mark 7:15, the very thing sinners lacked. Furthermore we can again see how easy it is to shift from Jewish sinners to Gentile sinners. In its Markan narrative context there is a further stressing of moral behavior, and, given the obvious narrative connections with Gentiles, it is no coincidence that the things which defile are interpreted in Mark 7:21–23 with a fairly standard list of bad behavior, stereotypically the kind of behavior expected of Gentiles. Perhaps Mark is also nervous that Gentiles will misbehave (cf. Mark 7:27–28). This is therefore another witness to the transmission of material on morality over against expanded purity concerns, the latter being largely irrelevant for Gentiles attracted to Christianity anyway. If my reading of Mark 7:1–23 is correct, then it must surely follow that the narrative function I have outlined here is also correct.

A final point can also be added. I argued that Gentile Christians would have been law observant in the 30s, at least when in the presence of Jewish Christians. Consequently these are also the kinds of Gentiles that I think would have been a part of Mark's first audience. A potentially significant aside can be added here. It has been *tentatively* suggested by Joel Marcus that the role of the Syro-Phoenician woman in Mark 7:27–28 parallels certain understandings of the ways that Gentiles were attracted to Judaism (e.g., *1 En.* 50:2; *Mek.* [Exod. 22:20]).[104] Marcus also notes that just as the Syro-Phoenician woman was called a "Greek ['Ελληνίς]," so too were Gentiles with some kind of attachment to Judaism and the synagogue in Josephus, Acts, and John's Gospel (*Ag. Ap.* 2.133; *Ant.* 3.217; *J.W.* 7.45; Acts 14:1; 16:1, 3; 17:4, 12; 18:14; John 12:20).[105] We might recall the reference to people coming from far away in Mark 8:3 reflecting the language of Gentile distance from, and Jewish closeness to, God and how it could be reapplied to Gentile converts to Judaism and Christianity (cf. *Mek.* [Exod. 18:15]; Eph. 2:13). Also notable in this respect are the continual references to bread in 6:30–8:21, combined with the obvious echoes of Moses and the exodus story (cf. also John 6:31–32) because the manna from heaven was interpreted as the Torah-Wisdom in certain Jewish texts.[106] Compare the following:

> Can you find any more trustworthy than Moses, who says that while other men receive their food from earth, the nation of vision alone has it from heaven? . . . the heavenly [food] is sent like the snow by God. . . . And indeed it says, "Behold I rain upon you bread from heaven" [Exod. 16:4]. Of what food can he rightly say that it is rained from heaven, save of the heavenly wisdom which is sent from above on souls which yearn for virtue by Him who sheds the gift of prudence in rich abundance, whose grace waters the universe, and chiefly so in the holy seventh which he calls the Sabbath. (Philo, *Names* 259–60)

But then there was always the perhaps unavoidable link between bread and Torah. Few good exegetes steeped in scriptural tradition would have missed the bread-Torah reference when reading what the personification of the Torah herself had to say: "Come, eat of my bread and drink of the wine I have mixed" (Prov. 9:5). In fact the Torah-based interpretation is, unsurprisingly, found in rabbinic literature and, in particular, *Genesis Rabbah*:

> . . . the bread of the Torah, as you read, *Come, eat of my bread* (Prov. 9:5) . . . (*Gen. Rab.* 54:1)

> . . . *brought forth bread and wine* (Gen. 14:18). . . . The Rabbis said: He revealed the Torah to him, as it is written, *Come, eat of my bread and drink of the wine I have mixed* (Prov. 9:5). (*Gen. Rab.* 43:6)

Significantly, this line of thought was adapted to suit the needs of interested Gentiles in *Genesis Rabbah*:

> *And will give me bread to eat and clothing to wear* (Gen. 28:20). Akilas the proselyte visited R. Eliezer and said to him: Does then all the benefit of the proselyte lie in what is said, *You shall love the stranger/proselyte* (Deut. 10:18)? Is then that a small thing in your eyes, replied he, for which our ancestor supplicated, praying, *And will give me bread to eat and clothing to wear* (Gen. 28:20) while He [God] comes and offers it to him [the proselyte] on a reed! Then he visited R. Joshua, who began to comfort him with words: *Bread* refers to the Torah, as it says, *Come, eat of my bread* (Prov. 9:5), while *clothing* means the [scholar's] cloak: when a man is privileged to [study the] Torah, he is privileged to perform God's precepts. (*Gen. Rab.* 70:5)

Of course it would be extremely pleasant if similar texts were known to be present some time very close to the 30s and 40s CE, but these texts do at least show that Jews were always liable to make such connections. Moreover, given the key theme of bread in Mark 6:30–8:21 and the central passage on the Torah in Mark 7:1–23—including a list of Gentile-like vices with echoes of the Decalogue—combined with the Philo text and Prov. 9:5, it can be legitimately suggested that the same kinds of arguments recorded in *Genesis Rabbah*, where bread is tied in with Jew and Gentile law observance, may also have been made in Mark 6–8. This would further support the argument that Mark 6:30–8:21 was a major justification of law observance among Jewish and Gentile Christians at the end of the 30s.

CONCLUSIONS

Jesus' mission to sinners, with its stress on law observance, provides a crucial link with the early concern for Gentile sinners and consequently the spread of earliest Christianity. We have seen that the Q legal material places great stress on justice, ethics, and so on, with some polemic aimed at Pharisaic interpretations of biblical law. While it is difficult to find an explicit concern for a Gentile mission in Q, the traditions were transmitted when Gentiles were attracted to the new Christian movement. Furthermore, it may be significant that Matthew and Luke incorporated the Q material when they were very much concerned with the rise of the Gentile mission. The implication is that Christians are expected to uphold good Jewish morality in exactly the way the caricatured

Pharisees of Q do not. This expectation must surely apply also to Gentile Christians. If the links between Jewish morality, law observance, and Gentiles are implied in Q, then in Mark 6–8 it is very much explicit. Once again there is a fierce attack on Pharisaic interpretations of biblical law coupled with allegations of supposed immoral behavior. What I argued was implicit in Q is explicit in Mark: Q implies that Christians should not behave in the ways attributed to Pharisees while Mark presents clear interpretation of what defiles morally; Q's implication would also apply to any Gentiles involved in the Christian movement while Mark's discussion of moral behavior is deliberately placed before Jesus' activities among Gentiles. Looking at the bigger picture, the slow-moving historical trends, we saw at the outset of the chapter that the social conditions were favorable for the spread of monotheism among Gentiles throughout the Roman Empire, particularly in the east. But it needed some kind of spark, and this is where chapters 2 and 3 come in: we can now see how Jesus' mission to *Jewish sinners*, itself sparked off by the socioeconomic conditions of 20s Galilee, provides a crucial link to the inclusion of the structurally similar *Gentile sinners*. If this analysis is anywhere near correct, then we must now account for the crucial shifts in law observance so obviously clear by the end of the 40s.

5

Recruitment, Conversion, and Key Shifts in Law Observance

The Origins of the Pauline Mission

> In researching many reports of religious conversion, I found it striking that a scholar or missionary might enthusiastically report hundreds or even thousands of converts, then in one throwaway sentence note that the percentage of converts was less than 10 percent. The truth is that enmeshment with old systems of religion, family, society, and politics seldom encourages movement to a new religious option. . . . Indeed seeking proselytes is extremely difficult and discouraging work. Evangelistic organizations continually have to build enthusiasm among members to preserve the momentum required to convert a relatively few others.[1]

So far we have seen that the Jesus movement began with a particular stress on the law that maintained the full validity of biblical law. We have also seen that this particular stress was important for interaction with Gentiles, especially those Gentiles who were converts or potential converts to the Christian movement. But it remains that by the mid-40s there were a noticeable number of Gentile Christians who were no longer observing major biblical laws and, in theory at least, even some Jewish Christians. This should raise an important further question: How did the Christian movement get from observance to nonobservance in such a short space of time? Put another way, how do we explain the gaps? This is where social-scientific approaches can be particularly effective in explaining historical change. Given that the issue of shifts in observance appears to involve the recruitment of Gentiles and given that Christianity was to become a religion in its own right, one particular approach lends itself to this problem: recruitment and conversion to (often new) religious movements.

The NT evidence is not always that helpful here.[2] There is increasing awareness that the stories of mass conversions (e.g., Acts 13) or conversions in response to a miracle (e.g., Acts 8:6–7; 13:7–12; 16:30) are extremely improbable or at the very least hugely exaggerated. This awareness is not just due to historical research but also to the increasing awareness of the importance of conversion through social networks, where the potentially interested (or, to use the technical jargon, the "structurally available") convert has a preexisting affective tie with at least one member of the religious movement. In particular, such an interdisciplinary approach to conversion was brought to the attention of a broad range of scholars working on Christian origins by Rodney Stark.[3] Indeed this approach was one aspect of a more totalizing model of conversion to new religious movements developed by Stark himself along with John Lofland in the 1960s.[4] This model, along with its subsequent modifications in sociological literature, has been used impressively in an important work on conversion and Christian origins by Jack T. Sanders as one aspect of his wide-ranging discussion of why Gentiles became Christians and why Christianity succeeded in the Greco-Roman world while other movements did not.[5]

There is always the ever-present danger of NT scholars poaching an approach from another discipline that has died a lonely death and rotted away on its home turf. Happily this seems not to be the case: scholarly analysis of conversion through social networks and affective ties is as sprightly as ever. With reference to the Lofland and Stark model as the "most important empirical study of conversion," Lewis Rambo argues that

> kinship and friendship networks are fundamental to most conversions, just as they are influential in resistance and rejection. . . . I would argue that relationships are important to most but not all conversions. . . . Virtually every social scientific study of conversion stresses the importance of relationships.[6]

In a critical testing of the Lofland-Stark model based on a comparison of adolescent converts and nonconverts, Willem Kox, Wim Meeus, and Harm 't Hart provide a notable conclusion: "It seems justified to suppose that religious groups have a twofold appeal: ideological, by offering a new perspective on life, and social, by providing a satisfactory social network."[7] In a recent reaction to the popular view that cults brainwash the lonely, isolated potential convert, Lorne L. Dawson, with reference to Stark, collaborators such as Lofland, and the subsequent scholarship based on this work, states, "Research has revealed otherwise, studies of conversion and case studies of specific groups have found that recruitment to NRMs [New Religious Movements] happens primarily through pre-existing social networks and interpersonal bonds."[8] Although not uncritical of the Lofland-Stark model, James T. Richardson summarizes its benefits for "the future of research on conversion" thanks to its focusing on the process of conversion and for recognizing that conversion has a definite organizational aspect and is a *social* event. One other key aspect of the model was the incorporation of subjects who would *self-define* themselves as religious *seekers* and take action to change by interacting with selected people and by allowing affective ties to develop with them.[9]

Conversion through social networks and affective ties no doubt played a crucial role in the spread of earliest Christianity. At least this view is accepted by Stark's critics. In a largely critical response to Stark's *The Rise of Christianity*, Todd Klutz says that in contrast to the view of mass conversions or responses to public miracles, "Stark proposes and ably defends a potentially more attractive explanation . . . the ordinary but effectual mechanisms of social networks."[10] In a more positive but far from uncritical review of Stark's account of Christian origins, Harry O. Maier adds an important but complementary qualification that will be developed in this chapter, namely, the importance of *ancient* social networks:

> Stark's own network analysis would have benefited from a closer study of the hierarchical structure of ancient society. In fact it appears that Paul's own mission was targeted in the first instance to more well-to-do members of society who offered a wider network of potential contacts than the more disenfranchised members: as went the householder, so the household with its slaves and associates.[11]

Clearly, then, this approach to conversion through social networks has the potential to command some support among scholars of Christian origins.

This general approach to the spread of Christianity through social networks forms the basis of this chapter. However, while Stark and Sanders, like Adolf Harnack, A. D. Nock, Robert M. Grant, Ramsay MacMullen, and others before them, sought to explain the success of Christianity in the wider Greco-Roman world and discuss Christianity well beyond the first century, my concern is less spectacular and has a different emphasis, which barely needs restating: the shifts in law observance in the first twenty years of Christianity. It will require another detailed look at social-scientific material on networks, recruitment, and conversion along with the ancient evidence in order to show how the social network model can be modified and adapted in a new way for my specific concerns.

SOCIAL-SCIENTIFIC APPROACHES TO RECRUITMENT AND CONVERSION TO RELIGIOUS MOVEMENTS

The pioneering work by Lofland and Stark on conversion to new religious movements through networks initially concentrated on the Unification Church, otherwise known as the Moonies.[12] The Korean Young Oon Kim, or "Miss Kim," arrived in America in 1959 to launch the U.S. mission, which involved talks, press releases, radio, and public meetings. Despite these efforts, they failed to bring in converts. Yet Lofland and Stark noticed that the movement did grow. The first converts were young housewives who lived next door to one another and whose friendship predated their conversion. They converted after Miss Kim had become a lodger with one of them. Husbands were to follow as were work colleagues of the husbands. Strangers were not liable to join. Converts were "people who formed close friendships with one or more members of the group." Lofland and Stark "soon realised that of all the people the Moonies encountered in their efforts to spread their faith, the only ones who joined were those *whose interpersonal attachments to members overbalanced their attachments to non-members.*"[13] Conversion was, effectively, "not about seeking or embracing an ideology; it is about bringing one's religious behaviour into alignment with that of one's friends and family members."[14] Other converts included people who came to San Francisco and formed strong friendships with group members just as they were physically removed from preexisting friendships and family ties. Concerned family members would try to intervene after a conversion, but if they lingered on they would convert also. A key conclusion is the following: "*Conversion to new, deviant religious groups occurs when, other things being equal, people have or develop stronger attachments to members of the group than they have to non-members.*"[15]

The Moonies were not able to grow that rapidly because they often relied on "befriending lonely newcomers" and thus new members did not open up ways in which the Moonies could spread.[16] Stark and William Sims Bainbridge point out similarities with a satanic cult studied by Bainbridge in which interpersonal bonds not only played a part in recruitment but were also crucial in the formation of the cult.[17] The group originated with two defectors from Scientology who tried to establish themselves as psychotherapists in London in 1963. The male member of the couple developed a clientele through his upper-middle-class friendship network. Individual therapy sessions led to group encounters and participants began to develop strong and deep bonds with one another far exceeding their relations with others outside the group. They soon found themselves in epic marathon sessions. Consequently their relations with those outside the group weakened, and the group become so inward looking that they engaged in exclusively intragroup relations. In this context their first religious ideas developed. It was not long before the group left for an isolated beach in Mexico to develop their beliefs in total isolation. From Mexico they then reentered society to seek recruits, but like the Moonies their success came when they had first developed strong personal ties. The group traveled across Europe and the United States but did not stay long enough in most places to establish close friendship networks. Their recruits thus tended to be socially isolated people, people who, significantly, had a lack of social ties and were geographically mobile.[18] But even here a crucial step to such people joining was the development of strong social ties.

Satan evidently needs similar methods to those of God if he wants to attract more and more dark hordes. In contrast to the Moonies and the satanic cult studied by Bainbridge, the Mormon approach, for instance, was infinitely more effective.[19] The Mormons have long recognized the importance of social networks in recruitment and would use such means whenever possible. This gained a significant degree of confirmation when Stark and Bainbridge obtained access to statistics for all the missionaries in the state of Washington during the year 1976–1977 and were "reliably informed that these data are typical of results reported for other states as well as for foreign missions." The results include the following: when Mormon missionaries simply went from door-to-door and lacked a preexisting social bond the success rate was only 0.1 percent yet when a Mormon friend or relative provided a home as the place of missionary contact the success rate rocketed up to 50 percent.[20] Stark and Bainbridge's conclusions, which are also based on Mormon missionary literature, follow naturally:

> Missionaries do not serve as the primary instrument of recruitment to the Mormon faith. Instead, recruitment is accomplished primarily by the rank and file of the church as they construct intimate interpersonal ties with non-Mormons and thus link them into a Mormon social network . . . from experience Mormons ratify the point made by observational studies—that interpersonal bonds come first, theology subsequently, not the reverse.[21]

David Snow and Cynthia Phillips critically tested the Lofland-Stark model against their own empirical study of the Nichiren Soshu Buddhist movement of America. The movement was formally introduced into America in 1960 as a foreign wing of *Sokagakkai*, a Japanese Buddhist movement, but since then Nichiren Shoshu started to establish its own separate identity in America. In 1960 the adherents of Nichiren Shoshu were less than five hundred; by the time of Snow and Phillips's 1980 article the number of variously committed members had reached 200,000.[22] While critical of much of the broader Lofland-Stark model, they noticed that their research tended to agree with it on the crucial issue of social networks and interpersonal bonds in conversion. They also point out that this bond was typically preexisting rather than emergent or movement specific, adding:

> Two of the fifteen members were recruited by a spouse, one by another relative, ten by friends or acquaintances, and only two by strangers. All but two of the most active members in the chanting cell were thus drawn into sustained contact with the movement by being linked to a member through a pre-existing, extramovement interpersonal tie.[23]

Further research into the Nichiren Shoshu also showed that this pattern was evident for the vast majority of members: 82 percent of their sample were recruited through a tie that was both preexisting and extramovement. The remaining 18 percent were recruited outside of social networks—especially from the streets by strangers—but even these conversions were dependent on the development of an affective bond with a member or members.[24] In fact, not only do Snow and Phillips accept Lofland and Stark's view that conversion involves "coming to accept the opinions of one's friends," they go a step further and argue that "it is rather unlikely in the absence of such an affective bond to one or more members" and so intensive interaction with the potential convert/newly converted is required.[25]

At the same time in another 1980 publication, and with a more extravagant sociological vocabulary, David Snow, Louis Zurcher Jr., and Sheldon Ekland-Olson listed ten studies of religious and political movements that demonstrate "the salience of social networks as a recruitment avenue." In each of these cases, with the exception of Hare Krishna, recruitment through social networking was strikingly high over against recruitment from outside (e.g., on the street, mass meetings, media, individuals joining on their own initiative). In five cases 90–100 percent of recruits were through social networks, and in two cases the percentage of recruits through social networks was in the 70s. In one case it was 59 percent, but there was no evidence of recruitment from outside, so the figure may have been even higher.[26] They also add a sample study of university students participating in various movements. In the case of political movements, 63 percent of the participating students were recruited through a preexisting, extramovement interpersonal tie to one or more members, 30 percent through media, and 7 percent in public places. In the case of religious movements 80 percent of participating students were recruited through a preexisting, extramovement interpersonal tie to one or more members and 20 percent through the media. Collectively these findings powerfully demonstrate the importance of preexisting social networks in movement recruitment. Thus Snow, Zurcher, and Ekland-Olson can reasonably suggest the following proposition:

> Those outsiders who are linked to one or more movement members through preexisting extramovement networks will have a greater probability of being contacted and recruited into that particular movement than will those individuals who are outside of members' extramovement networks.[27]

These findings were also complemented by reasons students did *not* participate in the various social groups, which, although used more for their discussion of structural availability of potential recruits, are also worth mentioning in passing. The main reason given (totals 71 percent: 73 percent for political; 66 percent for religious) was that the students did not know anyone involved. The other main reasons given are also complementary to the above: not enough time (totals 63 percent: for political 64 percent; for religious 61 percent) and was not asked (totals 54 percent: for political 57 percent; for religious 47 percent). More negative reasons, such as fear of reactions and simply not wanting to get involved, stay below 20 percent.[28]

But there was an exception. In the contrasting case of Hare Krishna, 97 percent of recruits were recruited "off the street" by strangers.[29] Snow, Zurcher, and Ekland-Olson attempt to explain this in several ways. For example, they observe that the recruitment efforts of Krishna devotees involve an initial step of getting prospects to the local temple and invited to attend a devotional session, to listen to a discussion of philosophy, or to attend a Sunday "love feast." In other words, it is not about initially joining the movement there and then but becoming a participant as soon as possible with justifications given for the initial act and for continuing participation.[30] Another reason for the lack of preexisting social networks in recruitment to Hare Krishna may have some relevance for present purposes. Core membership may depend on the severance of extramovement interpersonal ties due to a more ascetic communal lifestyle, so "the movement is structurally compelled to concentrate its recruitment efforts in public places. Consequently, most of its members are recruited 'off the streets.'" Snow, Zurcher, and Ekland-Olson therefore suggest two further propositions:

A. Movements requiring exclusive participation by their members in movement activities will attract members primarily from public places rather than from among extramovement interpersonal associations and networks.
B. Movements which do not require exclusive participation by their members in movement activities will attract members primarily from among extramovement interpersonal associations and networks, rather than from public places.[31]

What we know of earliest Christianity in the first few decades after Jesus' death most approximates to proposition B (cf. 1 Cor. 7:12–16, and see further below).

There are numerous other studies that could be used in support of religious conversion through social networks, but I will restrict myself to an example given by Lewis Rambo. Rambo provides a variety of examples of religious conversion through social networks and affective bonds,[32] including his own fieldwork and interviews he conducted, but he provides one notable example that may be deemed a rough parallel to conversion through households and similar social structures that were crucial in the spread of earliest Christianity, as we will be see below: conversion to Islam in certain parts of Africa. Using the work of W. Arens, Rambo records that one of the ways that Islam spread in sub-Saharan Africa is through a patronage system. Here a patron introduces a stranger to a village, and they both develop a close "father-son" relationship. The "father" sponsors the "son" and consequently the "son" becomes part of an extended kinship network. This also means the client takes on the religious affiliation of the sponsor: if the sponsor is Muslim, then the client also becomes Muslim, thereby opening up a network of social ties. Rambo notes that the conversion "may well owe more to material expedience than to deep emotional fervor," but we should not lose sight of the typical conversion process:

> Western Christians may harshly criticize such arrangements as clearly not being "genuine" conversions. I would argue, however, that many conversions in the missionary field, and also on our own shores (if we were willing to examine the issues objectively), reflect similar dynamics.[33]

There are also some notable parallels with broader network analyses in the social sciences that fill out all sorts of details underlying the assumptions in the discussions of "religious" conversion, in particular social network analysis.[34] Social network analysis was pioneered in the 1950s by John A. Barnes and studies the connections and ties between groups and/or individuals and how this can reflect social behaviors. Such studies, often illustrated with a whole host of exotic diagrams, cover the transmission of all kinds of things through social networks such as ideas, opinions, gossip, goods, kinship obligations, information, assistance, friendship, and so on. Additionally, people can be recruited to a network through a variety of connections, such as family, ethnic, friendship, and so on.[35] There is also an interesting parallel in the work of James C. Scott on "little tradition" among peasantry in Southeast Asia. Although Scott's analysis is based more on class and socioeconomic issues, it will become important here, for it highlights the shifting beliefs as we move from the center or the anchor of a given network. Scott notes that the political party arrives in the village "not as an abstract institution, but in the form of very concrete individuals embedded in the social structure." For example, in Thai elections, a vote for the ruling party was partly a vote for the community leader, who was also a distant cousin of the bodyguard of the Minister of Culture. In Burma, party factions were, at the village level, represented by local branches that generally followed village factional histories. So if a local notable urged a vote for a given faction, kin, friends, and retainers would follow. If a village was not split, it might support a single party backed by one important man. As Scott puts it, whatever vote was cast, "it was the local social structure which was decisive, not the national parties and what they stood for."[36]

SHIFTING LEVELS OF OBSERVANCE
AND COMMITMENT

We now need to see how such studies of conversion relate to shifting practices and commitment levels in the relevant scholarly literature. Lofland and Stark talk of two degrees of conversion: *verbal converts*, that is, fellow travelers and followers who accept beliefs and were accepted by core members as sincere but played no active role; and *total converts*, that is, converts who showed their commitment in deed as well as word.[37] It is therefore no surprise that there are examples of mixed behavior and loyalties among converts as a whole. Compare also the observations of Lofland and Stark:

> The development or presence of some positive, emotional, interpersonal response seems necessary to bridge the gap between first exposure to the D.P. [Divine Precepts] message and accepting its truth. That is, persons developed affective ties with the group or some of its members while they still regarded the D.P. perspective as problematic, or even "way out." In a manner of speaking, final conversion was coming to accept the opinions of one's friends.[38]

Indeed, even "Miss Lee"[39] when describing her own conversion initially "could not agree with the message intellectually" even if she found herself at "one with it spiritually," a view reflected by other recruits in the process of developing further bonds with the group.[40] But of course people did shift from verbal converts to total converts. Lofland and Stark refer to reminders/discussions of the importance of making more converts to the Moon cause. In fact, they noticed the stress on the necessity of supporting it in every way was among the main themes of verbal exchanges among the "tentatively accepting" and the "total converts," and even among the "total converts" themselves. They add,

> Away from this close association with those already totally committed, one failed to "appreciate" the need for one's transformation into a total convert. In recognition of this fact, the D.P. [Divine Precepts] members gave highest priority to attempts to persuade verbal converts (even the merely interested) to move into the cult's community dwellings.[41]

How could this mode of conversion affect earliest Christianity? Although there are a whole host of clear and obvious differences between the Moonies and the earliest Christians, the distinction between verbal and total convert is also useful in studying the latter. We cannot impose time limits on the length of a "total conversion" in earliest Christianity, but it can reasonably be suggested that conversions do take time for many people. If such conversions were going on in earliest Christianity in different places, then there would have been noticeable people connected in some way to the developing Christian movement who were not behaving in the ways expected of a total convert (see below).[42] But we have to engage in historical speculation for the situation a few years earlier than Paul's letters. Some interested Gentiles, for instance, may have been at one with Christianity spiritually but may have been puzzled over the relevance of certain commandments and could have taken time to come around, not least due to the non-Jewish social circles in which potential converts were active.

Take the issue of food laws. Avoidance of pork was seen by some Gentiles as distinctive if not a little odd (cf. Juvenal, *Sat.* 14.96–106). After all, for carnivores what else is there to do with a pig if not to eat it or hack off its various body parts for some use or other? Little surprise then that a question such as "Why do you refuse to eat pork?" could be reported as being raised when Philo's contingent had an audience with Caligula (*Legat.* 361–62). We will see that there were similar and powerful countervailing influences on the first Gentiles at the time when Christianity was largely law observant. Indeed, a God-fearing Gentile may eat with law-observant Jewish Christians one day and with lawless pagans the next. It is important to note just how powerful such influences would be. After all as early as the 50s those who wanted to keep the biblical food and Sabbath laws were no longer deemed normative in certain Christian contexts (e.g., Rom. 14:1–6).

Let us return to the interdisciplinary material and the argument that countervailing bonds are clearly important for understanding why levels of commitment to certain practices could notably differ. A particularly interesting example given by Lofland and Stark involves the spouse of a recruit to the developing Moon movement. The husband began tentatively to espouse the group beliefs and developed strong ties with key Moon figures. The wife struggled to accept and in the end "seemed nervous, embarrassed, and even ashamed" to be at the gatherings. One night the husband rushed in just before a prayer gathering and tearfully announced he would have nothing to do with the group even though he still thought the message was probably true. It was only a few months later before the husband lost his faith—not surprising given the approaches outlined here—and it is clear that the two affective bonds tore the man's loyalties.[43] Significantly, earliest Christianity would have close interaction with Gentiles attracted to Judaism; therefore the seeds of two strong, competing loyalties were already planted. But at least in its Pauline form it did not require such a stark choice to be made between spouse and religion (1 Cor. 7:12–16). It may therefore be generalized that this tension between competing loyalties was always going to be present in earliest Christianity but not necessarily to the extent of requiring a severing of the bond.[44]

However, the view that countervailing influences such as extramovement ties have to be neutralized or at least weakened for conversion to be consummated should not be raised to the level of some sociological "law." Indeed,

1 Cor. 7:12–16 already warns against this generalization. James T. Richardson and Mary Stewart, in a discussion of conversion and the Jesus Movement (the new religious movement as opposed to the first-century movement), accept the importance of affective ties with group members but also note that positive affective ties with nongroup members may also contribute towards conversion—for example, if a nongroup friend or relative had positive or at least neutral views of the group.[45] They also speculate that this effect is more likely to occur with groups closely related to the dominant culture, something we can say at least about some forms of Christianity reflected in the NT. Similarly, the findings of David Snow and Cynthia Phillips on Nichiren Shoshu also cast doubts on generalizing that extramovement ties need to be neutralized. Snow and Phillips argue that conversion could in fact lead to strengthening extramovement bonds because Nichiren Shoshu stresses that converts need to change themselves rather than others and improve and not worsen extramovement relations. They give examples of converts discussing personal problems in preexisting relationships and tell of how the converts came to realize that they themselves were often at fault for strains in the relationship and not the parents or the flatmate or the best friend. This stress on building the extramovement relations makes good sense if the movement wants to spread further, as Nichiren Shoshu realized.[46] Again this is not, as Snow and Phillips point out, a generalization for all religious movements, and much will depend on the characteristics of the given religious movement.

The significance of countervailing influences is not restricted to new religious movements or "cults" or anything else that may be regarded (rightly or wrongly) as nonmainstream. Kevin W. Welch analyzed commitment levels in what may be loosely called mainstream U.S. Protestant Christian denominations (e.g., Methodist, Episcopalian, American Lutheran, Southern Baptist, etc.).[47] He acknowledged that friendship and interpersonal attachments, crucial in the commitment to highly deviant groups, were important, but he then applied this approach to the maintenance of commitment levels to the norms established by the denomination to which the believer already belonged as opposed to being recently converted. For Welch it is increased social participation in the denomination (church groups, church-organized activities, attendance, etc.) which tends to strengthen adherence to constructed norms whereas increased extracongregational participation and exposure to secular influences, though limited due to the church links, tends to lead to a lower level of commitment to the denominational norms.[48] Flower arranging, cake baking, and regular barn dancing evidently go hand-in-hand with good theology.

These approaches to conversion through social networks are complemented by approaches to religious conversion that make the fairly obvious observation noted above that the ideology of a convert can often take some time to develop. Some converts may join with minimal knowledge of the group's observance levels and theology and gradually come to accept the ideology of the group. Compare the generalization given by Lewis Rambo:

> For people who continue with a new religious option after the initial encounter, their interaction with their adopted religious group intensifies. . . . The intensity and duration of this phase differs from one group to another. Some faiths insist on a very long period of education and socialization; others focus more on brief, intense periods during which potential converts are encouraged and/or required to make a decision.[49]

Lorne Dawson, whose study of cult conversion is grounded in studies of conversion through social networks, points out that conversions to new religious movements tend to be "gradual affairs, born of a search for spiritual insight or help and an interactive process of exchange and negotiation of commitments between the convert and the religious organization."[50] A similarly relevant discussion is that of John Lofland and Norman Skonovd on affectional conversion, commenting that "the process is relatively prolonged—a matter of at least several weeks" and pointing out that in this type of conversion "belief arises out of participation."[51] Indeed, as Kox, Meeus, and 't Hart observe, the Lofland-Stark model itself indicates that the conversion process can extend over a long period.[52] In studies of conversion in earliest Christianity we get similar uncontroversial comments. Jack Sanders remarks that "most of what Paul writes in all his letters involves the assumption that Christians are in process—that they have become Christians, but that they still need to learn what it means to be Christian" and that the idea of converts growing into faith "confirms the sociological distinction between recruitment (joining a movement) and conversion (coming to share the ideology and goals of the movement)."[53]

However, one might object and say that the relevance of most of this material on conversion through social networks is dubious because most of the movements discussed above were attracting converts to change from their old ways to the new. Such a change would seem quite the opposite to Christianity shifting from a law-observant movement to one that no longer saw the need for various commandments to be observed. But cultural influences are not one way, even in the case of conversions, and there are always historical particularities to take into account. In the case of earliest Christianity one historical particularity is that we have an initially law-observant Jewish movement that involved a notable interaction with interested Gentiles. With the increased number of interested Gentiles, and friends of friends of friends, arises the historically particular situation of a significant number of interested Gentiles not particularly bothered about keeping the commandments. This had to lead to a decision one way or another.

In fact such cultural mixtures are a fairly standard feature in discussions of conversion. Lewis Rambo synthesizes examples from a variety of studies based on different groups and different places. Building on Steven Kaplan's research on missionaries in Africa, he notes that Kaplan's idiosyncratic labeling of six types of missionary change (tolerance, translation, assimilation, Christianization, acculturation, and incorporation) "may be considered relevant around the world,"[54] to which I might add that it would hardly be controversial to say that some of these types are paralleled in the spread of earliest Christianity and differing legal practices of converts. So what precisely are the key types? Well, "tolerance," for one, is pragmatics in action. Missionaries may be confronted with unpalatable beliefs but have to tolerate them in the hope persuasion will eventually work. "Assimilation" involves the realization by the missionary that such indigenous practices may actually have some value; indeed, indigenous practices may in fact be assimilated into the missionary's worship practices. A more radical form of this is "acculturation" whereby the missionary even acts to preserve and promote indigenous cultures. This is surely a common sense (for what that term is worth) observation by Rambo. After all, it is well documented that the broader concepts of tolerance, assimilation, and acculturation are extremely common features of groups in a whole range of societies, picking and choosing aspects they accept, reject, or wish to modify, with early Judaism and Christianity being no exceptions.[55]

Lest this seem too abstract, Rambo has provided several other empirical examples of mixing and syncretism in religious conversion. Rambo provides discussion of research on the conversion of the Uraon people in Chotanagpur, India, by Lutheran and then Roman Catholic missionaries. In the early stages of encounter the first converts swung between their previous beliefs and the new Christian beliefs, with nominal affiliation to and little knowledge of Christianity. The main benefits of conversion were material, such as legal help in the face of oppressive landlords. Yet despite these benefits the new converts remained strongly attached to their previous traditions. Rambo reports that 83 percent of Catholic converts and 93 percent of Lutheran converts still held belief in witchcraft and sorcery.[56] An even more relevant example is dancing, which was an important part of local Uraon culture. Just as Ned Flanders's worst fears were realized when his buttocks accidentally came into contact with the buttocks of another young man after being talked into doing a dance called "The Bump," so some of the Western missionaries were concerned that dancing stimulated "inappropriate sexual activity." But after a period of conflict a compromise was reached with missionaries accepting dancing as an integral part of the culture.[57]

Another example is Rambo's reference to research done on the response of the Igbo people in Nigeria to Christianity. Noting that it was often marginalized figures (e.g., slaves, accused witches) who were most likely to attach themselves to a new movement, he points out that their "mode of conversion involved a syncretism that mixed old and new in a fashion that was determined by their own values, assumptions, and rituals." It is perhaps also worth noting that after constant missionary educational activity there was even a secularizing impact of Western ideas and ideals.[58] Rambo refers to research done on the development of Islam in Africa where "mixing" occurs in the context of conversion in the sense of "adhesion" to Islam. He notes that it is "not uncommon in Africa for a person to be involved in multiple cults and to engage in various ritual activities." In such contexts becoming a Muslim is "fairly easy" and the admission ritual is simply to confess, "There is one God and Mohammad is God's prophet."[59]

One highly relevant example from analysis of conversion through social networks sheds further light on the shift in law observance among the earliest Christians. Jack Sanders points to the work done on Nichiren Shoshu and compares a conference of the American-based group with its roots in Japanese Buddhism with the Jerusalem conference (Gal. 2:1–10; Acts 15). The Nichiren Shoshu conference was held to discuss the issue of accommodation and a decision was reached: "foreign practices," such as the flying of the American flag and statues of the Virgin Mary at home, were permitted so long as the "essence of the religion" remained.[60] This example is particularly apt as it clearly illustrates what is to be expected in the spread of earliest Christianity when faced with the obvious countervailing cultural influences.

We might also compare similar points arising out of social-network analysis and related social studies that do not (always) explicitly concern religious conversion. One important feature of broader social-network analysis is the observation that people's behavior in a network will differ according to different social contexts. In the course of fieldwork in Ndola, A. L. Epstein recorded that ever-recognizable case of a man caught lying where he ought not to be before fleeing the bedroom of the wife of another man. What Epstein showed was how different gossip groups modified and adapted the story to suit different social tastes and self-identities.[61] James Scott's studies of radical parties who were (potentially) promising revolutionary change in Indonesia also provides a useful comparison. One particular example Scott gives is the Communist Party of Indonesia (PKI) from approximately 1951 to 1965, where access for the peasantry appeared to be largely through social networks of patronage, kinship, and traditional respect. PKI leaders regularly denounced this practice, and when by 1955 peasants were the majority of PKI membership, party leaders were even complaining that local wealthy elements were preventing certain decisions. This is a good example of the shifting practices when moving away from the "center" as in this case the localized interest group created some serious problems for class militancy. Indeed, this discontinuity between localism and national politics could even lead to a mutilation or even complete disjunction of issues when they shifted from the national to the local level. But commonly the case would be that "issues are simply transformed and syncretized as we move from the centre to the periphery."[62] Scott argues that this discontinuity helps explain why nationalism had limited appeal in Southeast Asian villages, and where it did develop (e.g., Vietnam), it was intimately linked with issues of local importance or even took on a millennial tone with elements of folk religion, in notable contrast to the nationalist intelligentsia.[63] This, of course, may be said to reflect a broader and culturally widespread phenomenon.

These provide useful analogies for understanding the spread of earliest Christianity. When we start getting to the level of "friends of friends of friends," we can no doubt include pagans becoming attracted to the Christian movement but with little attachment to the center or the anchor and with some or many Gentile Christians still having strong connections with pagan movements. There was always the major possibility that people's behavior would differ according to different social contexts in a given social network, something echoed in Paul's missionary work (1 Cor. 9:19–23; cf. Acts 16:1–3). It is also telling that, at a slightly later time, 1 John 5:21 feels the need to warn believers to keep themselves from idols (cf. Gal. 4:8) or that Paul has to deal with the issue of eating food sacrificed to idols when Christians were in different social contexts (1 Cor. 8–10). In fact none of this was necessarily uncommon. Philip Harland points out that the polemic aimed at honoring the emperor in Revelation would have been aimed at a relatively common practice among Christians of the time: participation in everyday social life.[64]

Dennis Duling has provided a useful application of network analysis in the social sciences to the wandering charismatic Jesus movement famously nurtured by Gerd Theissen. One aspect of Duling's approach is the development of the "ego-centred" network. An ego-centered network does exactly what it says on the tin: it is a network with a focal person or Ego at the center. Ego-centered networks tend to be structurally diverse networks composed of different persons from different activity fields. Relationships between the Ego and other people in the network "vary in intensity" according to "interactional criteria." Duling illustrates this concept by concentric circles or "zones of intensity": the first-order zone or intimate network interacts closest to the Ego; the second-order zone or effective network is important but not as close—"friends of friends," to apply a well-worn phrase; the third-order zone or extended network are not close but are distant and often unknown though (crucially) potentially knowable—"friends of friends of friends."[65]

Duling points out the similarities of this approach with Theissen's different levels of charismatic followers of Jesus: the primary charismatic (Jesus) parallels the Ego; the secondary charismatics are the followers of Jesus, especially the Twelve; tertiary charismatics include a wider circle of community sympathizers who did not leave house and home and the people as a whole (i.e., people who listened to Jesus, possibly attracted to his message but did not become sympathizers or supporters), all notably similar to the intimate network, effective network, and extended network. Of course we can equally apply this approach to Christianity in its first twenty years—say, the network where the Jerusalem church is around the center, with "zones of intensity" spreading out. But what makes the application to Christianity in the 30s and 40s most significant for present purposes is that a movement which now includes a significant number of Gentiles is going to have a notable number of connections with non-Christian pagans in or close to the social network. This would inevitably have raised issues of worship: whether the Sabbath is worth observing at all, whether pork or shellfish can be eaten, whether many of the commandments are relevant at all, and so on.[66] What is also important, and we will return to this in more detail below, is that Judaism already had what may be loosely classed as social networks for this practice: as Shaye Cohen has detailed, there is good evidence of Gentiles attracted to Judaism in varying degrees.[67] In contrast, the Jesus movement was a Jewish renewal movement largely focused on Jews alone and would not have these kinds of problems; nor indeed to any significant degree would any other Palestinian Jewish movement of Jesus' time.

We may now make some generalizations for our study of earliest Christianity. It is most likely that conversion would involve some kind of social network. It is likely that, with more and more converts and all the cultural influences they would bring, there would be differing degrees of commitment that would inevitably lead to the need for compromise and accommodation. This kind of approach can help explain the shift from observance to nonobservance among some Christians. We now need to see how this idea ties in with the evidence from around the time of Christian origins.

ANCIENT SOCIAL NETWORKS AND GENTILES ATTRACTED TO JUDAISM

Social networks in the ancient world have been discussed by scholars of earliest Christianity for some time. In a seminal social history that in some ways anticipates Stark and Sanders, Wayne Meeks provided valuable insight concerning the role of social networks underlying the Pauline mission.[68] Families, households, work, and trade are all shown to have played a significant role. The ancient cities connected with the Pauline mission were densely populated, with privacy being rare. News and rumor could spread like wildfire, and riots could be provoked in an instance (cf. Philo, *Flacc.* 25–43; Acts 19:23–41). Peddlers could take advantage of such networks by having word spread around once first contacts were made. Locations of and connections with artisans and ethnic quarters in a city were easily made (cf. Acts 16:13; 18:2–3). Meeks and others have even suggested that the workplace may have provided an important network for Paul's preaching.[69] This picture may be necessarily speculative in parts, but its overall validity can hardly be doubted. We can now add Philip Harland's important work, based on a great deal of archaeological and inscriptional evidence. Harland also develops the idea of conversion though networks like households, workplaces, marketplaces, neighborhoods, and so on, and provides ancient parallels, such as the spread of Mithraism through the military.[70] One of Harland's particularly important emphases is on dual or multiple affiliations to different associations.[71] Harland also notes that

> associations, synagogues, and congregations were small noncompulsory groups that could draw their membership from several possible social network connections within the polis . . . all could engage in at least some degree of external contacts, both positive and negative, with other individuals, benefactors, groups, or institutions in the civic context.[72]

This interconnectedness and possibility of dual and multiple membership is important because it can be adapted to provide one feature of countervailing influences in the social networks described above. What is now necessary for present purposes is to see what aspects of the ancient evidence are useful for explaining the shift in practice of the law in earliest Christianity. I will discuss the importance of households later, but I turn first to what may be loosely defined as a preexisting network available to the first Christians: Gentiles attracted to Judaism or behaving like Jews.[73]

There is scriptural justification for Jews accepting Gentiles who would become more intimately involved with the covenant and the commandments, most notably from Isaiah (e.g., Isa. 42:1–7; 49:1–6; 56:1–8). Jewish literature from roughly the right period makes some generalizing and at times idealizing comments on the popularity of the law among Gentiles.[74] Josephus, for instance, spoke of the attractiveness of Jewish practices in grandiose terms: "As God permeates the universe, so the Law has found its way among all humankind" (*Ag. Ap.* 2.284). Philo also makes similar comments on the law in general:

> Not only Jews but almost every other people, particularly those which take more account of virtue, have so far grown in holiness as to value and honour our laws. In this they have received a special distinction which belongs to no other code. (*Mos.* 2.17; cf. *Ag. Ap.* 2.123, 280)

In a more concrete situation, Josephus says that the post-Antiochus IV Jewish community in Antioch "were constantly attracting to their religious ceremonies multitudes of Greeks, and these they had in some measure incorporated with themselves" (*J.W.* 7.45). It may also be of some relevance that early in the Jewish war there were Syrian-based "Judaizers" who aroused suspicion of advocating the Jewish cause in "each city" (*J.W.* 2.463). Moreover, there are specific practices that attracted Gentiles mentioned in Jewish literature. Isaiah 56:1–8, for example, looks to a time when Gentiles will keep the Sabbath and give offerings in the Temple. More relevant of course is material from around the time of Christian origins, such as the following:

> The masses have long since shown a keen desire to adopt our religious observances; and there is not one city, Greek or barbarian, nor a single nation, to which our custom of abstaining from work on the seventh day has not spread, and where the fasts and the lighting of the lamps [cf. *m. Šabb.* 2.6–7; Tertullian, *Nat.* 1.13] and many of our prohibitions in the matter of food are not observed. (*Ag. Ap.* 2.282–283)

In addition are Gentile texts that also mention the attraction of specific Jewish practices, such as the famous passage from Juvenal:

> Some who have had a father who reveres the Sabbath, worship nothing but the clouds, and the divinity of the heavens, and see no difference between eating swine's flesh, from which their father abstained, and that of man; and in time they take to circumcision. Having been wont to flout the laws of Rome, they learn and practise and revere the Jewish law, and all that Moses handed down in his secret tome, forbidding to point out the way to any not worshipping the same rites, and conducting none but the circumcised to the desired fountain. For all which the father was to blame, who gave up every seventh day to idleness, keeping it apart from all the concerns of life. (Juvenal, *Sat.* 14.96–106)

It is not clear to what extent Gentiles were observing such practices in the presence of Jews in these passages or simply assimilating what they had seen. But close association is clearer elsewhere, as a few examples should show. The *Letter of Aristeas* and Daniel, for example, show that this was at least a theoretical possibility, even if the situations are massively idealized. In John's Gospel we are told that "Greeks" were among those who went up to worship at Passover (John 12:20).[75] As we will see below, Josephus provides evidence of Gentiles looking to Jewish figures on areas of law and conversion—or at the very least it is evidence of Gentiles interested in Jewish practices—such as the interaction between the house of Adiabene and the Jewish merchant Ananias, not to mention the strict Galilean Jew Eleazar (*Ant.* 20.34–48). There are of course rabbinic stories of rabbis in debate with Gentiles and Gentiles interested in some Jewish practice or other. Perhaps the most famous is a Gentile approaching the unwelcoming Shammai and then the accepting Hillel and asking to be made a proselyte while standing on one foot (*b. Šabb.* 31a). Of course it would not be easy to prove that this rabbinic story reflects a histori-cal event, but it does work with the assumption of possible Jewish-Gentile interaction over issues of law observance. There is also the later "God-fearer" inscription from Aphrodisias that has Gentiles with different relationships to the Jewish community. On Side A there are two "God-fearing" Gentiles with a close relationship to proselytes and Jews through birth, similar to God-fearers in the sense of the Gentiles at synagogues in Acts. On Side B, in contrast, there appear to be Gentile "God-fearers" who play a more general supportive role.[76] In all these cases the assumption that gentiles would have been behaving like law-observant Jews in such contexts is surely, well, assumed.

There is no restricting where such Gentiles might be found and where Jews or Jewish Christians might come into contact with them. The Greek Magical Papyri with, among other things, their references to Israel's God in one form or other and traces of Jewish theology also point to some kind of social inter-action. The workplace, social meetings, or associations would be more concrete examples (cf. Philo, *Flacc.* 57; *Corpus Inscriptionum Judaicarum* 745, 755, 777).[77] There should be no doubt that the earliest Jewish Christians used the preexist-ing social networks established by Jews to spread the message. A major advan-tage the early Christians had if they wanted their message spread was this sizeable hinterland of preexisting social networks without the difficult problem of always having to create new social bonds, although no doubt the Christians did this too. It may even have been synagogues that proved particularly useful in the spread of the earliest Christian message among such Gentiles attracted to Judaism, as has often been suggested (cf. Acts 2:10–13; 6:5; 8:27–28; 10:2, 22, 35; 13:16, 26, 43).[78] Luke has references to Gentiles with some connection to the synagogue (e.g., Acts 13:16, 26), but the historical accuracy of these sto-ries has been doubted because, among other reasons, they fit too neatly with Lukan theological concerns and are not paralleled in Paul's letters. Yet even if Luke did completely invent these stories and even though they indeed do fit his theological motivations, it is possible that the very writing of the Lukan stories requires the existence of such people forming a section of the earliest Christian movement. As for Paul not having any parallels, that is understandable because Paul is addressing specific issues in specific churches and he may simply have had no need to bring up the issue of Gentiles attracted to the synagogue. More-over, it is also *possible* that use of Scripture in the Pauline letters implies that at least some Gentiles in the audience could follow such complicated arguments and that this skill was honed in a synagogue context.[79] None of this proves much either way, but the idea of Gentiles being attracted to synagogues as Luke describes should not be ruled out just yet.

And there is more. There is some non-NT evidence that might support the general view of Gentile god-fearers at synagogues. Steven Fine notes a degree of socioreligious interaction between Jews and Gentiles in Roman Palestine and notably after the destruction of the Temple. There were some Jews who were open in supporting Gentile rulers, as suggested by the Qazyon inscription from Upper Galilee (cf. *y. Meg.* 3.1–3, 73d–74a), and some Jews would happily buy a Torah scroll from a Gentile (e.g., *t. 'Abod. Zar.* 3.6–7). But most important for present purposes were Gentiles said to have donated and contributed to the physical well-being of synagogues (e.g., *t. Meg.* 2.16).[80] Of course, these are not quite the Lukan god-fearers, but such examples of socioreligious interaction from post-70 Roman Palestine suggest that while the Lukan view of Gentiles at synagogues may (or may not) have been exaggerated, it is sociologically likely for such connections to have existed in the more multicultural urban settings in the Mediterranean Diaspora and before the Temple was destroyed. Again, Harland's discussion of dual and multiple affiliations may also point toward a more mixed scenario in certain cases. As noted above, Harland gives evidence of Jews attached to synagogues interacting with the broader Gentile world and belonging to different associations (cf. Philo, *Flacc.* 57; *Corpus Inscriptionum Judaicarum* 745, 755, 777). It may be suggested then that Gentiles attracted to Judaism and attached to some association may also have been linked to a synagogue. Indeed given Harland's analysis and given the varying levels of accommodation and acculturation among Jews in the ancient world, this would hardly have been unusual. If we now combine the insights of Fine and Harland with the evidence from Acts (irrespective of whether Luke invented the stories) then Jew-Gentile synagogue links become more than just a speculative guess. If this is anywhere near correct, we would have not only an important social network but one with preexisting countervailing influences.

Based on the approach to conversion discussed above, Gentiles attracted to Judaism would be among those "structurally available" for conversion, or even "religious seekers," to use another term from conversion studies. With the connections through social networks it may be possible that friends of friends of friends of these Gentiles with looser attachments to Judaism were the people with little care for major parts of the law. However, here we may now be getting too speculative for the tastes of the more empirically minded. It is now necessary to sharpen the focus and supply some stronger evidence.

ANCIENT SOCIAL NETWORKS AND THE CONVERSION OF HOUSEHOLDS

Meeks's analysis of households provides important evidence for the purposes of this book.[81] Here we have one powerful witness to conversion of households and the spread of earliest Christianity: Paul. Paul says that he baptized "the household of Stephanas [τὸν Στεφανᾶ οἶκον]" (1 Cor. 1:16), who were, tellingly, "the first converts of Achaia" (1 Cor. 16:15–16). Also from 1 Corinthians Paul speaks of "Chloe's people [τῶν Χλόης]" (1:11). It is worth noting that Philippians even ends with the following greeting: "All the saints greet you, especially those of the emperor's household [οἱ ἐκ τῆς Καίσαρος οἰκίας]" (Phil. 4:22). Although not as strong a witness, Luke clearly knows that such a practice happened. A good example is that of Cornelius's household, who were dedicated to God (Acts 10:2), and later (Acts 11:14) Peter is said to bring the message to save the entire household (πᾶς ὁ οἶκός σου]. Lydia, a purple cloth dealer from the city of Thyatira, became baptized, along with the household (Acts 16:14–15). In the conversion of the jailer in Philippi (16:31–34), Paul and Silas speak of saving "you and your household [οἶκός σου]" before baptizing him and his family. There is also the example of Crispus, the synagogue official in Corinth, who became a believer along with "all his household [ὅλῳ τῷ οἴκῳ αὐτοῦ]" (Acts 18:8). Finally, we should also mention that in John 4:46–54 Jesus heals the son of a royal official in Capernaum and so the royal official and his household then believe. Of course several of these examples may be entirely fictional, but they almost certainly reflect one very practical way of converting several people at once.

It may be argued then that the head of the household might convert to or show a degree of interest in Christianity when it was largely law observant but that the members of the household were not necessarily going to have the same degree of commitment. More generally but with obvious relevance for my purposes, Meeks suggests,

> If the existing household was the basic cell of the mission, then it follows from the motivational bases for becoming part of the *ekklēsia* would likely vary from one member to another. If a household became Christian more or less en bloc, not everyone who went along with the new practices would do so with the same understanding or inner participation. Social solidarity might be more important in persuading some members to be baptized than would understanding or convictions about specific beliefs. Differential qualities and degrees of engagement with the group would not be surprising.[82]

In the NT there is some useful evidence in the shape of Onesimus, slave of the Christian Philemon, who does not appear to have converted until Paul took him under his wing (Phlm. 10). Nicholas Taylor makes a potentially useful qualification entirely in line with the view of conversion taken throughout this chapter:

> Onesimus was initiated into the church with the rest of Philemon's household, but without having acquired Christian convictions. His flight from Philemon would have severed his connection with the church as with the household. What changed, presumably through

Onesimus's encounter with Paul, was the quality of this Christianity, from involuntary incorporation into a Christian community and conformity therewith, to commitment to the Christian faith. His return to Philemon would combine conviction with socialization and observance, and so complete Onesimus' conversion.[83]

The example of Onesimus provides an important and early example of a household member initially attached to Christianity in a very loose way. If the situation of households converting was happening when Christianity was essentially a law-observant movement, then we must surely expect instances where members of the household were not going to be fully committed to law observance.

As we have already seen in part, there is also evidence of problems with converting to Christianity elsewhere in Paul's letters, which do in fact discuss the issue of law, though unfortunately not quite in the precise context of the ongoing relevance of the validity of commandments. When Paul discusses the issue of Christians divorcing nonbelieving partners (1 Cor. 7:12–16), he not only allows the possibility of their staying together but also raises the possibility of future conversion of the nonbelieving partner, something Paul may well have had previous direct experience of in his missionary and pastoral work. Again we see differing levels of commitment and the potential for a future combination of conviction with socialization to echo Taylor. Although 1 Corinthians was written at a time when a notable number of Christians were not fully observing major parts of biblical law, the situation in 1 Cor. 7 is not only fifteen years or so after the time when I suggest Christianity was largely law observant but is defended with what is clearly a legal-style argument.[84] Moreover, we also have evidence of wives devoted to Judaism where husbands were not. Josephus gives one important example in Damascus at the beginning of the war. The men of Damascus were bent on destroying the Jewish populace but, Josephus adds, "their only fear was of their own wives who, with few exceptions, had all become converts to the Jewish religion, and so their efforts were mainly directed to keeping the secret from them" (*J.W.* 2.560–61). So again it is historically and sociologically plausible or even probable that when Christianity first emerged in the 30s it would have faced the problem of partners with differing socioreligious affiliations.

For the issue of law observance and conversion we need to turn to more Jewish evidence where there is some mention of household conversion. Noting Meeks's work that Christianity grew partly through household conversions, Shaye Cohen notes parallels in Jewish sources and makes the following and almost certainly accurate claim: "We may be sure that the involuntary members of the household had substantially less enthusiasm, at least at first, for the new religion than did the chieftain who initiated the conversion, but all alike became members of the new community."[85] There is only a small amount of recorded Jewish discussion on this issue, but the few examples remain vital, for they provide the most important thematic parallels to the first law-observant Christians. *T. Qidd.* 5:11–12, for example, raises the following situation:

> R. Meir did say, "There is a husband and a wife who produces five castes." How so? "A gentile man who has a slave-boy and a slave girl, and they have two children, and one of them is converted—Lo, [1] one is a proselyte, and [2] one is a gentile. [If] their master converted and converted the slaves, and they produced a son, then [3] the offspring is a slave. [If] the slave-girl is freed, and that slave boy had sexual relations with her, and they produced a son, the son is [4] a *mamzer*. And [if] both of them are freed, and they produce a son, then the son is [5] a freed slave."

This is no doubt an abstract discussion, but it does assume the validity of the conversion of households. Also in later Judaism some Jews found a scriptural precedent for this in Jonah 1:16, where the sailors feared God and even made sacrifices and vows to God. *Pirqe de Rabbi Eliezer* 10, very aware of the problems involved in proselytes' making sacrifices, has the sailors' being circumcised after seeing the miracles and wonders of God and turning away from their idols, their useless lower-case gods. In fact circumcision is what is *really* meant by sacrifice in Jonah 1:16. And in addition to circumcision we get the accompanying conversion of the household: "And they made vows every one to bring his children and all belonging to him to the God of Jonah." As this passage may imply, there is also the relevant issue of Jews converting slaves. There is some scriptural justification in Exod. 12:48 ("If an alien who resides with you wants to celebrate the passover to the Lord, all his males shall be circumcised . . . he shall be regarded as a native of the land") and the various issues arising from circumcising a slave for Passover are discussed in, for example, *Mek.* (Exod. 15). The conversion or socialization of a slave is also assumed in Mishnaic texts where the freed slave parallels the status of proselyte.[86] Note too the ambiguous status of such a person:

> R. Eliezer b. Jacob says, A woman who is the daughter of proselytes may not marry a priest, unless her mother was an Israelite. The same [law] applies to proselytes and freed slaves, [and holds] even to the tenth generation: [she may not marry a priest] unless her mother is an Israelite. An executor, agent, slave, woman, person of doubtful sex, and an androgynous [person] bring first fruits but do not recite, because they are not able to say, "[And behold, now I bring the first of the firstfruit of the ground], which you, O Lord, have given me" (Deut. 26:10). (*m. Bik.* 1:5)

> R. Eliezer b. Jacob says, An Israelite who married a female proselyte—his daughter is suitable for marriage into the priesthood. And a proselyte who married an Israelite girl—his daughter is valid for marriage

into the priesthood. But a male proselyte who married a female proselyte—his daughter is invalid for marriage into the priesthood. All the
same are proselytes and freed slaves, even down to tenth generations—
[the daughters cannot marry into the priesthood] unless the mother is
an Israelite. (*m. Qidd.* 4:7).

Or again notice the theoretical possibility of circumcising Gentile slaves
recorded in the Palestinian Talmud: "R. Isaac bar Nahman in the name of
R. Joshua b. Levi: A man once bought a city of uncircumcised slaves from a gentile on condition that he would circumcise them, but they retracted" (*y. Yebam.*
8, 8d). In a more down-to-earth context, the circumcision of slaves and their
status as proselytes may be assumed in the following piece of Roman law with
a ruling dating to Antioninus Pius and attributed to Modestinus:

> MODESTINUS, *Rules, book* 6: By a rescript of the deified Pius it is
> allowed only to Jews to circumcise their own sons [*Circumcidere Iudaeis
> filios suos tantum rescripto Divi Pii permititur*]; a person not of that reli-
> gion who does so suffers the penalty of one carrying out a castration.
> (*Digesta* 48.8.11)

As Stern notes, the Jewish circumcision seems to have been an exceptional
concession and if "the ban on circumcision was then of general validity, the
Jews would have been prohibited from performing circumcision on non-Jews
even if allowed to circumcise Jewish males."[87] And one of the most obvious
ways a Jew could circumcise a male of course would be if the male was a slave.
Given what we have already seen on household conversions, we must surely
assume that if a master was converted and converted the slaves, full-blown conversion of all individuals would not have taken place and commitment levels
would vary. Of course, it is difficult to know for sure what the levels of observance were and what degrees of dedication there might have been, but once
again it is difficult to dispute what Cohen says about converted slaves: "These
slaves, even if they assented to their conversion . . . cannot have been moti-
vated by a deep or sincere love for the God of Abraham. They were converted
to Judaism for the religious convenience of their owners."[88]

An outstanding example of a conversion of a household through a social network is the famous conversion of Izates and the house of Adiabene (*Ant.*
20.34–48).[89] A Jewish merchant called Ananias, no doubt with good connections to the royal household, taught the king's wives to worship the Jewish god.
Josephus tells us that it was through their actions that Ananias was brought to
the attention of Izates, "whom he similarly won over with the co-operation of
the women." When Izates was summoned by his father, Ananias went along too.
Furthering the influence of the social network, Izates's mother Helena had also
been converted to Jewish laws. This prompted Izates to take on more aspects

of Judaism, even to the extent of circumcision because he considered this to be the defining aspect of becoming a Jew. What is particularly significant is the countervailing influence of his mother, who vigorously pressured him not to be circumcised because the people would not tolerate such an overt show of Jewish identity. Here we have an excellent example of the problems of conversion and differing levels of observance in the light of social and political influences in a given household, albeit an untypical one. This required a decision one way or another. Ananias, for personal and practical reasons (he might get the blame) agreed strongly with Helena: no, he should not be circumcised. After all, does not devotion to the Jewish god mean even more than circumcision? And does not God also realize the everyday political problems a ruler faces? Although this held some sway for a while, the strict Galilean Jew Eleazar, on a visit to pay his respects, urged him to become circumcised. Is it not a bit hypocritical to follow the law and skip the trickier commandments? Circumcision is, after all, a fairly major one.[90] Eleazar's arguments got through. Josephus adds that while there were indeed threats to Izates and his children, God fortunately protected them.

We must assume that there were similar competing influences on members of households who converted to earliest Christianity. These influences would vary according to gender, class, or whatever, but they would no doubt be present and would require decisions on some tough issues. Let us not forget that the example just given had a Gentile population hostile towards this circumcision, so we should not underestimate the pressure on the earliest converts not to circumcise. It is, presumably, no coincidence that there are a notable number of women with interest in converting to Judaism in the primary sources (cf. Josephus, *J.W.* 2.560; *Ant.* 18.81–84; 20.35).[91] It is surely not too speculative to suggest that a lot of the first males attracted to Christianity were simply not going to want to be circumcised. On the other hand, we should recall that some of the converts from areas neighboring or close to Palestine may already have been circumcised (cf., e.g., Philo, *QG* 3.48; Herodotus 2.104.2–4; *Mek.* [Exod. 15]; *b. Yeb.* 71a), even if not circumcised correctly (cf. *Jub.* 15:33), so this may not have been an immediate problem for all the first male converts. Still, they would have had other socioreligious pressures, as the proposed marriage of the handsome Syllaeus, an Arab governor under Obadas, king of Arabia, to the besotted Salome shows:

> But when they asked Syllaeus to be initiated into the customs of the Jews before the wedding—otherwise, they said, marriage would be impossible—he would not submit to this but took his departure, saying that if he did submit, he would be stoned to death by the Arabs. (Josephus, *Ant.* 16.225)

As Syllaeus was an Arab and as the issue of circumcision is not mentioned, it appears that Josephus assumes he was circumcised.[92] Even so, Syllaeus could not face going all the way over to observance of Jewish customs in general because of social, political, and religious influences. Granted, this is at court level, but the broad nature of the opposition again suggests the wider problems of fully endorsing the practices of another group.

There are other stories in Josephus of family members converting to certain degrees and, once again, social and political influences play a major role in defining the relationships.[93] One example of people with different ideas about what they were prepared to do is that of Agrippa's giving his sister Drusilla in marriage to Azizus, king of Emesa, who had agreed to be circumcised. On the other hand "Epiphanes, son of King Antiochus, had rejected the marriage since he was not willing to convert to the Jewish religion, although he had previously contracted with her father to do so" (*Ant.* 20.139). Again it is possible that the same kinds of countervailing influences Syllaeus experienced prevented Epiphanes from doing the same. Another notable example is of Berenice. After the death of her "uncle and husband" Herod of Chalcis, Berenice was a widow but still had a taste for incest. Perceptions of her widowed state changed when rumors were rife that she had a liaison with her brother. Berenice lured Polemo, king of Cilicia, to be not only married but also circumcised in order to falsify the reports of her scandalous behavior. Polemo was no mug, however, and Berenice's wealth appears to have been, if anything, more alluring than Berenice herself. Like many celebrity weddings of the *Heat* variety, the marriage did not last long, and Josephus adds that Polemo "was relieved simultaneously of his marriage and of further adherence to the Jewish way of life" (*Ant.* 20.145–47). It can be assumed, then, that Polemo's heart was not in Judaism whilst married to Berenice. But if, somehow, they had stayed together . . . who knows? Perhaps they may even have gone along the same lines as Paul hoped in the case of believing and nonbelieving partners: the unbeliever may indeed come round and the children could at least be saved (1 Cor. 7:12–16). Whatever, the marriage of Berenice and Polemo was one of convenience, and although once again this is court level, the timeless principle that people do not always convert with all their hearts is well known and would hardly have been wholly uncommon. Consequently there is the potential for a lesser degree of consistency in observance levels than might be expected in such converts.

A loose but potentially useful parallel to group conversion and its differing commitment levels is the "conversion" of the Idumeans under John Hyrcanus:[94]

> Hyrcanus also captured the Idumean cities of Adora and Marisa, and after subduing all the Idumeans, permitted them to remain in their

country so long as they had themselves circumcised and were willing to observe the laws [νόμοις, var. νομίμοις] of the Jews. And so out of attachment to the land of their fathers, they submitted to circumcision and to making their manner of life conform in all other aspects to that of the Jews. And from that time on they have continued to be Jews. (*Ant.* 13.257–58)

From what can be gleaned from Josephus, this was a slightly unusual situation because there does not seem to have been a major rebellion against Jewish customs or indeed Jewish rule. There are also statements in other sources that at least do not imply any problems with the conversion of the Idumeans, whether it is described as forced or willing:

As for Judea, its western extremities towards Casius are occupied by the Idumeans. . . . The Idumeans are Nabateans, but owing to a sedition they were banished from there, joined the Judeans, and shared in the same customs with them. (Strabo, *Geogr.* 16.2.34)

Jews and Idumeans differ, as Ptolemy states in the first book of the History of King Herod. Jews are those who are so by origin and nature. The Idumeans, on the other hand, were not originally Jews and having been forced to undergo circumcision, so as to be counted among the Jewish nation and keep the same customs, they were called Jews.[95]

Indeed there are times when Idumeans seemed quite content to be associated with Jews. Idumeans (20,000 according to Josephus) became involved in the Jewish infighting when during the Jewish war they initially helped "the zealots" (*J.W.* 4.224–355; cf. *J.W.* 2.72–79). There is, however, other evidence that not all Idumeans were simply going to go Jewish. Costobarus is the most notable:

Costobarus was of Idumean race and was one of the first rank among them, and his ancestors had been priests of Koze, whom the Idumeans believe to be a god. Now Hyrcanus had altered their way of life and made them adopt the customs and laws of the Jews. When Herod took over royal power, he appointed Costobarus governor of Idumea and Gaza . . . he gradually exceeded all bounds. For he did not think that it was proper for him to carry out the orders of Herod, who was his ruler, or for the Idumeans to adopt the customs of the Jews and be subject to them. (*Ant.* 15.253–54)

This is several decades after the conversion of the Idumeans, and it implies that there had been at least some reaction to assimilation, something that is to be expected in the light of conversion studies. Clearly it was still possible for an Idumean to talk of the old ways and want people to revert back to them.

Herod the Great might be an example of someone with Idumean roots who was not the most faithful Jew.[96] But there is a history of polemic against Herod the Great and his Idumean background which has no doubt tampered with the common perception of his behavior. For all the genuine evidence Herod looks no more or less brutal than any other such ruler, and he seems to have attempted a presentation of himself as a good Jew. He is also regarded as an Ἰουδαῖος in different sources.[97] He was associated with the rebuilding of the Jerusalem Temple, which was so massive some scholars have been tempted to call it the Third Temple. Josephus records Herod speaking as a spectacularly faithful Jewish "insider" to the crowd in Jerusalem when he proposed to rebuild the Temple (*Ant.* 15.383–87). To add to the show of piety, Herod himself had restricted access to the Temple as it was being built, and the priests were made responsible for the rebuilding of the most important areas (*Ant.* 15.420). Despite this, Josephus still manages to tell his audience that Herod was more interested in building temples, theaters, and baths for Gentile cities "whereas there was not a single city of the Jews on which he deigned to bestow even minor restoration or any gift worth mentioning" (*Ant.* 19.328–30)! Once again, despite Josephus's spin, it seems that there were Jews quite prepared to accept Herod's "Jewishness" in certain contexts. Compare the following report of a dispute in Caesarea on the eve of the Jewish war:

> There arose also a quarrel between the Jewish and Syrian inhabitants of Caesarea on the subject of equal civic rights. The Jews claimed that they had the precedence because the founder of Caesarea, their king Herod, had been of Jewish descent; the Syrians admitted what they said about Herod but asserted that Caesarea had been called Strato's Tower, and that before Herod's time there had not been a single Jewish inhabitant in the city. (*Ant.* 20.173)

However, the parallel report makes particularly interesting reading because now we start to see the ambiguities in Herod's "Jewish" behavior:

> Another disturbance occurred at Caesarea, where the Jewish portion of the population rose against the Syrian inhabitants. They claimed that the city was theirs on the ground that its founder, King Herod, was a Jew. Their opponents admitted the Jewish origin of its second founder, but maintained that the city itself belonged to the Greeks, since Herod would never have erected the statues and temples which he had placed there had he destined it for Jews. (*J.W.* 2.266)

It might just be significant that, despite there being no denial of Herod's Jewish background in the Caesarea episode, there remained a perception that he did not always behave the way a good Jew should. Herod may be suspect on a specific law (*Ant.* 16.1–5), but idolatry is the main problem. Josephus is quite clear that when Herod gave his gifts to Gentile cities, he was acting contrary to Jewish custom and for his own glorification. But Josephus also notes that he could not have gotten away with the same practice in Jewish cities and that Herod gave the excuse that he was doing such things to satisfy the Romans (*Ant.* 15.326–30). Josephus mentions the problems Herod had when establishing such pagan practices as a theater and amphitheater in the area of Jerusalem. Josephus is very clear that Herod has acted contrary to Jewish law although it is telling that Herod still manages to remove offensive items and convince Jews that he was doing nothing wrong (*Ant.* 15.326–30). So even if there was a perception that Herod was not a good Jew, Herod certainly tried to make out that he actually was to his Jewish subjects. And some believed him.

It is possible that this perception of Herod as a not-always-good-Jew was due to his Idumean background.[98] There are, for example, some problems with the background of Herod's father, Antipater, in Josephus's account (*Ant.* 14.8–10; cf. *J.W.* 1.123). While Josephus claims Antipater was an Idumean, Nicolas of Damascus recorded that Antipater belonged to the leading Jews who had returned from Babylon. Josephus regards this as an invention by Nicolas to please Herod, and given that the Babylonian connection seems too good to be true, he is probably right. But even in the fabulously unlikely scenario of the Babylonian connection not being a piece of Herodian propaganda, the problematic Idumean perception remained. Herod was even described in derogatory terms due to his Idumean background:

> But Antigonus . . . told Silo and the Roman army that it would be contrary to their own notion of right if they gave kingship to Herod who was a commoner and an Idumean, that is, a half-Jew [ἡμιιουδαίῳ],[99] when they ought to offer it to those who were of the royal family, as was their custom.

It is most likely that in reality when Herod acted in a way that seemed contrary to Jewish custom, it was due not so much to his Idumean influences but rather, as can be seen even through Josephus's spin, due to his wanting to keep his Gentile subjects pacified, please Rome, and glorify himself. However, the *perception* that his Idumean background was a problem in identifying Herod as a good Jew must have been present for some (but not necessarily all), and it was not entirely groundless with people like Costobarus around. This perception has proven difficult in establishing Herod's reputation as a true Jew right up to the present.

The Idumean issue is not a strong parallel by itself. Its strength lies in that it reflects certain perceptions of a group of people who were seemingly forced into conversion but who were not always thought to behave in the way a good convert perhaps ought to. Though not the most directly relevant evidence, the case of the Idumeans does once again show the varying degrees of commitment stemming from what might have been forced group conversion, real or perceived. This in fact reflects broader suspicions about the seriousness of Gentile conversion and adherence to Jewish practices in rabbinic literature (e.g., *m. Nid.* 7:3; *Exod. Rab.* 42:6; *b. B. Meṣiʿa* 59b; *b. Yeb.* 47b). But this is also reflected in first-century material. As Josephus puts it, "The Greeks . . . many of them have agreed to adopt our laws; of whom some have remained faithful, while others, lacking the necessary endurance, have again seceded" (*Ag. Ap.* 2.123).

IMPLICATIONS AND CONCLUSIONS

The view of conversion to earliest Christianity through social networks has the potential to gain a great deal of scholarly agreement. It has a strong base in the social sciences and religious studies, and there is unambiguous evidence of conversion of households in earliest Christianity. One implication is that it can lead to changing beliefs and practices or, more specifically, provide a powerful explanation of the shift from a law-observant movement to a movement that included increasing numbers of friends of friends of friends who did not feel obliged to observe major commandments, such as food laws and the Sabbath, or to be circumcised.

There would also be strong countervailing influences on Gentiles already observing major commandments not to do so, at least in certain social settings and especially if they participated in one group one day and another group the next. Moreover, it is quite probable that even if the first Gentile converts were observing major commandments such as Sabbath and food laws in front of Jewish Christians, many (most? all?) were not prepared to go so far as to be circumcised. I do not use the term "proselyte" to describe the Gentiles because I argue that the earliest Christian movement of the 30s and possibly early 40s was largely law observant. When in the company of the first law-observant Jewish Christians, these Gentiles would have appeared law observant also. But it does not necessarily mean that they were circumcised or perhaps even that some would continue to observe major commandments in different social contexts. It is these kinds of links with different social settings that would have provided the shift in law observance. Of course the lack of hard evidence from the 30s and early 40s requires the use of historical imagination, but given the strong parallels I have shown, this approach is surely a highly plausible one.

These implications and conclusions take us back to the concerns of the first chapter and in particular the secular approach to Christian origins grounded in social history. The results of this chapter suggest that we should not put too much weight on the history of ideas. There still remain strong tendencies in NT studies to see Paul's theology almost purely as the act of a personal genius who found "something wrong" with Jewish intellectual thought. The approach of this chapter would suggest, however, that the earliest Christian movement was faced with people who were attracted to the new movement with varying commitment levels. Something needed to be done about these people, hence the Jerusalem conference somewhere around the year 50 CE. Figures such as Paul come to the fore in this general context. Paul's views on the law and justification by faith can thus be seen as an intellectual reaction to and justification of a very down-to-earth and messy social problem.

Conclusion

The persistence of monotheism, like the demise of polytheistic paganism, owed much to economic as well as to psychological and cultural conditions.[1]

In chapter 4—to start towards the end rather than the beginning—it was argued that at least some sections of the ancient world were exhibiting strongly monotheistic tendencies and that the Jesus movement satisfied the conditions to spark off a major spread of a universalistic monotheistic religion. Chapters 2, 3, and 5 show that these conditions were "satisfied." Chapter 2 provided the various socioeconomic reasons that contributed to the "spark," namely, the rise of the Jesus movement and its specific approach to the law. Land alienation and increased commercialization led to a variety of movements hostile to the prevailing social, economic, and political order. These could range from violent to nonviolent reactions, but one way or another there would be change: if humans could not do it then God would. This hostility clearly left its mark on Jesus' teaching, and there should be little doubt that the socioeconomic conditions of 20s Galilee were collectively a major causal factor in the emergence of not only Jesus' specific view of the law but the Jesus movement as a whole.

If the rich oppressors were going to be damned then what should be done? Put crudely, there were two choices available: let them burn or try to make them repent. For good or for ill Jesus went for the latter, as chapter 2 and chapter 3 both showed, although to what degree they gave up their previous lifestyles is impossible to know. But it did mean that the Jesus movement had to accommodate a very broad range of people, from the poor to the rich. In the case of the stereotypically oppressive rich, otherwise derogatorily known as the "sinners," this meant associating with people no better than lawless Gentiles.

This provided a crucial connection to associating with Gentiles themselves whilst still remaining law observant, as chapter 4 shows. Both the Q legal traditions and Markan legal traditions, both of which I would regard as the earliest traditions we have in the NT and earliest Christianity, give some indication of what kinds of material could be used in a context where Christianity was still largely and visibly law observant (30s CE and early 40s CE). There is not only a concern for the law but a concern for the practice of proper moral conduct, something that, stereotypically, Gentiles were infamous for not practicing. Mark 6–8 makes this point, I would argue, abundantly clear.

But if the Christians of the 30s were largely and visibly observant of major biblical laws, how do we get to situations like Paul's having to justify nonobservance of Gentile and perhaps even Jewish Christians and a council in Jerusalem gathering to deal with this situation sometime close to 50 CE? Here social-network analysis has proven to be a useful tool. In chapter 5 it was argued that conversion to Christianity through social networks (work, households, etc.) was crucial for the spread of earliest Christianity. Yet when more and more Gentiles were being converted this way, a number of factors contributed to the rise of nonobservance. To begin with, some Gentiles interested in the Christian form of Judaism would have been fully observant when at a worship gathering (bringing a gift of pork chops or taking time out of the Sabbath service to whack a hammer would not go down well), but who knows what kinds of nonkosher behavior certain converts exhibited when in more pagan settings? Obviously, participation in non-Christian social circles provided an influence that would have run counter to some of the important practices of the law. Misunderstanding and puzzlement over the strangeness of Jewish behavior is well documented in the primary sources. Some partners would not have converted, thus creating a tension in the household. Some people would have converted without initially knowing too much about the details of what they were converting to. Conversion of a household would inevitably leave some members as converts in name only: converts who did not really love God with all their heart, mind, and soul. There would have been loose attachments—friends of friends of friends—whose commitment levels would have varied. And so on . . .

This, in other words, is a secular account of one aspect of Christian origins, the importance of which I advocated in chapter 1. It is also an account that while not omitting the importance of history of ideas and ideology, does downplay their causal significance and give greater emphasis to broader socioeconomic factors. Ideology still has an important place—for example, in explaining *historical* particularities—but surely the time has come for a more *widespread* scholarly approach to the causal factors involved in the spread of earliest Christianity. An approach is needed that does not merely look at such topics or questions as the textual ways in which Jesus was thought of as divine, whether the resurrection happened or not, precisely what Jesus said, when this or that Gospel was written, what this or that source looked like, what some passage in Paul or a Gospel *really* means, what the experiences of the early Christians were, or how exegetical study can provide relevance for the modern world. Indeed one criticism I would aim at this present work is that it is too heavily based on the NT texts. Another project along these lines would involve a further step back from the textual action, something I am attempting elsewhere.[2] Don't get me wrong: these textual issues listed above are important in their own right, and most are important for the bigger picture. But an increase of widespread scholarly energy on the question of *why* this movement or these movements happened would provide some big answers to some big, big questions. While there have been attempts at grand causal explanations without resorting to Christian superiority, it has still not caught on in a major way, and it is not because of the emergence of that usual coverall target, postmodernism. No, this has always been a problem in NT studies. To change this I suspect it may require a greater number of non-Christians working in the field, as I advocated in chapter 1. Whether NT scholars will do anything about this problem in the near future is unlikely in my view, given the ideological makeup of the discipline, but there is no harm in some of us at least trying.

There is, of course, much more work to be done on providing a comprehensive account of Christian origins. Some suggestions can be made. For instance, if the Jesus movement did meet the conditions for the emergence of another monotheistic faith that would develop widely, then it may have something to say on the full deification of Jesus, particularly as a means to identify the new religion over against Judaism and pagan religions, and consequently to be seen as a new religion in its own right in the Greco-Roman world. This appears to have happened relatively early: something close to the full deification of Jesus appears to be present towards the end of the first century in John's Gospel. The universalism required for the wide-ranging spread of a monotheistic faith probably emerged thanks to the establishment of a massive travel-and-communication network along with long-established monotheistic Jewish networks in a Gentile world increasingly accepting of monotheism. If this did contribute to the spread of earliest Christianity, then it would suggest that very broad, slow-moving social, geographical, and economic factors have something important to tell us about the emergence of Christianity. This is nothing new to conventional historians, of course, not least due to the pioneering work of Braudel on "geo-history." Serious interaction with such approaches and how they can be applied to the ancient Mediterranean and Christian origins has the potential to provide a wealth of insights. If these and other such insights are not exploited, NT studies will retain its dubious academic status as being nothing more than the pious scholarly wings of the Christian churches, with their scholars often plying their trade in secular universities.

Notes

Introduction

1. I still use the term "Christianity" for nothing more than convenience to denote the followers of Jesus in the 30s even if no such term was then in use and even though the movement had not yet split from Judaism. I do not imply anything more than that. It should be obvious that this is how I use the label.

2. J. G. Crossley, *The Date of Mark's Gospel: Insight from the Law in Earliest Christianity* (London: Continuum/T. & T. Clark, 2004), 82–205.

3. E.g., P. R. Davies, *In Search of 'Ancient Israel'* (Sheffield: Sheffield Academic Press, 1992), e.g., 43–45; P. R. Davies, *Whose Bible Is It Anyway?* (Sheffield: Sheffield Academic Press, 1995); J. Berlinerblau, "'Poor Bird, Not Knowing Which Way to Fly': Biblical Scholarship's Marginality, Secular Humanism, and the Laudable Occident," *BibInt.* 10 (2002): 267–304; J. Berlinerblau, *The Secular Bible: Why Nonbelievers Must Take Religion Seriously* (Cambridge: Cambridge University Press, 2005).

4. For those who are not specialists in biblical studies, New Testament histories are not histories of the New Testament through the ages but rather something akin to the history of the first-century movement that would become Christianity, usually with reference to its general historical context, and often a history of first-century Christian theological ideas.

Chapter 1: Toward a Secular Approach to Christian Origins

1. J. Berlinerblau, *The Secular Bible: Why Nonbelievers Must Take Religion Seriously* (Cambridge: Cambridge University Press, 2005), 110.

2. P. R. Davies, *In Search of 'Ancient Israel'* (Sheffield: JSOT, 1992), 44–45.

3. N. T. Wright, *The Resurrection of the Son of God* (London: SPCK, 2003).

4. Cf. J. H. Elliott, *What Is Social Scientific Criticism?* (Minneapolis: Fortress, 1993), 18–20.

5. Two prominent examples: D. G. Horrell, "Social-Scientific Interpretation of the New Testament: Retrospect and Prospect," in *Social-Scientific Approaches to New Testament Interpretation*, ed. D. G. Horrell (Edinburgh: T. & T. Clark, 1999), 3–27 (9–11); H. J. Kaye, *The British Marxist Historians* (Cambridge: Polity, 1984), 1–7.

6. So also e.g., L. Stone, "History and the Social Sciences in the Twentieth Century," in *The Past and the Present* (London: Routledge, 1981), 3–44 (23, 27).
7. A. Deissmann, *Paulus: Einer kultur—und religious—geschichtliche Skizze* (Tübingen: J. C. B. Mohr, 1911); A. Deissmann, *Paul: A Study in Social and Religious History*, trans. W. E. Wilson (New York: Harper & Bros., 1957); A. Deissmann, *Licht vom Osten*, 4th ed. (Tübingen: J. C. B. Mohr, 1923); A. Deissmann, *Light from the Ancient East: The New Testament Illustrated by Recently Discovered Texts of the Graeco-Roman World*, trans. L. R. M. Strachan (London: Hodder & Stoughton, 1927); E. Troeltsch, *Die Soziallehren der christichen Kirchen und Gruppen, Gesammelte Schriften I* (Tübingen: J. C. B. Mohr, 1912); E. Troeltsch, *The Social Teaching of the Christian Churches, Vol. I*, trans. O. Wyon (London: Allen and Unwin, 1931); A. Harnack, *The Mission and Expansion of Christianity in the First Three Centuries*, 2 vols. (London: Williams Norgate, 1904–5). For analysis and overview see R. Hochschild, *Sozialgeschichtliche Exegese: Entwicklung, Geschichte und Methodik einer neutestamentlichen Forschungsrichtung* (Göttingen: Vandenhoeck & Ruprecht, 1999), 45–206.
8. F. Engels, "On the History of Earliest Christianity (1894)," in *Collected Works Volume 27, Engels: 1890–95*, K. Marx and F. Engels (London: Lawrence & Wishart, 1990), 447–69; K. Kautsky, *Der Ursprung des Christentums: Eine historische Untersuchung* (1908); K. Kautsky, *Foundations of Christianity: A Study in Christian Origins* (London: Orbach & Chambers, 1925).
9. S. J. Case, *The Social Origins of Christianity* (Chicago: University of Chicago Press, 1923); *The Social Triumph of the Ancient Church* (New York: Harper & Bros., 1933); F. C. Grant, *The Economic Background of the Gospels* (London: Oxford University Press, 1926, 1973).
10. R. W. Funk, "The Watershed of the American Biblical Tradition: The Chicago School, First Phase, 1892–1920," *JBL* 95 (1976), 4–22; H. C. Kee, *Christian Origins in Sociological Perspective* (London: SCM, 1980), 17.
11. Horrell, "Social-Scientific Interpretation," 6.
12. G. Theissen, *Social Reality and the Early Christians: Theology, Ethics and the World of the New Testament* (Edinburgh: T. & T. Clark, 1993), 9–13.
13. O. Cullmann, "Les récentes etudes sur la formation de la tradition évangélique," *Revue d'histoire et de philosophie religieuses* 5 (1925): 564–79 (573).
14. P. F. Esler, *Community and Gospel in Luke-Acts: The Social and Political Motivations of Lucan Theology* (Cambridge: Cambridge University Press, 1987), 3.
15. S. Heschel, "Nazifying Christian Theology: Walter Grundmann and the Institute for the Study and Eradication of Jewish Influence on German Church Life," *Church History* 63 (1994): 587–605; M. Casey, "Some Anti-Semitic Assumptions in *The Theological Dictionary of the New Testament*," *NovT* 41 (1999): 280–91; P. Head, "The Nazi Quest for an Ayrian Jesus," *JSHJ* 2 (2004): 55–89.
16. W. Grundmann, *Jesus der Galiläer und das Judentum* (Leipzig: Wigand, 1940).
17. Casey, "Anti-Semitic Assumptions."
18. G. Vermes, *Jesus and the World of Judaism* (London: SCM, 1983), 64–66.
19. E. Käsemann, *New Testament Questions of Today* (London: SCM, 1969), 186.
20. D. Boyarin, *A Radical Jew: Paul and the Politics of Identity* (Berkeley: University of California Press, 1994), 213.
21. It should be added that antisemitism, anti-Judaism, and sympathy for Nazism were not of course restricted to Germany. A. C. Headlam, for example, was Regius Professor of Divinity at Oxford, the Bishop of Gloucester, and, most disturbingly perhaps, chair of the Church of England Council on Foreign Rela-

tions. He had some respect for Hitler, sympathized with the Nazi Deutsche Christen movement, and criticized those who thought Christianity and National Socialism were incompatible. See further, e.g., R. C. D. Jasper, *Arthur Cayley Headlam: Life and Letters of a Bishop* (London: Faith, 1960), 290–301; A. Hastings, *A History of English Christianity 1920–1990* (London: SCM, 1991), 320–24.

22. For detailed discussion of the *Annales* movement see P. Burke, *The French Historical Revolution: The* Annales *School 1929–1989* (Cambridge: Polity, 1990).

23. M. Bloch, *Les rois thaumaturges* (Strasbourg: Istra, 1924, new ed., 1983). M. Bloch, *The Royal Touch*, trans. J. E. Anderson (London: Routledge & Kegan Paul, 1973).

24. Burke, *French Historical Revolution*, 18.

25. E.g., *Life in Renaissance France* (ET; Cambridge, MA: Harvard University Press, 1977). Other important works for present concerns are *A Geographical Introduction to History* (New York: Knopf, 1925); *A New Kind of History*, trans. P. Burke (New York: Harper & Row, 1973).

26. E. Hobsbawm, "British History and the *Annales*: A Note," in *On History* (London: Weidenfeld & Nicolson, 1997), 236–45 (239–41). First printed in *Review* 1 (Winter-Spring, 1978): 157–62.

27. The book was revised and enlarged in 1966. The ET was published later still: *The Mediterranean and the Mediterranean World in the Age of Philip II*, trans. S. Reynolds (London: Collins, 1972–73).

28. Burke, *French Historical Revolution*, 38.

29. See M. Perry, *Marxism and History* (Basingstoke: Palgrave, 2002).

30. F. Engels, "Engels to Conrad Schmidt in Berlin (London, 5 August, 1890)," in *Collected Works Volume 49, Engels: 1890–1892*, K. Marx and F. Engels (London: Lawrence & Wishart, 2001), 6–9 (7–8).

31. H. Kaye, "Political Theory and History: Antonio Gramsci and the British Marxist Historians," *Italian Quarterly* 25 (1984): 145–66. For Gramsci's work see A. Gramsci, *Selections from Prison Notebooks* (London: Lawrence & Wishart, 1971) and *Selections from Cultural Writings: Language, Linguistics and Folklore* (London: Lawrence & Wishart, 1985).

32. On the CPHG see, e.g., E. Hobsbawm, "Communist Party Historians' Group 1946–56," in *Rebels and Their Causes: Essays in Honour of A. L. Morton*, ed. M. Cornforth (London: Lawrence & Wishart, 1978), 21–48; B. Schwarz, "The People in History: The Communist Party Historians Group 1946–56" in *Making Histories: Studies in History Writing and Politics*, ed. R. Johnson (London: Hutchinson, 1982), 44–95; D. Parker, "The Communist Party Historians' Group," *Socialist History* 12 (1997): 33–58; S. Ashman, "Communist Party Historians' Group," in *Essays on Historical Materialism*, ed. J. Rees (London: Bookmarks, 1998), 145–59 (154–57); Perry, *Marxism and History*, 88–94. On the prominent figures of the CPHG see Kaye, *British Marxist Historians*, which also includes an overview of the CPHG (10–18).

33. R. Hilton, "The Origins of Robin Hood," *Past and Present* 14 (1958): 30–44.

34. In addition to those bibliographical references already given, these works include, e.g., W. E. B. Du Bois, *Black Reconstruction* (New York: Harcourt, 1935); I. Deutscher, *Stalin: A Political Biography* (London: Oxford University Press, 1949); I. Deutscher, *Prophet Armed: Trotsky, 1879–1921* (London: Oxford University Press, 1954), *Prophet Unarmed: Trotsky, 1921–1929* (London: Oxford University Press, 1959), *Prophet Outcast: Trotsky, 1929–1940* (London: Oxford University Press, 1963); E. P. Thompson, *William Morris: Romantic to Revolutionary*, 2d

ed. (London: Merlin Press, 1977); G. Rudé, *The Crowd in the French Revolution* (London: Oxford University Press, 1959); A. Soboul, *The Parisian Sans Culottes and the French Revolution* (Oxford: Clarendon, 1964); G. Lefebvre, *The French Revolution*, trans. E. M. Evanson, 2 vols. (London: Routledge & Kegan Paul, 1964); D. Torr, *Tom Mann and His Times* (London: Lawrence & Wishart, 1936).

35. K. Thomas, "History and Anthropology," *Past and Present* 24 (1963): 3–24 (7).

36. E.g., G. E. M. de Ste. Croix, "Karl Marx and the History of Classical Antiquity," *Arethusa* 8 (1975): 7–41; G. E. M. de Ste. Croix, *The Class Struggle in the Ancient Greek World from the Archaic Age to the Arab Conquests* (London: Duckworth, 1981).

37. Stuttgart: Kreuz-Verlag, 1972; London: Darton, Longman & Todd, 1976. Other Marxist/Marxist-influenced approaches include H. Kreissig, "Zur sozialen Zusammensetzung der frühchristlichen Gemeinden im ersten Jahrhundert u.Z," *Eirene* 6 (1967): 91–100; M. Robbe, *Der Ursprung des Christentums* (Leipzig: Urania-Verlag, 1967); F. Belo, *Lecture matérialiste de l'évangile de Marc* (Paris: Cerf, 1974); F. Belo, *Materialist Reading of the Gospel of Mark*, trans. M. J. O'Connell (Maryknoll: Orbis, 1981); A. Meyer, *Der zensierte Jesus: Soziologie des Neuen Testaments* (Olten: Walter Verlag, 1983). On other Marxist approaches to Christian origins that effectively stand outside the scholarly canon and have consequently made no impact in "mainstream" NT studies see, e.g., P. Kowalinski, "The Genesis of Christianity in the Views of Contemporary Marxist Specialists of Religion," *Antonianum* 47 (1972): 541–75.

38. L. Schottroff, "'Not Many Powerful': Approaches to a Sociology of Early Christianity" in *Social-Scientific Approaches to New Testament Interpretation*, ed. D. G. Horrell (Edinburgh: T. & T. Clark, 1999), 277–86 (286). Orig. German: "'Nicht viele Mächtige': Annäherungen an eine Soziologie des Urchristentums," *Bibel und Kirche* 1 (1985): 2–8.

39. Cf. J. G. Gager, "Shall We Marry Our Enemies? Sociology and the New Testament," *Int* 36 (1982): 256–65 (257): "Though such anti-religious aims had nothing whatsoever to do with the social scientific methods themselves, one can hardly blame biblical scholars, the vast majority of whom were also pious believers, for their doubts about the usefulness of these methods."

40. Cf. N. K. Gottwald, *The Tribes of Yahweh: A Sociology of the Religion of Liberated Israel 1250–1050 BCE* (New York: Orbis, 1981), 8–11.

41. E.g., S. C. Barton, "Historical Criticism and Social-Scientific Perspectives in New Testament Study," in *Hearing the New Testament: Strategies for Interpretation*, ed. J. B. Green (Grand Rapids: Wm. B. Eerdmans, 1995), 61–89 (76). For similar comments elsewhere, e.g., see D. J. Harrington, "Sociological Concepts and the Early Church: A Decade of Research," *Theological Studies* 41 (1980): 181–90 (189); Gager, "Shall We Marry Our Enemies?" 257; B. Holmberg, *Sociology and the New Testament: An Appraisal* (Minneapolis: Fortress, 1990), 145–50.

42. O. Chadwick, *The Christian Church in the Cold War*, 2d ed. (London: Penguin, 1993), 3–7, quote on 7. See further Otto Dibelius, *In the Service of the Lord*, trans. M. Ilford (London: Faber, 1965).

43. Hastings, *English Christianity 1920–1990*, 320; and on fear of or hostility to communism in English Christianity cf. 173, 312, 320 ("Clergy as a whole were anything but inclined to Communism"), 406–7, 411, 424.

44. Theissen, *Social Reality*, 3–8.

45. For further discussion of the Kongress in relation to social-scientific interpretation of the NT see, e.g., S. J. Friesen, "Poverty in Pauline Studies: Beyond the So-called New Consensus," *JSNT* 26 (2004): 323–61 (323–37).

46. There are also parallels to this in England at the turn of the twentieth century and the development of working-class education. Callum Millard has pointed out to me that the founding of the Workers Education Association (WEA) was set against the backdrop of Christians like Albert Mansbridge, on the one hand, who Christianized socialist principles and downplayed class divisions and class-based analysis, and the more radical wings of the Labor and trade union movements, on the other, which were influenced by revolutionary Marxism.

47. Kautsky and Kalthoff are criticized in *Light*, 403. Footnote 3 on 403 contrasts Kautsky with Troeltsch, the latter worthy of more praise for having "real familiarity with the modern scientific study of antiquity." The 4th edition of *Light* also includes Appendix 11, which fires at Kautsky.

48. Deissmann, *Light*, 404.

49. Schottroff, "Not Many Powerful," 278–79.

50. Judge, *Social Pattern*, 51.

51. E. Lohse, "Das Evangelium für die Armen," *ZNW* 72 (1981): 51–64 (54).

52. Schottroff, "Not Many Powerful," 285–86.

53. G. Bornkamm, *Jesus of Nazareth* (London: Hodder & Stoughton, 1960), 102.

54. Ibid., 102.

55. Ibid., 223.

56. Cf. Friesen, "Poverty in Pauline Studies," 323–37. Roland Boer also notes the ignoring and downplaying of Marxist literary criticism, which is not unconnected to social-scientific criticism, in biblical studies (esp. of the Hebrew Bible). See R. Boer, *Marxist Criticism of the Bible* (London: Continuum/T. & T. Clark/SAP, 2003), 4–5.

57. J. D. G. Dunn, *Jesus Remembered* (Grand Rapids: Wm. B. Eerdmans, 2003), 522, 524. Quote on 522.

58. G. Theissen, *Sociology of Early Palestinian Christianity* (Philadelphia: Fortress, 1978), 125, n. 40.

59. Chadwick, *Christian Church*, 119–21.

60. Hobsbawm, "Communist Party Historians' Group," 30–31; Ashman, "Communist Party Historians' Group," 148–49; Perry, *Marxism and History*, 91–93.

61. E. Hobsbawm, *Interesting Times: A Twentieth Century Life* (London: Abacus, 2002), 207–9.

62. Perry, *Marxism and History*, 92. Cf. Kaye, *British Marxist Historians*, 17–18; Ashman, "Communist Party Historians' Group," 148. Here Ashman also comments strongly on the lack of a critical attitude among the CPHG towards the Communist Party, claiming, "They were all, whether they liked it or not, apologists for Stalinism."

63. Ashman, "Communist Party Historians' Group," 148.

64. Thompson, *William Morris*, 769.

65. E.g., a letter from Communist Party historians (including Dobb and Hobsbawm) published in *New Statesman* (1 Dec. 1956) and *Tribune* (1 Dec. 1956). The letter was rejected by the *Daily Worker* when sent on 18 Nov. 1956 (Hobsbawm, *Interesting Times*, 207, 425, n. 7).

66. Hobsbawm, *Interesting Times*, 207.

67. Letter from E. J. Hobsbawm, *World News* (26 Jan. 1957), 62; Hobsbawm, *Interesting Times*, 204, 424, n. 4.

68. Iulia de Beausobre, *The Woman Who Could Not Die* (London: Chatto & Windus, 1938). See further C. B. Smith, *Iulia de Beausobre: A Russian Christian in the West* (London: Darnton, Longman & Todd, 1983); Hastings, *English Christianity*, 329.

69. Chadwick, *Christian Church*, 15.

70. See, e.g., E. A. Judge, "The Social Identity of the First Christians: A Question of Method in Religious History," *JRH* 11 (1980): 201–17; C. S. Rodd, "On Applying a Sociological Theory to Biblical Studies," *JSOT* 19 (1981): 95–106.

71. R. Scroggs, "The Sociological Interpretation of the New Testament: The Present State of Research," *NTS* 26 (1980): 164–79 (177).

72. For a useful overview see R. J. Evans, *In Defence of History*, 2d ed. (London: Granta, 2000), 129–90.

73. Braudel, *Mediterranean*, vol. 1, 21.

74. Burke, *French Historical Revolution*, 40.

75. For some even the charismatic leader provides a theological problem. Cf. Barton, "Social-Scientific Perspectives," 74: "The effect can be that text and world of the NT lose their revelatory otherness and particularity. Jesus becomes just another charismatic leader."

76. B. J. Malina, *The Social World of Jesus and the Gospels* (London: Routledge, 1996), 123; cf. 124–42, 217–41.

77. Scroggs, "Sociological Interpretation," 165–66.

78. P. L. Berger, *The Sacred Canopy: Elements of a Sociological Theory of Religion* (New York: Doubleday, 1969), 47. Cf. R. Stark and W. S. Bainbridge, "Networks of Faith: Interpersonal Bonds and Recruitment to Cults and Sects," *American Journal of Sociology* 85 (1980): 1376–95 (1383).

79. E.g., Scroggs, "Sociological Interpretation," 166–67; B. J. Malina, "The Social Sciences and Biblical Interpretation," *Int* 37 (1982): 229–42 (237–38); Gager, "Shall We Marry Our Enemies?" 257; T. F. Best, "The Sociological Study of the New Testament: Promise and Peril of a New Discipline," *SJT* 36 (1983): 181–94 (189–94); O. C. Edwards Jr., "Sociology as a Tool for Interpreting the New Testament," *Anglican Theological Review* 65 (1983): 431–46 (445); W. A. Meeks, *The First Urban Christians: The Social World of the Apostle Paul* (New Haven, CT: Yale University Press, 1983, 2003), 2–7; Esler, *Community and Gospel*, 137–38; Holmberg, *Sociology*, 149–50; Barton, "Social-Scientific Perspectives," 74–76; Theissen, *Social Reality*, 187–88.

80. Holmberg, *Sociology*, 145–57.

81. P. F. Esler, "Introduction: Models, Context and Kerygma in New Testament Interpretation," in *Modelling Early Christianity: Social-Scientific Studies of the New Testament in Its Context*, ed. P. F. Esler (London: Routledge, 1995), 1–20 (3–4, 14–19). See now P. F. Esler, *New Testament Theology: Communion and Community* (Minneapolis: Fortress, 2005). The opening of Esler's book also includes some refreshingly inclusive remarks concerning secular and non-Christian scholars (1–2). Cf. Meeks, *Urban*, 7.

82. Barton, "Social-Scientific Perspectives," 76.

83. Theissen, *Social Reality*, 2–3.

84. Similar critiques have been made of other early examples of social-scientific approaches, such as those of G. Uhlhorn (*Christian Charity in the Ancient Church* [1882; ET: trans. S. Taylor (Edinburgh: T. & T. Clark, 1883)]), Harnack, and Troeltsch. See, e.g., Schottroff, "Not Many Powerful," 277–78; S. J. D. Cohen, "Adolph Harnack's 'The Mission and Expansion of Judaism': Christianity Succeeds Where Judaism Fails," in *The Future of Early Christianity: Essays in Honour of Helmut Koester*, ed. B. A. Pearson, A. T. Kraabel, G. W. E. Nickelsburg, and N. R. Petersen (Minneapolis: Fortress, 1991), 162–69; Theissen, *Social Reality*, 5–6; J. T. Sanders, *Charisma, Converts, Competitors: Societal and Sociological Factors in the Success of Early Christianity* (London: SCM, 2000), 1–2.

85. Cf. Hochschild, *Sozialgeschichtliche Exegese*, 79–96; J. H. Schütz, "Introduction" in G. Theissen, *The Social Setting of Pauline Christianity* (Edinburgh: T. & T. Clark, 1982), 1–23 (10).
86. Burke, *French Historical Revolution*, 96–97.
87. Hobsbawm, *On History*, 238–39.
88. Evans, *Defence*, 192.
89. E. Fox-Genovese and E. Genovese, *Fruits of Merchant Capital: Slavery and Bourgeois Property in the Rise and Expansion of Capitalism* (Oxford: Oxford University Press, 1983), 188.
90. Burke, *French Historical Revolution*, 50.
91. E. Hobsbawm, "Marx and History," in *On History*, 207–25 (208). First published in *New Left Review* 143 (Feb. 1984): 39–50.
92. Anonymous, "Historian of the Mediterranean," *TLS* (Feb. 15, 1968): 156.
93. E. H. Carr, *What Is History?* (London: Penguin, 1961, 2d ed., 1987), 65–66.
94. See further, e.g., V. Mehta, *Fly and the Fly-Bottle: Encounters with British Intellectuals* (London: Penguin, 1963), 106–7, 111–12, 149–54 ; E. H. Carr, "The Russian Revolution and the West [an interview with E. H. Carr]," *New Left Review* 111 (1978): 25–36; N. Stone, "Grim Eminence," *London Review of Books* 5, no. 1 (1983): 3–8; R. W. Davies, "From E. H. Carr's Files: Notes towards a Second Edition of *What Is History?*" in Carr, *What Is History?* 157–83 (176–82); C. Jones, *E. H. Carr and International Relations: A Duty to Lie* (Cambridge: Cambridge University Press, 1998); M. Cox, ed., *E. H. Carr: A Critical Appraisal* (London: Palgrave, 2000); J. Haslam, *The Vices of Integrity: E. H. Carr, 1892–1982* (London: Verso, 2000).
95. Stone, "Grim Eminence," 8.
96. Ibid., 6.
97. E.g., Kee, *Christian Origins*, 17; S. C. Barton, "The Communal Dimension of Earliest Christianity: A Critical Survey of the Field," *JTS* 43 (1992): 399–427 (esp. 401, 426); Theissen, *Social Reality*, 16–18; Horrell, "Social-Scientific Approaches," 6–7; Hochschild, *Sozialgeschichtliche Exegese*, 207–29.
98. E.g., Scroggs, "Sociological Interpretation," 165; Horrell, "Social-Scientific Approaches," 6.
99. B. J. Malina, "Dedication," in *The Social Setting of Jesus and the Gospels*, ed. W. Stegemann, B. Malina, and G. Theissen (Minneapolis: Fortress, 2002), vii–viii.
100. Thomas, "History and Anthropology," 7.
101. Stone, "History and the Social Sciences," 13. Cf. Kee, *Christian Origins*, 17.
102. J. H. Schütz, "Charisma and Social Reality in Primitive Christianity," *Journal of Religion* 54 (1974): 51–70; J. H. Schütz, *Paul and the Anatomy of Apostolic Authority* (Cambridge: Cambridge University Press, 1975); J. G. Gager, *Kingdom and Community: The Social World of Early Christianity* (Englewood Cliffs, NJ: Prentice-Hall, 1975); R. Scroggs, "Earliest Christian Communities as Sectarian Movement," in *Christianity, Judaism and Other Greco-Roman Cults: Studies for Morton Smith at Sixty. Part Two: Early Christianity*, ed. J. Neusner (Leiden: E. J. Brill, 1975), 1–23; B. Holmberg, *Paul and Power: The Structure and Authority in the Primitive Church as Reflected in the Pauline Epistles* (Lund: C. W. K. Gleerup, 1978); Kee, *Christian Origins*, 54–73.
103. G. Vermes, *Jesus the Jew: A Historian's Reading of the Gospels* (London: SCM, 1973), 58–82; G. Vermes, *The Religion of Jesus the Jew* (London: SCM, 1993), 70–75.
104. E.g., R. J. Evans, *In Hitler's Shadow: West German Historians and the Attempt to Escape from the Nazi Past* (New York: Tauris, 1989); *Defence*, 2d ed. (London:

Granta, 2000), 37–38; cf. R. J. Evans, *Rereading German History: From Unification to Reunification 1800–1996* (London: Routledge, 1997), 3, 12, 16, 48–49,
72–73, 77–78, 238–45.

105. M. Hengel, *Nachfolge und Charisma: Eine exegetisch-religionsgeschichtliche Studie
zu Mt 8 21f. und Jesu Ruf in die Nachfolge* (Berlin: Alfred Töpelmann, 1968); ET:
M. Hengel, *The Charismatic Leader and His Followers*, trans. James C. G. Greig
(Edinburgh: T. & T. Clark, 1981). Cf. M. Hengel, *Judentum und Hellenismus*,
2 vols. (Tübingen: Mohr Siebeck, 1969); ET: M. Hengel, *Judaism and Hellenism*, trans. J. Bowden (London: SCM, 1974).

106. E.g., G. Theissen, "Wanderradikalismus. Literatursoziologische Aspekte der
Überlieferung von Worten Jesu im Urchristentum," *ZTK* 70 (1973): 245–71;
The First Followers of Jesus (London: SCM, 1978); *Studien zur Soziologie des
Urchristentum* (Tübingen: Mohr Siebeck, 1979); *The Social Setting of Pauline
Christianity* (Edinburgh: T. & T. Clark, 1982).

107. P. Novick, *That Noble Dream: The 'Objectivity Question' and the American Historical Profession* (Cambridge: Cambridge University Press, 1988).

108. T. Haskell, "Objectivity Is Not Neutrality: Rhetoric vs. Practice in Peter
Novick's *That Noble Dream*," *History and Theory* 29 (1990): 129–57 (132).
Updated in T. Haskell, *Objectivity Is Not Neutrality: Explanatory Schemes in His-
tory* (Baltimore: John Hopkins University Press, 1998), 145–73.

109. Haskell, "Objectivity Is Not Neutrality," 135.

110. E. Hobsbawm, "On Partisanship," in *On History*, 164–85.

111. Evans, *Defence*, 222–23.

112. Compare the comments of Gerd Theissen, which are of course applicable
beyond social-scientific exegesis: university teachers are members of
"the bourgeoisie, the middle class" who have been confronted with "a great
many challenges" in the last 100 years and so it is "probable on the face of it
that we shall find the history of the middle-classes, and the deadlocks in which
they are involved, reflected in the history of sociological exegesis" (*Social Reality*, 2).

113. Of course, individual scholars may not be Christians but the overall result is
effectively Christian. It could be argued that one of the reasons for the lack of
acceptance for the Cynic thesis is its theological uselessness; cf. J. S. Kloppenborg Verbin, *Excavating Q: The History and Setting of the Sayings Gospel* (Edinburgh: T. & T. Clark, 2000), 420–26. This may be so, but it is hardly
incompatible with the liberal Christian worldview of those associated with the
Cynic thesis and the not-unrelated Jesus Seminar.

114. M. Casey, "Who's Afraid of Jesus Christ? Some Comments on Attempts to
Write a Life of Jesus," in *Writing History, Constructing Religion*, ed. J. G. Cross-
ley and C. Karner (Aldershot: Ashgate, 2005), 129–46 (129–30). Cf. Gager,
"Shall We Marry Our Enemies?" 257.

115. There are of course other examples. Again, at the Sept. 2005 British New Testament Conference at Liverpool Hope, the college tradition of saying grace
before the evening meal was continued. I should stress that I am *not* saying that
religious believers should not be allowed to congregate and worship among
themselves at such conferences.

116. For similar comments to mine but with a broader frame of reference see, e.g.,
Davies, *Search*, 44–46; Berlinerblau, *Secular Bible*, 5–7, 10, 52, 58–59, 139.

117. Esler, "Models, Context and Kerygma," 18–19.

118. Barton, "Social-Scientific Perspectives," 76.

119. D. C. Allison, "Explaining the Resurrection: Conflicting Convictions," *JSHJ* 3 (2005), 117–33 (132).

120. G. O'Collins, SJ, "The Resurrection: The State of the Question," in *The Resurrection: An Interdisciplinary Symposium on the Resurrection of Jesus*, ed. S. T. Davis, D. Kendall, and G. O'Collins (Oxford: Oxford University Press, 1997), 5–28 (16).

121. J. G. Crossley, "Against the Historical Plausibility of the Empty Tomb Story and the Bodily Resurrection: A Response to N. T. Wright," *JSHJ* 3 (2005): 153–68.

122. For similar comments of spectacular events recorded in the Hebrew Bible and ANE literature see L. L. Grabbe, "'The Comfortable Theory', 'Maximal Conservatism' and Neo-Fundamentalism Revisited," in *Sense and Sensitivity: Essays on Reading the Bible in Memory of Robert Carroll*, ed. A. G. Hunter and P. R. Davies (Sheffield: Sheffield Academic Press, 2002), 174–93 (181, 186).

123. Wright, *Resurrection*, 196. But cf. the rendering in the Soncio edition.

124. Cf. J. D. Crossan, *The Birth of Christianity: Discovering What Happened in the Years Immediately After the Execution of Jesus* (New York: HarperCollins; Edinburgh: T. & T. Clark, 1998), 26–29.

125. Dunn's review is in *JTS* 55 (2004): 629–32. For other sympathetic reviews that do not take issue with the argument in favor of Jesus' bodily resurrection, see M. Bockmuehl, "Compleat History of the Resurrection: A Dialogue with N. T. Wright," *JSNT* 26 (2004): 489–504, and L. W. Hurtado's reviews in *ExpT* (2004): 83–86 and L. W. Hurtado, "Jesus' Resurrection in the Early Christian Texts: An Engagement with N. T. Wright," *JSHJ* 3 (2005): 197–208.

126. So, e.g., Evans, *Defence*, 83.

127. Similarly Jacques Berlinerblau comments with reference to the rise of pro-gay biblical interpretations in an era that has seen the rise of gay rights and queer studies, "Social conditions certainly do make possible, or at least facilitate, given readings of the Bible and their dissemination" (*Secular Bible*, 114).

128. G. Vermes, *Providential Accidents: An Autobiography* (London: SCM, 1998), 10–17.

129. Vermes, *Jesus the Jew*, 17.

130. Vermes, *Providential Accidents*, 211.

131. Vermes, *Jesus the Jew*, 17.

132. Vermes, *Providential Accidents*, 210.

133. See, e.g., Vermes, *Religion*, 208–15.

134. Vermes, *Providential Accidents*, 211.

135. Ibid., 220.

136. For a recent example of the latter see, e.g., H. Maccoby, *Jesus the Pharisee* (London: SCM, 2003).

137. Cf. the influence in two very different portraits of Jesus: E. P. Sanders, *The Historical Figure of Jesus* (London: Penguin, 1993) and J. D. Crossan, *The Historical Jesus: The Life of a Mediterranean Jewish Peasant* (Edinburgh: T. & T. Clark, 1991).

138. Sanders, *Jesus and Judaism*, 334.

139. E. P. Sanders, "Comparing Judaism and Christianity: An Academic Autobiography" (April–May 2004), available at http://www.duke.edu/religion/home/EP/Intel%20autobiog%20rev.pdf. The original paper was read at "New Views of First-Century Jewish and Christian Self-Definition: An International Conference in Honor of E. P. Sanders" (April, 2003).

140. Sanders, "An Academic Autobiography," 2–5.
141. Ibid., 6–7.
142. Ibid., 20–21.
143. Ibid., 26–27.
144. Sanders, *Historical Figure*, 2.
145. Ibid., 5. See also 6–8.
146. Cf. ibid., xiii: reconstructing the life of the historical Jesus is "extremely hard work" but work that nevertheless "pays off in the modest ways that are to be expected in the study of ancient history."
147. Sanders, "An Academic Autobiography," 5–7.
148. Ibid., 11.
149. J. D. G. Dunn, "The New Perspective on Paul," *BJRL* 65 (1983): 95–122.
150. See, e.g., S. J. Gathercole, *Where Is Boasting? Early Jewish Soteriology and Paul's Response in Romans 1–5* (Grand Rapids: Wm. B. Eerdmans, 2002).
151. Evans, *Defence*, 202–3.
152. Burton Mack, *The Christian Myth: Origins, Logic, and Legacy* (New York & London: Continuum, 2001).
153. Ibid., 215. See now R. Cameron and M. P. Miller, eds., *Redescribing Christian Origins* (Atlanta: SBL, 2004).
154. A similar point comes through in Berlinerblau, *Secular Bible*, 138–39. There is not space to enter the debate on whether or not biblical studies as a whole should be grounded in a more secular or more confessional approach. It should be clear from the above discussion that while I approach biblical studies from a secular perspective, I do not think it should be demanded of its participants, and the more perspectives, the better. See further, e.g., H. Räisänen, *Beyond New Testament Theology: A Story and a Programme*, 2d ed. (London: SCM, 1990, 2000); F. Watson, *Text, Church and World: Biblical Interpretation in Theological Perspective* (Grand Rapids: Wm. B. Eerdmans, 1994); P. R. Davies, *Whose Bible Is It Anyway?* (Sheffield: Sheffield Academic Press, 1995); F. Watson, "Bible, Theology and the University: A Response to Philip Davies," *JSOT* 71 (1996): 3–16; R. B. Matlock, "Beyond the Great Divide? History, Theology, and the Secular Academy," in *Prospects for a Story and Programme: Essays on Räisänen's* Beyond New Testament Theology, ed. T. Penner and C. Vander Stichele (Finnish Exegetical Society, forthcoming).
155. For suggestions on how an openly secular approach to biblical and religious studies might be achieved, see Berlinerblau, *Secular Bible*, 138–39. There is also potential for increased secular approaches to biblical studies from radical and Marxist movements. For example, Roland Boer (*Marxist Criticism*, 2–3) reports that a session on "Marxism and the Bible" at the Marxism 2000 conference, Amherst, Massachusetts, had one of the highest attendances of the whole conference, with plenty of interdisciplinary interest.

Chapter 2: Peasant Unrest and the Emergence of Jesus' Specific View of the Law

1. J. D. Crossan, *The Birth of Christianity: Discovering What Happened in the Years Immediately After the Execution of Jesus* (New York: HarperCollins; Edinburgh: T. & T. Clark, 1998), 151–235; G. E. Lenski, *Power and Privilege: A Theory of Social Stratification* (New York: McGraw-Hill, 1966); J. H. Kautsky, *The Politics of Aristocratic Empires* (Chapel Hill: University of North Carolina Press, 1982). See also J. D. Crossan, *The Historical Jesus: The Life of a Mediterranean Jewish*

Peasant (New York: HarperCollins; Edinburgh: T. & T. Clark, 1991), e.g., 43–46. Crossan is not of course the only one to have applied Lenski and Kautsky to the study of Christian origins. See, e.g., D. A. Fiensy, *The Social History of Palestine in the Herodian Period: The Land Is Mine* (Lewiston, NY: Edwin Mellen, 1991), 155–76; K. C. Hanson and D. E. Oakman, *Palestine in the Time of Jesus: Social Structures and Social Conflicts* (Minneapolis: Augsburg Fortress, 1998), 67–70, 84, 100–120; E. W. Stegemann and W. Stegemann, *The Jesus Movement: A Social History of Its First Century* (Edinburgh: T. & T. Clark, 1999). More generally, B. J. Malina, "Social Scientific Methods in Historical Jesus Research," in *The Social Setting of Jesus and the Gospels*, ed. W. Stegemann, B. J. Malina, and G. Theissen (Minneapolis: Fortress Press, 2002), 3–26 (4), even goes so far as to say, "What has been done with the social sciences is significant, much of it important enough to be plagiarized by John Dominic Crossan"!

2. E. J. Hobsbawm, "Peasants and Politics," *Journal of Peasant Studies* 1 (1973): 3–22, and E. J. Hobsbawm, "Peasant Land Occupations," *Past and Present* 62 (1974): 120–52, reprinted in *Uncommon People: Resistance, Rebellion and Jazz* (London: Abacus, 1998), 196–222 and 223–55, respectively. All subsequent references will be to the reprinted versions.

3. See, e.g., D. G. Horrell, "Models and Methods in Social-Scientific Interpretation: A Response to Philip Esler," *JSNT* 78 (2000): 107–13; J. G. Crossley, "Defining History," in *Writing History, Constructing Religion*, ed. J. G. Crossley and C. Karner (Aldershot: Ashgate, 2005), 9–29 (20–21).

4. For a related discussion with reference to the work of the famous sociologist of religion Bryan Wilson, see A. Aldridge, "Postmodernism Before and After: The Fate of Secularization," in Crossley and Karner, eds., *Writing History, Constructing Religion*, 65–84.

5. Crossan, *Birth of Christianity*, 154.

6. Kautsky (*Politics of Aristocratic Empires*, 17) makes the importance of this point quite clear.

7. For a general introduction to agrarian societies, see G. E. Lenski and J. Lenski, *Human Societies: An Introduction to Macrosociology* (New York: McGraw-Hill, 1970), 164–208; P. Nolan and G. Lenski, *Human Societies: An Introduction to Macrosociology*; 9th ed. (Boulder, CO: Paradigm, 2004), 141–80. Cf. Hobsbawm, "Peasants and Politics," 198–200.

8. As 20s Galilee was effectively a satellite territory where Rome cast its shadow through its sheer surrounding presence, there should be no problem regarding it in the same broad socioeconomic context as the agrarian Roman Empire. On the agrarian characteristics of the Roman Empire and ancient Mediterranean world, see, e.g., Lenski and Lenski, *Human Societies*; Lenski, *Power and Privilege*; G. Alföldy, *The Social History of Rome* (Totowa: Barnes & Noble, 1985); and Stegemann and Stegemann, *Jesus Movement*, 7–14, 21–22, 42–52.

9. Lenski, *Power and Privilege*, 190–92.

10. Ibid., 194.

11. Ibid., 210.

12. Kautsky, *Politics of Aristocratic Empires*, 74.

13. Ibid., 274.

14. P. A. Harland, "The Economy of First-Century Palestine: The State of the Scholarly Discussion," in *Handbook of Early Christianity: Social Science Approaches*, ed. A. J. Blasi, J. Duhaime, and P.-A. Turcotte (Walnut Creek, CA:

AltaMira Press, 2002), 511–27 (515). See also Stegemann and Stegemann, *Jesus Movement*, 104–25; D. E. Oakman, *Jesus and the Economic Questions of His Day* (Lewiston, NY: Edwin Mellen, 1986); Fiensy, *Social History of Palestine*.

15. Lenski, *Power and Privilege*, 271.

16. On this and the following, see Lenski, *Power and Privilege*, 198–206. On the urban in the Roman Empire, cf. A. Wallace-Hadrill, "Elites and Trade in the Roman Town," in *City and Countryside in the Ancient World*, ed. J. Rich and A. Wallace-Hadrill (New York: Routledge, 1991), 241–72, e.g. 249: "When it came to imposing order on the barbarians, the Romans left no doubt of their commitment to the town as an instrument of civilisation. Urbanisation is the unmistakable result of Roman control"; Moses Finley speaks of "the growth of towns as the regular and relentless accompaniment of the spread of Graeco-Roman civilisation; eastward after the conquests of Alexander as far as the Hindu Kush, to the west from Africa to Britain with the Roman conquests, until the number of towns rose to the thousands . . . the Graeco-Roman world was more urbanised than any other society before the modern era." See M. I. Finley, "The Ancient City: From Fustel de Coulanges to Max Weber and Beyond," in *Economy and Society in Ancient Greece* (London: Chatto & Windus, 1981), 3–23 (3, 20). Orig. printed in *Comparative Studies in Society and History* 19 (1977): 305–27.

17. Lenski, *Power and Privilege*, 201.

18. Kautsky, *Politics of Aristocratic Empires*, 39.

19. For a selection see M. I. Finley, *The Ancient Economy*, 2d ed. (London: Penguin, 1985 [1973]), esp. 123–49; Finley, "The Ancient City"; P. Anderson, *Passages from Antiquity to Feudalism* (London: NLB, 1974), 19; T. F. Carney, *The Shape of the Past: Models and Antiquity* (Lawrence, KS: Coronado, 1975); G. E. M. de Ste. Croix, *The Class Struggle in the Ancient Greek World from the Archaic Age to the Arab Conquests* (London: Duckworth, 1981), 9–19; D. A. Edwards, "First Century Urban/Rural Relations in Lower Galilee: Exploring the Archaeological and Literary Evidence," *SBL Seminar Papers* (1988): 169–82; Oakman, *Economic Questions*; H. Moxnes, *The Economy of the Kingdom: Social Conflict and Economic Relations in Luke's Gospel* (Philadelphia: Fortress, 1988); Fiensy, *Social History of Palestine*, 168–70; A. Wallace-Hadrill, "Introduction," in Rich and Wallace-Hadrill, eds., *City and Countryside*, ix–xviii (x, xiv–xvii); S. Freyne, "Urban-Rural Relations in First Century Galilee: Some Suggestions from the Literary Sources," in *The Galilee in Late Antiquity*, ed. L. I. Levine (New York: Jewish Theological Seminary, 1992), 75–91; R. L. Rohrbaugh, "The Preindustrial City," in *The Social Sciences and New Testament Interpretation*, ed. R. L. Rohrbaugh (Peabody, MA: Hendrickson, 1996), 107–25 (115–18); Crossan, *Birth of Christianity*; Stegemann and Stegemann, *Jesus Movement*, 7, 12–14, 29–30, 35–37. Cf. Hobsbawm, "Peasants and Politics," 200–201; J. C. Scott, "Protest and Profanation: Agrarian Revolt and the Little Tradition, *Part I*," *Theory and Society* 4 (1977): 1–38 (4, 16); J. C. Scott, "Protest and Profanation: Agrarian Revolt and the Little Tradition, *Part II*," *Theory and Society* 4 (1977): 211–46 (213–15).

20. Finley, *Ancient Economy*, on which cf. S. Freyne, "Herodian Economics in Galilee: Searching for a Suitable Model," in *Modelling Early Christianity: Social-Scientific Studies of the New Testament in Its Context*, ed. P. F. Esler (London: Routledge, 1995), 23–46 (25).

21. See Hobsbawm, "Peasants and Politics," 205–9.

22. Here the similarity with Kautsky is doubly important given the problems that have emerged when imposing models of, for example, the modern European-style

nation-state on ancient political systems. See esp. K. W. Whitelam, *The Invention of Ancient Israel: The Silencing of Palestinian History* (London: Routledge, 1996).
23. Hobsbawm, "Peasants and Politics," 207.
24. Ibid., 211. Cf. Hobsbawm, "Peasant Land Occupations," 245–46.
25. Hobsbawm, "Peasant Land Occupations," 224 (italics mine). For empirical examples see 230–46, esp. 234 and note also the reference to outside assistance.
26. Kautsky, *Politics of Aristocratic Empires*, 5.
27. Stegemann and Stegemann, *Jesus Movement*, 13.
28. On the Roman Empire cf. Wallace-Hadrill, "Elites and Trade in the Roman Town," 267: "My argument has sought to break down some of our assumptions about the ideological and physical distance between the elite of the Roman town and commercial activity. My concern has been with attitudes, not with the economy. None of the evidence here discussed undermines the proposition that agriculture was dominant in the economy or that agricultural interests were dominant among a landowning political elite."
29. Kautsky, *Politics of Aristocratic Empires*, 38. Cf. the discussion of Kautsky in Stegemann and Stegemann, *Jesus Movement*, 9 (cf. 33–34): "Nonetheless, it is as least controversial whether agriculture or trade and business were more important economically in these societies. Here we are inclined toward the view . . . [that] the land was by far the most important producer of wealth, but at the same time the cities had a close symbiotic relationship with rural regions." I see nothing in this that would contradict Kautsky's main position.
30. Kautsky, *Politics of Aristocratic Empires*, 5.
31. Ibid., 35; cf. 273, 291.
32. Ibid., 273; cf. Stegemann and Stegemann, *Jesus Movement*, 28–29. Compare also Finley, *Ancient Economy*, 188: "It is generally accepted that the main (and favoured) form of wealth throughout antiquity was the land. It should follow automatically that exploitation of the land normally involved deployment of the available resources for purposes of self-enrichment or self-advancement in social status and power in a variety of ways, including not only profits in the narrow sense but also, for example, expansion of the manpower under a landowner's personal influence or direct control."
33. Kautsky, *Politics of Aristocratic Empires*, 278–92. Cf. ibid., 48: "Most of the pertinent literature does not draw the distinction between traditional aristocratic empires and commercialized ones, a distinction that . . . can be crucial in accounting for some phenomena, like peasant revolts, that are often simply ascribed to traditional aristocratic empires."
34. Ibid., 288. On "early stages" cf. ibid., 289: "That peasant revolts seem to break out within a century or two of the transition from traditional aristocratic empire to commercialization is obviously no coincidence. The interrelated growth of agricultural production of trade, of a money and a market economy, of towns, and of populations has a deeply unsettling effect on peasants."
35. Ibid., 281.
36. Ibid., 289. The following points are taken from 288–92, 302–3. Cf. Carney, *Shape of the Past*, 146–52, 201.
37. Hobsbawm, "Peasants and Politics," 210.
38. Kautsky, *Politics of Aristocratic Empires*, 307–19.
39. Ibid., 308. Cf. R. A. Horsley with J. S. Hanson, *Bandits, Prophets, and Messiahs: Popular Movements in the Time of Jesus* (Minneapolis: Winston, 1985), 50–51; Crossan, *Birth of Christianity*, 223.

40. Kautsky, *Politics of Aristocratic Empires*, 308.

41. Ibid., 309.

42. Ibid., 318. Cf. R. H. Hilton, "Peasant Society, Peasant Movements and Feudalism in Medieval Europe," in *Rural Protest: Peasant Movements and Social
   Change*, ed. H. A. Landsberger (New York: Macmillan, 1973), 67–94 (89): "The
   egalitarian and libertarian outlook which is strongly marked in most movements, whether social-political or religious in overt motivation . . ." Eric Hobsbawm makes a similar point concerning social banditry in *Bandits* (London:
   Penguin, 1969, 1985), 29, ch. 7. See also Scott, "Protest and Profanation, *Part
   I*," 17: "The theme of a world without class distinctions has always been an integral part of popular Christianity and millennial movements in the West. South
   East Asia is no exception to this pattern. Persistent beliefs in a golden age or in
   the return of a just king have supplied the ideological basis for many rebellions.
   Often the rebels made use of the egalitarian strains within the major religions
   of Islam, Buddhism, and Christianity to confront a social order in which all
   believers were decidedly not equal." Scott provides numerous cross-cultural
   examples of the role of symbolic reversals of the social order along with utopian
   and millenarian beliefs in peasant unrest, usually in the context of significant
   economic change in agrarian contexts. See Scott, "Agrarian Revolt and the Little Tradition, *Part II*," 217–19, 224–42.

43. Hobsbawm, "Peasants and Politics," 212. Cf. Hobsbawm, "Peasant Land Occupations," 252–53.

44. Kautsky cites various examples from primary and secondary literature as does
   Crossan, *Birth of Christianity*, 168. On Marx and peasant leadership see K. Marx,
   "Eighteenth Brumaire of Louis Bonaparte," in *Collected Works Volume 11, Marx
   and Engels: 1851–53*, K. Marx and F. Engels (London: Lawrence & Wishart,
   1979), 101–97; Hobsbawm, "Peasants and Politics," 221–22.

45. Kautsky, *Politics of Aristocratic Empires*, 304.

46. Ibid., 304, 306.

47. Hobsbawm, "Peasants and Politics," 208–9, quote 209. See also "Peasant Land
   Occupations," 246–51.

48. Carney, *Shape of the Past*.

49. Freyne, "Herodian Economics in Galilee," 46.

50. J. F. Strange, "First-Century Galilee from Archaeology and from the Texts,"
   SBL Seminar Papers (1994): 81–90 (81, 82, 84).

51. For cautious comments on trade in Galilee see R. A. Horsley, "The Historical
   Jesus and Archaeology of the Galilee: Questions from Historical Research to
   Archaeologists," *SBLSP* (1994): 91–135 (102, 105); Stegemann and Stegemann,
   Jesus Movement, 9, 33–34. For an overview of the role of trade in Roman Pales-
   tine, including a review of scholarly discussion, see Harland, "Economy of First
   Century Palestine," 517–20.

52. As with the broader Roman world, the precise nature of the degree of urbanization and the urban/rural relationship in Galilee has been vigorously debated.
   See, e.g., Horsley, "Historical Jesus and Archaeology of the Galilee";
   P. Richardson and D. Edwards, "Jesus and Palestinian Social Protest: Archaeological and Literary Perspectives," in Blasi, Duhaime, and Turcotte, eds., *Handbook of Early Christianity*, 247–66 (254–55).

53. For a convenient overview of the various issues and scholarly opinion concerning Jesus and Sepphoris, see J. L. Reed, *Archaeology and the Galilean Jesus:
   A Re-examination of the Evidence* (Harrisburg, PA: Trinity Press International,

2000), 100–114. For what it is worth, I am not convinced by the argument that Galilee and Sepphoris in particular had undergone a high degree of hellenization and were fully immersed in Gentile culture. For recent, convincing, and hugely important works on Galilee at the time of Jesus see M. Chancey and E. M. Meyers, "How Jewish Was Sepphoris in Jesus' Time?" *BAR* 26, no. 4 (2000): 18–33; M. Chancey, "The Cultural Milieu of Ancient Sepphoris," *NTS* 47 (2001): 127–45; E. P. Sanders, "Jesus' Galilee" in *Fair Play: Diversity and Conflicts in Early Christianity. Essays in Honour of Heikki Räisänen*, ed. I. Dunderberg, C. Tuckett, and K. Syreeni (Leiden: E. J. Brill, 2002), 3–41; M. A. Chancey, *The Myth of a Gentile Galilee* (Cambridge: CUP, 2002).

54. This should not be taken to mean that Judas or his father Hezekiah were social bandits in the Robin Hood sense (see below), even if they had followers from the peasantry. S. Freyne ("Bandits in Galilee: A Contribution to the Study of Social Conditions in First-Century Palestine," in *The Social World of Formative Christianity and Judaism: Essays in Tribute to Howard Clark Kee*, ed. J. Neusner, P. Borgen, E. S. Frerichs, and R. Horsley [Philadelphia: Fortress, 1988], 50–68 [55–58]), points out it does not look as if the motives of the leader at the very least was one of looking out for the oppressed peasantry but "the last efforts of a dying social class to regain its former position of wealth and status within Palestinian life" (58) in opposition to the emerging Herodian dynasty.

55. J. F. Strange, "Tiberias," *ABD* 5 (1992): 547–49 (547).

56. In the context of peasant revolts, Kautsky argues that disgruntled outsiders are most likely to provide leadership for peasant revolts and unrest. This will be discussed in detail below.

57. Cf. Reed, *Archaeology and the Galilean Jesus*, 136.

58. Stegemann and Stegemann, *Jesus Movement*, 112.

59. Cf. Sanders, "Jesus' Galilee," 26–34.

60. Cf. Stegemann and Stegemann, *Jesus Movement*, 95: "Unrest in the populace could have either ethnic or economic causes." Or again, 100: "Socio-economic antagonism is naturally also reflected in *religious* antagonism." Richard Horsley has strongly emphasized the importance of combining socioeconomic concerns with nationalistic, religious, or ethnic concerns. See, e.g., R. A. Horsley, *Archaeology, History, and Society in Galilee: The Social Context of Jesus and the Rabbis* (Valley Forge, PA: Trinity Press International, 1996). A good example of this combination of concerns would be the Caligula crisis.

61. E.g., Freyne, "Herodian Economics in Galilee," 44. Cf. Horsley, "Historical Jesus and Archaeology of the Galilee," 98, "Considering that in a relatively limited area one city had been rebuilt and another new city founded within two decades, 'urban-rural' relations in Galilee during the lifetime of Jesus would not have fit normal patterns known from later Galilee or from cross-cultural material. The 'cultural influences' as well as social-economic impact would have been dramatically new."

62. D. R. Edwards, "The Socio-Economic and Cultural Ethos of the Lower Galilee in the First Century: Implications for the Nascent Jesus Movement," in *The Galilee in Late Antiquity*, ed. L. I. Levine (New York: Jewish Theological Seminary of America, 1992), 53–73. On the point of the archaeological finds, Reed claims (*Archaeology and the Galilean Jesus*, 112) that Edwards is "perhaps exceeding the limits of the archaeological data." For further criticisms, see, e.g., Freyne, "Urban-Rural"; Horsley, "Archaeology, History, and Society in Galilee," 118–30.

63. So, e.g., M. Goodman, "The First Jewish Revolt: Social Conflict and the Problem of Debt," *JJS* 33 (1982): 417–27; Horsley, "The Historical Jesus and Archaeology of the Galilee," 109–10; Freyne, "Herodian Economics in Galilee," 44; Stegemann and Stegemann, *Jesus Movement*, 111–13.

64. See further Fiensy, *Social History of Palestine*, 55–60, 77–79.

65. E.g., Strange, "First Century Galilee," 89. Crossan, through a critical engagement with David Adan-Bayewitz's work on pottery in Roman Galilee and Dean Arnold's cross-cultural anthropological work on ceramics, also argues that the pottery production associated with Kefar Hananya in Galilee is due to population pressure and a lack of available or useful agricultural land, which meant people were forced to turn to ceramic resources. See Crossan, *Birth of Christianity*, 223–30. Cf. D. E. Arnold, *Ceramic Theory and Cultural Process* (Cambridge: Cambridge University Press, 1985); D. Adan-Bayewitz and I. Perlman, "The Local Trade of Sepphoris in the Roman Period," *IEJ* 40 (1990): 153–72; D. Adan-Bayewitz, *Common Pottery in Roman Galilee: A Study of Local Trade* (Ramat-Gan: Bar Ilan University Press, 1992). See also Horsley, "Historical Jesus and Archaeology of the Galilee," 106–8, 111.

66. N. K. Gottwald, "Social Class as an Analytic and Hermeneutical Category," *JBL* 112 (1993): 3–22 (18–21).

67. Stegemann and Stegemann, *Jesus Movement*, 134.

68. For an analysis of the relevant passages on the death of John the Baptist, see J. G. Crossley, "History from the Margins: The Death of John the Baptist," in Crossley and Karner, eds., *Writing History, Constructing Religion*, 147–61.

69. On banditry in Roman Palestine see, e.g., B. Isaac, "Bandits in Judea and Arabia," *Harvard Studies in Classical Philology* 88 (1984): 172–203; Horsley with Hanson, *Bandits, Prophets, and Messiahs*, 48–87; Freyne, "Bandits in Galilee," 50–68; Crossan, *Historical Jesus*, 174–206; N. T. Wright, *Jesus and the Victory of God* (London: SPCK, 1996), 155–60; Richardson and Edwards, "Jesus and Palestinian Social Protest," 259–62; K. C. Hanson, "Jesus and the Social Bandits," in Stegemann, Malina, and Theissen, eds., *Social Setting of Jesus and the Gospels*, 283–300. Cf. Kautsky, *Politics of Aristocratic Empires*, 275–76.

70. B. D. Shaw, "Bandits in the Roman Empire," *Past and Present* 105 (1984): 5–52; Richardson and Edwards, "Jesus and Palestinian Social Protest," 256–59.

71. E.g., E. J. Hobsbawm, *Primitive Rebels* (New York: Norton, 1965); "Social Banditry: A Reply," *Comparative Studies in Society and History* 14 (1972): 503–5; "Social Banditry," in Landsberger, ed., *Rural Protest*, 142–57; *Bandits* (London: Penguin, 1969, 1985). See also the important early critique by A. Blok, "The Peasant and the Brigand: Social Banditry Reconsidered," *Comparative Studies in Society and History* 14 (1972): 494–503.

72. Stegemann and Stegemann, *Jesus Movement*, 173–74.

73. Cf. ibid., 176: "'Ordinary robbers' are probably meant in Luke 10:30."

74. Hobsbawm, "Social Banditry," 151.

75. M. Hengel, *The Zealots*, 2d ed. (Edinburgh: T. & T. Clark, 1989), 34; M. Hengel, "Zeloten und Sikarier," in *Josephus-Studien: Festschrift für Otto Michel*, ed. O. Betz, M. Hengel, and K. Haacker (Göttingen: Vandenhoeck & Ruprecht, 1971), 175–96 (181–82); Hobsbawm, "Social Banditry," 143, 145, 149–50; Freyne, "Bandits in Galilee," 62–64; Horsley with Hanson, *Bandits, Prophets, and Messiahs*, 49–63, 67, 85; Crossan, *Historical Jesus*, 168–74; Isaac, "Bandits in Judaea and Arabia," 178–79; Shaw, "Bandits in the Roman Empire," 352ff.;

Fiensy, *Social History of Palestine*, 96; Stegemann and Stegemann, *Jesus Movement*, 173.

76. Shaw, "Bandits in the Roman Empire."
77. Isaac, "Bandits in Judaea and Arabia," 179; cf. Shaw, "Bandits in the Roman Empire," 36–43.
78. Cf. Josephus, *Ant.* 15.342–48 and *J.W.* 1.398–400.
79. Horsley with Hanson, *Bandits, Prophets, and Messiahs*, 67.
80. Hanson and Oakman, *Palestine in the Time of Jesus*, 74.
81. Horsley with Hanson, *Bandits, Prophets, and Messiahs*, 85.
82. Cf. ibid., 71: "For him to have sustained a twenty-year career obviously required the protection of the peasantry."
83. Cf. Josephus, *J.W.* 2.238: "All these were threatened with destruction merely for the object of avenging the blood of a single Galilean."
84. Josephus, *Ant.* 20.121 is more generalized in the portrayal of violence, but it is violent nonetheless. Note also that Crossan (*Historical Jesus*, 182, 184) sees this event in 52 CE as almost leading to a full-scale revolt started among the peasantry and bandits rather than retainers and aristocrats. See, e.g., Josephus, *Ant.* 20.120 (cf. *J.W.* 2.239–46; *Ant.* 20.125–36; Tacitus, *Ann.* 12.54).
85. See, e.g., Freyne, "Bandits in Galilee," 55–65; Fiensy, *Social History of Palestine*, 166–67; Crossan, *Historical Jesus*, 169–72.
86. Cf. Freyne, "Bandits in Galilee," 63.
87. Cf. Josephus, *J.W.* 2.278–79: "He stripped whole cities, ruined entire populations, and almost went the length of proclaiming throughout the country that all were at liberty to practise brigandage, on condition that he received his share of the spoils."
88. It should be noted that the extent to which Sepphoris can be called "pro-Roman" is controversial. See, e.g., E. Meyers, "Sepphoris on the Eve of the Great Revolt (67–68 C.E.): Archaeology and Josephus," in *Galilee through the Centuries*, ed. E. Meyers (Winona Lake, IN: Eisenbrauns, 1999), 109–22.
89. Freyne, "Bandits in Galilee," 61.
90. On the role of oil and related liquids in purity and other laws, see J. G. Crossley, *The Date of Mark's Gospel: Insight from the Law in Earliest Christianity* (London: Continuum/T. & T. Clark, 2004), 193–97.
91. It is possible that Cumanus may not have been so innocent himself: cf. Josephus, *Ant.* 20.113–15.
92. So, e.g., Crossan, *Historical Jesus*, 196–206.
93. Richardson and Edwards, "Jesus and Palestinian Social Protest," 263; M. Goodman, *The Ruling Class of Judaea: The Origins of the Jewish Revolt against Rome AD 66–70* (Cambridge: Cambridge University Press, 1987), 38–42, 139–40. See further, R. Fenn, *The Death of Herod: An Essay in the Sociology of Religion* (Cambridge: Cambridge University Press, 1992).
94. Stegemann and Stegemann, *Jesus Movement*, 177.
95. Cf. Lenski, *Power and Privilege*, 256–63. For application of Lenski and Kautsky on class to first-century Palestine see, e.g., Fiensy, *Social History of Palestine*, 155–76; Crossan, *Birth of Christianity*, 154–57. For a discussion of the use of the term "class" in aristocratic empires, see Kautsky, *Politics of Aristocratic Empires*, 73–75; de Ste. Croix, *Class Struggle*.
96. For a vigorous defense of his definition of "peasant" see Crossan, *Birth of Christianity*, 216–18.

97. Kautsky, *Politics of Aristocratic Empires*, 280.

98. Ibid., 304, n. 26.

99. A. Millard, *Reading and Writing in the Time of Jesus* (Sheffield: Sheffield Academic Press, 2000). In contrast, Crossan (*Birth of Christianity*, 234–35) draws on cross-cultural estimates of literacy and argues that "peasants, almost by definition, are illiterate . . . Jesus was a peasant from a peasant village. Therefore, for me, Jesus was illiterate until the opposite is proven." Millard's detailed arguments were of course published after Crossan's *Birth of Christianity*.

100. Crossley, *Date*, 82–124. This largely concerns the presentation in the Synoptics, but I also suggested that much of this could well reflect the historical Jesus.

101. J. D. G. Dunn, "Jesus, Table-Fellowship, and Qumran," in *Jesus and the Dead Sea Scrolls*, ed. J. H. Charlesworth (New York: Doubleday, 1992), 254–72 (264–67).

102. Kautsky, *Politics of Aristocratic Empires*, 304, n. 26, also notes that Emiliano Zapata's peasant uprising "remained relatively localised in Morelos and might have been more so had it not become involved in the larger and non-peasant-led Mexican Revolution." Although Christianity did not emerge into a full-blown revolutionary movement, it might be said that the Jesus circle may have died out had it not been for an increase in support from urbanized figures. Cf. W. A. Meeks, *The First Urban Christians: The Social World of the Apostle Paul* (New Haven, CT: Yale University Press, 1983, 2003); G. Theissen, *The Social Setting of Pauline Christianity* (Edinburgh: T. & T. Clark, 1982). See also Crossan, *Birth of Christianity*, 235, "*Jesus' kingdom-of-God movement began as a movement of peasant resistance but broke out from localism and regionalism under scribal leadership*" (Crossan's italics). As we will see in the next chapter, it may be significant that Jesus' mission itself was partially aimed at people of some wealth who were connected with the aristocracy that also prevented it from dying out.

103. Hilton, "Peasant Society"; Kautsky, *Politics of Aristocratic Empires*, 304, n. 26.

104. Hilton, "Peasant Society," 90. Recall also Hobsbawm, "Peasants and Politics," 209, cited above.

105. Hilton, "Peasant Society," 91.

106. Crossan, *Birth of Christianity*, 346–50.

107. D. Daube, "Responsibilities of Master and Disciples in the Gospels," *NTS* 19 (1972–73): 1–16.

108. M. Casey, *Aramaic Sources of Mark's Gospel* (Cambridge: Cambridge University Press, 1998), 142.

109. Lenski, *Power and Privilege*, 265.

110. Ibid., 263, 265; cf. Hilton, "Peasant Society," 89–90.

111. Lenski, *Power and Privilege*, 264.

112. L. J. Hoppe, *There Shall Be No Poor among You: Poverty in the Bible* (Nashville: Abingdon Press, 2004). Cf. Horsley with Hanson, *Bandits, Prophets, and Messiahs*, 59–60; Crossan, *Birth of Christianity*, 177–208.

113. Cf. N. T. Wright, *The Resurrection of the Son of God* (London: SPCK, 2003), 162: "Judgment must fall, because the wicked have been getting away with violence and oppression for far too long."

114. G. W. E. Nickelsburg, "Riches, The Rich, and God's Judgment in 1 Enoch 92–105 and the Gospel according to Luke," *NTS* 25 (1979): 324–44 (326–32).

115. T. E. Schmidt, *Hostility to Wealth in the Synoptic Gospels* (Sheffield: Sheffield Academic Press, 1987). Schmidt also tries to apply this to the Gospel tradition with some reference to the socioeconomic background, which he did not think was

particularly harsh in the sense that it would give rise to a more literal understanding of the harder sayings. Hopefully I have shown that the opposite is the
case. It would be pointless and unfair to critique Schmidt's analysis of the
socioeconomic background to the Gospel tradition, for it is now out of date as
much significant work has been done since 1987.

116. Crossan, *Historical Jesus*, 174.
117. R. J. Bauckham, "Rich Man and Lazarus: The Parable and the Parallels," *NTS*
37 (1991): 225–46 (230).
118. Crossley, *Date*, 82–124, 159–205.
119. J. G. Crossley, "The Damned Rich (Mark 10.17–31)," *ExpT* 116 (2005):
397–401.
120. See Crossley, "The Damned Rich," 399–400, for further reasons in favor of
general historicity.
121. See especially Bauckham, "Rich Man and Lazarus," 225–46. On the pagan
background see, e.g., K. Grobel, "'. . . Whose Name Was Neves,'" *NTS* 10
(1963–1964): 373–82; R. F. Hock, "Lazarus and Micyllus: Greco-Roman Backgrounds to Luke 16:19–31," *JBL* 106 (1987): 448–55.
122. J. B. Green, *Gospel of Luke* (Grand Rapids: Wm. B. Eerdmans, 1997), 605, noting Lenski, *Power and Privilege*, 281–84.
123. For a list of scholars advocating these unrealistic views and an effective rebut-
tal, see Bauckham, "The Rich Man and Lazarus," 228, 232–33, 235–36. Green
(*Gospel of Luke*, 604–5, n. 326) criticizes Bauckham on this point: "The rich man
is condemned for not taking seriously his scriptural responsibility to use his
wealth on behalf of the needy." But where does Luke say this? Scripture is certainly mentioned in 16:29, but it does not say that rich people should responsi-
bly use wealth. Luke 16:25 gives the reason: the rich man had good things in
this life while Lazarus did not. Therefore there is a role reversal in the afterlife.
It ultimately boils down to "the inexcusable injustice of the co-existence of rich
and poor" and not the moral qualities of the men (Bauckham, "The Rich Man
and Lazarus," 246).
124. See Green, *Gospel of Luke*, 605.
125. M. Hengel, *The Charismatic Leader and His Followers* (ET; Edinburgh: T. & T.
Clark; New York: Crossroad, 1981), 3–15. But see also the qualifications in
M. Bockmuehl, "Let the Dead Bury Their Dead (Matt. 8.22/Luke 9.60): Jesus
and the Halakah," *JTS* 49 (1998): 553–81. Also available in M. Bockmuehl, *Jewish Law in Gentile Churches: Halakhah and the Beginning of Christian Public Ethics*
(Edinburgh: T. & T. Clark, 2000).
126. The dichotomy between early tradition and Lukan redaction may be overdone.
Luke may have been most impressed with this tradition and so included it, possibly with little alteration. Theissen suggests that as Luke makes the time of
Jesus "a special era, in which special, different ethical rules applied," in contrast
to Luke's own time when "he unmistakably disassociates himself from the rad-
icalism of the early Christian itinerants," he is able to "preserve Jesus' words
most faithfully of all" (G. Theissen, *Social Reality and the Early Christians* [Edin-
burgh: T. & T. Clark, 1993, 58]). Cf. Dunn, *Jesus Remembered*, 524–25.
127. J. A. Fitzmyer, *The Gospel according to Luke II* (New York: Doubleday, 1985),
1125, 1127.
128. R. W. Funk, R. W. Hoover, and the Jesus Seminar, *The Five Gospels: The Search
for the Authentic Words of Jesus* (San Francisco: HarperCollins, 1993), 36.
129. Ibid., 362.

130. Bauckham, "The Rich Man and Lazarus," 236–44.
131. Ibid., 243.
132. J. G. Crossley, "The Semitic Background to Repentance in the Teaching of John the Baptist and Jesus," *JSHJ* 2 (2004): 139–58. See also the next chapter.
133. See Crossley, *Date*, 83–84.
134. So, e.g., J. D. G. Dunn, *Jesus, Paul and the Law* (London: SPCK, 1990), 61–86; M. Hengel and R. Deines, "E. P. Sanders' 'Common Judaism', Jesus, and the Pharisees," *JTS* 46 (1995): 1–70; Casey, *Aramaic Sources*, 190–91; Crossley, *Date*, 132–33.
135. See, e.g., C. A. Evans, "Jesus' Action in the Temple: Cleansing or Portent of Destruction?" *CBQ* 51 (1989): 237–70; *Jesus and His Contemporaries: Comparative Studies* (Leiden: E. J. Brill, 1995), ch. 9.
136. Crossley, *Date*, 62–74.
137. P. Doble, "Something Greater than Solomon: An Approach to Stephen's Speech," in *The Old Testament in the New Testament: Essays in Honour of J. L. North*, ed. S. Moyise (Sheffield: Sheffield Academic Press, 2000), 181–207 (192–201); cf. Crossley, *Date*, 127–29.
138. See Evans, "Predictions," 106 for other possible allusions, including Ruth 2:12; Pss. 17:8; 36:7; 57:1; 61:4.
139. Ibid., 106–7.
140. This is even more relevant to some versions of Matt. 23:38: "See, your house is left to you, desolate [ἔρημος]."
141. Cf. Schmidt, *Hostility to Wealth*, 156; Crossley, *Date*, 27–29.
142. Kautsky, *Politics of Aristocratic Empires*, 306. It is perhaps worth *speculating* on the presence of the female followers with help from Kautsky, Hobsbawm, and numerous others. As noted above, sometimes radical egalitarianism is a feature of social unrest, and it might be noted that in revolution after revolution throughout history there has been a concern for a more prominent role for women. Indeed, in the context of the Jewish war Simon bar Giora was said to have a female following, which was deemed strange enough by the bandits he joined at Masada to have them sectioned off of the fortress (Josephus, *J.W.* 4.505; cf. *J.W.* 4.538). This may prove to be a useful analogy with Jesus' female following.

Chapter 3: Jesus and the Sinners

1. For a selection of differing views see, e.g., J. Jeremias, "Zöllner und Sünder," *ZNW* 30 (1931): 293–300; J. Jeremias, *New Testament Theology, Part One: The Proclamation of Jesus* (London: SCM, 1971), e.g., 108–13; E. P. Sanders, "Jesus and the Sinners," *JSNT* 19 (1983): 5–36; E. P. Sanders, *Jesus and Judaism* (London: SCM, 1985), 174–211; E. P. Sanders, *The Historical Figure of Jesus* (London: Penguin, 1993), 226–37; J. D. G. Dunn, "Pharisees, Sinners and Jesus," in *The Social World of Formative Christianity and Judaism: Essays in Tribute to Howard Clarke Kee*, ed. P. Borgen, J. Neusner, E. S. Frerichs, and R. Horsley (Philadelphia: Fortress, 1988), 264–89; J. D. G. Dunn, *Jesus, Paul and the Law: Studies in Mark and Galatians* (London: SPCK, 1990), 61–88; J. D. G. Dunn, "Jesus, Table-Fellowship, and Qumran," in *Jesus and the Dead Sea Scrolls*, ed. J. H. Charlesworth (New York: Doubleday, 1992), 254–72; J. D. G. Dunn, *Jesus Remembered* (Grand Rapids: Wm. B. Eerdmans, 2003), 526–33; N. T. Wright, *Jesus and the Victory of God* (London: SPCK, 1996), 264–68. Cf. R. Horsley, *Jesus and the Spiral of Violence: Popular Jewish Resistance in Roman Palestine* (San Francisco: Harper & Row, 1987), 217–21, for important qualifications. For a still

very useful review of older scholarship see D. A. Neale, *None but the Sinners: Religious Categories in the Gospel of Luke* (Sheffield: JSOT, 1991), 69–75. For a more recent survey of scholarship with broader reference to Jesus' meals see C. L. Blomberg, *Contagious Holiness: Jesus' Meals with Sinners* (Downers Grove, IL: InterVarsity, 2005), 19–31. See also the criticisms of the sinners and the so-called "despised trades" in Horsley, *Spiral*, 219–20.

2. Sanders, *Jesus and Judaism*, 198–99.

3. Ibid., 177–78.

4. See, e.g., Pss. 7:9; 31[32]:10; 33[34]:21; 57[58]:10; 67[68]:2; 74[75]:8; 96[97]:10; 111[112]:10; 140[141]:5; 145[146]:9; Prov. 11:31; cf. Dan. 12:10.

5. See the similar conclusions after an analysis of the Greek Psalms in Neale, *None but the Sinners*, 75–81.

6. See also Ps. 36[37]:10, 14, 17, 20; 57[58]:10; 90[91]:8; 91[92]:7; 100[101]:8; 105[106]:18; 144[145]:20; 145[146]:9; 146[147]:6; Prov. 11:31; 24:19; Isa. 14:5; Ezek. 33:8. On judgment of sinners in the Greek Psalms see also Neale, *None but the Sinners*, 82–83.

7. Curiously ἁμαρτωλός appears to be absent from Josephus and Philo.

8. Cf. Wis. 4:10; Sir. 2:12; 3:27; 5:9; 8:10; 15:12; 16:6; 21:6; 23:8; 41:5; *1 En.* 1:9; 5:6; 22:10–13; 98:6; *T. Ab.* [A]11:11; 12:10; 14:11; *Ps. Sol.* 12:6; 17:23, 25, 36.

9. E.g., Wis. 4:10; Sir. 13:17; 19:22; 36[33]:14; *T. Ab.* [A] 13:3, 9; 17:8; *T. Ab.* [B—MS "E"] 13:20; *Ps. Sol.* 3:9; 4:8; 14:6; 15:7–8.

10. For similar comments on the sinners as wealthy and oppressive in *1 Enoch* see G. W. E. Nickelsburg, "Riches, The Rich, and God's Judgment in *1 Enoch* 92–105 and the Gospel according to Luke," *NTS* 25 (1979): 324–44 (326–27).

11. E.g., Dunn, *Jesus, Paul and the Law*, 73–77; Dunn, "Table-Fellowship," 259.

12. E.g., Sir. 5:6; 7:16; 12:6; 16:13–14; 25:19; 40:8; 41:5; 1 Macc. 2:62; *1 En.* 1:9; 22:10, 12, 13; 97:7; 100:2–3, 9; 102:3, 5–6; *T. Ab.* [A] 11:11; 12:10; 13:3, 9, 12; 14:11; 17:8; *T. Ab.* [B—MS "E"] 13:20; *T. Jud.* 25:5; *Pss. Sol.* 2:34–35; 3:11–12; 4:2, 8, 23; 12:6; 13:2, 5–8, 11; 14:6; 16:5; 17:23, 25, 36. Compare also Horsley, *Spiral*, 218–19; Neale, *None but the Sinners*, 83–85.

13. E.g., 1Q34 3 II, 5; 4Q510 II, 1; 11Q5 XXIV, 6; 11Q10 VII, 4; XXIV, 1; cf. 1Qap Genar I, 2; 4Q511 18 II, 6; 4Q506 CXXXI–CXXXII, 14.

14. E.g., 1Q27 1, I, 5–6; 1Q34 3, I, 2, 5; CD I, 19; XX, 21; 4Q171 II, 9–16; 4Q212 IV, 16; 4Q 185 1–2 II, 9; 4Q508 I, 1; 11Q5 XVIII, 12–15; 11Q10 III, 6; VII, 4; 11Q13 1 II, 11.

15. E.g., 1QpHab V, 5; 1QM I, 2; 1Q27 I, 1, 5–6; CD I, 19; II, 3; XI, 21; 4Q171 III, 12; 4Q174 1 I, 14; 4Q511 63, III, 4; 11Q5 XVIII, 12–15; 4Q504 1–2 II, 10; 4Q504 1–2 V, 19. Cf. M. Casey, *An Aramaic Approach to Q* (Cambridge: Cambridge University Press, 2002), 139.

16. E.g., 1QpHab V, 5; XIII, 4; 1QM IV, 4; 1QS VIII, 7; 1Q34 3 I, 5, II, 5; CD I, 19; IV, 7; VII, 9; XIX, 6; XX, 26; 4Q171 III, 12; 4Q212 IV, 16; 4Q398 XI–XIII, 5; 4Q511 63 III, 4; 11Q10 III, 6; VII, 4; XI, 3; XXXIV, 8; cf. 1QM XIV, 7; XV, 2; 1Q28a I, 3.

17. E.g., 1QpHab XIII, 4; 1QM I, 2; XI, 14; CD VIII, 8–12; 4Q169 3 I, 1–2; cf. 1QM XIV, 7; XV, 2.

18. E.g., 1QM XI, 12–14; 1Q27 I, 1, 11; 4Q169 3 IV, 1, 5; 4Q171 II, 18; 4Q544 II, 3; 11Q10 III, 6; VII, 4; XI, 3; XXV, 6; XXXIV, 8; cf. 1QS X, 19; CD VI, 15; XIX, 17; 4Q204 5, II, 25–28; 4Q510 I, 7; 4Q511 X, 3; XXXV, 1, 9; 11Q10 II, 7.

19. Cf. Sanders, *Historical Figure*, 227, with reference to רשעים: "I shall refer to them as the 'wicked', since that it almost certainly is the word that was used by Jesus

and his critics. (They spoke Aramaic rather than Hebrew, but the word is the same.)" See also Sanders, *Jesus and Judaism*, 177.

20. B. D. Chilton, "Jesus and the Repentance of E. P. Sanders," *TynBul* 39 (1988), 1–18 (9).
21. E.g., Pesh. Pss. 7:9; 9:17; 9:23–25 [10:2–4]; 33[34]:21[22]; 36[37]:10, 14, 17, 20, 21; 57[58]:10[11]; 67[68]:2[3]; 72[73]:3; 74[75]:8[9]; 81[82]:2, 4; 90[91]:8; 91[92]:7; 93[94]:3, 13; 96[97]:10; 100[101]:8; 111[112]:10.
22. E.g., Pesh. Pss. 105[106]:18; 119:61, 95, 155; 144[145]:20; 145[146]:9; 146[147]:6.
23. E.g., Pesh. Pss. 9:36 [10:15]; 49[50]:16; 119:53, 110.
24. Chilton, "Repentance," 9–10.
25. M. Black, *An Aramaic Approach to the Gospels and Acts*, 3d ed. (Oxford: Oxford University Press, 1967), 140; Chilton, "Repentance," 10–12. For positive evaluations of the language of debtor-sinner see also M. Casey, *Aramaic Sources of Mark's Gospel* (Cambridge: Cambridge University Press, 1998), 60, 85; Casey, *Aramaic Approach*, 139.
26. Cf. Chilton, "Repentance."
27. Cf. Dunn, "Table-Fellowship," 257–60.
28. Cf. Sanders, *Historical Figure*, 227–29.
29. This stands even if we accept Horsley's argument (*Spiral*, 212–17) that the evidence in favor of Jesus' associating with tax collectors and them forming a part of his following is at best weak because it remains that the tradition still associated tax collectors with sinners. In other words, first-century Christians placed them side by side.
30. J. G. Crossley, "The Semitic Background to Repentance in the Teaching of John the Baptist and Jesus," *JSHJ* 2 (2004): 138–57.
31. Cf. Neale, *None but the Righteous*, 90–95.
32. Chilton, "Repentance," 10.
33. E.g., E. Würthwein, "μετανοέω, μετάνοια: B. Repentance and Conversion in the Old Testament," *TDNT* 4 (1933–79): 980–89 (989). Cf. the qualifications in R. H. Bell, "Teshubah: The Idea of Repentance in Ancient Judaism," *Journal of Progressive Judaism* 5 (1995): 22–52 (24).
34. Cf. Crossley, "Repentance," 145.
35. Cf. ibid., 147.
36. Crossley, *Date*, 82–124, 159–205.
37. Sanders, *Historical Figure*, 233–34, notes the differences in Matt. 18:12–14 par. Luke 15:3–7, between the shepherd going after the lost sheep (Matthew) and the lost sheep deciding to come back (Luke). For Sanders, Matthew's emphasis is on God's search and is more reflective of Jesus' own view. But against this the parabolic language should not be taken too literally (Wright, *Victory*, 254). Moreover, as I argued elsewhere, the *teshubah* ideal of repentance can cover both the sinner returning and another seeking out a sinner (cf. Ezek. 33:7–9, 11, 19; 4Q393 1–2 ii, 4–7; *T. Abr.* 10.14 [A]; Tob. 13:6). See further Crossley, "Repentance," 141, n. 8.
38. Sanders, *Jesus and Judaism*, 106–13; Sanders, *Historical Figure*, 230–35.
39. See further, e.g., Allison, "Jesus and the Covenant," 70–71; Chilton, "Repentance," 1–18; Wright, *Victory*, 246–58.
40. Cf. E. P. Sanders, *Paul and Palestinian Judaism: A Comparison of Patterns of Religion* (Philadelphia: Fortress; London: SCM, 1977), 176–79.
41. Sanders, *Historical Figure*, 236.

42. See, e.g., Dunn, *Jesus, Paul and the Law*, 61–86; M. Hengel, and R. Deines, "E. P. Sanders' 'Common Judaism', Jesus, and the Pharisees," *JTS* 46 (1995): 1–70; J. G. Crossley, *The Date of Mark's Gospel: Insight from the Law in Earliest Christianity* (London: Continuum/T. & T. Clark, 2004), 131–33. With this in mind, a passage such as the following is double edged: "Whosoever causes the multitude to be righteous, through him shall no sin be brought about, but one that leads the many to sin, to him shall not be given the means to repentance" (*m. 'Abot.* 5:18).

43. E.g., Dunn, "Table-Fellowship," 254–55, 259–68.

44. Cf. the much later *b. Sanh.* 25b: "A usurer: this includes both lender and borrower. And when are they judged to have repented? When they tear up their bills and undergo a complete reformation, that they will not lend [on interest] even to a gentile."

45. Sanders, *Jesus and Judaism*, 206.

46. Cf. Crossley, *Date*, 62–76, 83–84, 87–98, 107–10, 115–23. It is also common to claim that John the Baptist bypassed the Temple system too despite the lack of evidence. But, as with Jesus, John is never criticized for neglecting the law in any way and only remembered as stressing Jewish pieties and certain commandments (Mark 6:17–20; Luke 3:10–14; Josephus, *Ant.* 18.116–19). Surely one of these sources would have mentioned John overriding biblical law if he did such an unlikely thing. Moreover, there is also a close parallel to John's teaching in Sir. 5:5–8 that reflects similar concerns to those of John and, naturally, assumes a situation of traditional Jewish piety.

47. See further Dunn, *Jesus, Paul and the Law*, 19–20. Note Sanders's argument on tax collectors: "No one would have objected if Jesus persuaded tax collectors to leave the ranks of the wicked: everybody else would have benefited. If he were *a successful reformer* of dishonest tax collectors, Jesus would not have drawn criticism. But in fact he was criticised *for associating with them*" (*Historical Figure*, 236, my italics). Is there not an important difference between *association with* tax collectors and sinners/the wicked and *the reforming of* sinners/the wicked?

Chapter 4: From Jewish Sinners to Gentile Sinners

1. See further J. G. Crossley, *The Date of Mark's Gospel: Insight from the Law in Earliest Christianity* (London: Continuum/T. & T. Clark, 2004), 22, 34.

2. Crossley, *Date*, 125–58.

3. P. Nolan and G. Lenski, *Human Societies: An Introduction to Macrosociology*, 9th ed. (Boulder, CO: Paradigm, 2004), 169–72 (italics original). This is a revised version of G. E. Lenski and J. Lenski, *Human Societies: An Introduction to Macrosociology* (New York: McGraw-Hill, 1970), 252–53.

4. R. Riesner, *Paul's Early Period: Chronology, Mission Strategy, Theology* (Grand Rapids: Wm. B. Eerdmans, 1998); M. B. Thompson, "The Holy Internet: Communication between Churches in the First Christian Generation," in R. Bauckham, ed., *The Gospel for All Christians: Rethinking the Gospel Audiences* (Edinburgh: T. & T. Clark, 1998), 49–70.

5. M. Stern, ed., *Greek and Latin Authors on Jews and Judaism* (3 vols.; Jerusalem: Israel Academy of Sciences & Humanities, 1974), 2:206–10.

6. P. Athanassiadi and M. Frede, "Introduction," in *Pagan Monotheism in Late Antiquity*, ed. P. Athanassiadi and M. Frede (Oxford: Oxford University Press, 1999), 1–20 (1–2, quotes 1); see also M. L. West, "Towards Monotheism," in Athanassiadi and Frede, eds., *Pagan Monotheism*, 21–40.

7. See, e.g., L. W. Hurtado, *One Lord, One God: Early Christian Devotion and Ancient Jewish Monotheism* (Philadelphia: Fortress, 1988), 17–69; M. Casey, *From Jewish Prophet to Gentile God: The Origins and Development of New Testament Christology* (Louisville, KY: Westminster John Knox; Cambridge: James Clarke, 1991), 78–96; J. J. Collins, *The Scepter and the Star: The Messiahs of the Dead Sea Scrolls and Other Ancient Literature* (New York: Doubleday, 1995), 136–94.

8. S. Mitchell, "The Cult of Theos Hypsistos between Pagans, Jews and Christians," in Athanassiadi and Frede, eds., *Pagan Monotheism*, 83–148. Documentary evidence is collected on 128–48.

9. Mitchell, "Theos Hypsistos," 128. Cf. the similar comments made in the introduction to Athanassiadi and Frede, eds., *Pagan Monotheism*, 20: "Christianity did not convince because it was monotheistic; rather it would appear that in order to convince, it had to become monotheistic in a society which was fast moving in that direction."

10. This is obviously a massive issue. The point of the biblical suppression of magic in the Persian period in relation to developments in monotheism I owe to discussion with Diana Edelman. I remain entirely responsible for any error on this point. On the suppression of magic in certain Pentateuchal traditions, see, e.g., T. Römer, "Competing Magicians in Exodus 7–9: Interpreting Magic in Priestly Theology," in *Magic in the Biblical World: From the Rod of Aaron to the Ring of Solomon*, ed. T. Klutz (London: Continuum/T. & T. Clark, 2003), 12–22. On the broader issues see, e.g., D. V. Edelman, ed., *The Triumph of Elohim: From Yahwisms to Judaisms* (Kampen: Kok Pharos, 1995). On first-century monotheism see, e.g., L. W. Hurtado, "First-Century Jewish Monotheism," *JSNT* 71 (1998), 3–26.

11. The secondary literature on this debate is vast. For a selection see P. Fredriksen, "Judaism, the Circumcision of Gentiles, and Apocalyptic Hope: Another Look at Galatians 1 and 2," *JTS* 42 (1991): 533–42; S. McKnight, *A Light among Gentiles* (Minneapolis: Fortress, 1991); S. J. D. Cohen, "Was Judaism in Antiquity a Missionary Religion?" in *Assimilation and Accommodation: Past Traditions, Current Issues and Future Perspectives*, ed. M. Mor (Lanham, MD: University Press of America, 1992), 14–23; M. Goodman, "Jewish Proselytizing in the First Century," in *Jews among Pagans and Christians in the Roman Empire*, ed. J. Lieu, J. L. North, and T. Rajak (London: Routledge, 1992), 53–78; M. Goodman, *Mission and Conversion: Proselytizing in the Religious History of the Roman Empire* (Oxford: Oxford University Press, 1994); L. Feldman, *Jews and Gentiles in the Ancient World: Attitudes and Interactions from Alexander to Justinian* (Princeton, NJ: Princeton University Press, 1993); A. T. Kraabel, "Immigrants, Exiles, Expatriates and Missionaries," in *Religious Propaganda and Missionary Competition in the New Testament World: Essays Honoring Dieter Georgi*, ed. L. Bormann, K. Del Tredici, and A. Strandhartinger (Leiden: E. J. Brill, 1994), 71–88; J. Carleton Paget, "Jewish Proselytism at the Time of Christian Origins: Chimera or Reality?" *JSNT* 62 (1996): 65–103. For a useful overview of the main issues surrounding the possibilities of Jewish proselytism, see Carleton Paget, "Chimera or Reality?" 65–75.

12. S. C. Barton, *Discipleship and Family Ties in Mark and Matthew* (Cambridge: Cambridge University Press, 1995).

13. On fictive kinship being compatible with actual kinship in the Synoptic Gospel tradition, see Crossley, *Date*, 86–87, 105–7, 113–14.

14. Some recent arguments against Q as a fixed literary document have come from Michael Goulder and Mark Goodacre. See, e.g., M. D. Goulder, *Luke—A New*

Paradigm (Sheffield: Sheffield Academic Press, 1989); M. D. Goulder, "Is Q a Juggernaut?" *JBL* 115 (1996): 667–81; M. Goodacre, *The Case against Q: Studies in Markan Priority and the Synoptic Problem* (Harrisburg, PA: Trinity Press International, 2002); M. Goodacre and N. Perrin, eds., *Questioning Q: A Multidimensional Critique* (Downers Grove, IL: InterVarsity, 2004). For useful but inevitably brief critiques of Goodacre and the Goodacre and Perrin volume see C. M. Tuckett, "Review of Mark Goodacre, *The Case against Q: Studies in Markan Priority and the Synoptic Problem*," *NovT* 46 (2004): 401–3; J. Verheyden, "Review of M. Goodacre and N. Perrin (eds.), *Questioning Q: A Multidimensional Critique*," *Review of Biblical Literature* (Sept. 3, 2005), available at http://www.bookreviews.org/bookdetail.asp?TitleId=4655&CodePage=2436,46 55,1932,3214. For a respectful critique of Goulder see M. Casey, *An Aramaic Approach to Q* (Cambridge: Cambridge University Press, 2002), 44–47. See also P. Foster, "Is it Possible to Dispense with Q?" *NovT* 45 (2003): 313–37; J. S. Kloppenborg, "On Dispensing with Q? Goodacre on the Relation of Luke to Matthew," *NTS* 49 (2003): 210–36.

15. R. A. Horsley and J. A. Draper, *Whoever Hears You Hears Me: Prophets, Performance and Tradition in Q* (Harrisburg, PA: Trinity Press International, 1999); Casey, *Aramaic Approach*.

16. I am aware this is not the conventional dating of these Gospels, which are usually placed somewhere closer to the end of the century. So here, briefly, are my reasons:

I suspect Matthew was written sometime close to 70 CE (whether before or after the fall, I leave open) because of additions made to a Q passage that heightens Jerusalem's destruction (Matt. 22:7). I do not think it could have been very long after 70 because of the heightening of the imminence of Mark 9:1 and making it refer to the second coming of Jesus within the lifetime of those standing by (Matt. 16:28). This gives us an upper date of around 70. Note too that in Matt. 24:34 he retains the emphasis in Mark 13:30 on the second coming and "end times" within a generation (30–40 years).

I suspect Luke was written sometime shortly after 70 CE. The explicit additions to Mark 11 stressing the fall of Jerusalem (Luke 19:41–44) and the direct alteration of Mark 13:14 stressing likewise (Luke 21:20–24) are surely not coincidental, irrespective of whether these were earlier sources. Note too that Luke makes subtle changes to Mark 9:1 (Luke 9:27) and Mark 13:30 (Luke 21:32) but does not go so far as to remove all traces of imminent eschatology, which may suggest that it is not too far after 70 CE.

If either Luke or Matthew were written much later than this we might reasonably expect the serious problems found with imminent eschatology in later documents. John's Gospel, for instance, drops all the references to the imminently coming kingdom and replaces them with a couple of kingdom references in a very different context (John 3:1–10). John 21 also shows the problems of the nonappearance of Jesus. This is also a problem in 2 Pet. 3. None of these problems are found in Matthew and only small hints of downplaying are found in Luke. Moreover, both these Gospels contain significant-enough eschatological material that they clearly edit. For further discussion of the problems with eschatology and the nonappearance of Jesus, see Crossley, *Date*, 19–43.

17. For a selection see, e.g., S. Schultz, *Q—Die Spruchquelle der Evangelisten* (Zürich: TVZ, 1971), 94–141; R. A. Wild, "The Encounter between Pharisaic and Christian Judaism: Some Early Gospel Evidence," *NovT* 27 (1985), 105–24;

C. M. Tuckett, "Q, the Law, and Judaism," in *Law and Religion: Essays on the Place of the Law in Israel and Early Christianity*, ed. B. Lindars (Cambridge: James Clark, 1988), 90–101; C. M. Tuckett, *Q and the History of Early Christianity: Studies on Q* (Edinburgh: T. & T. Clark; Peabody, MA: Hendrickson, 1996), 393–424; D. R. Catchpole, *The Quest for Q* (Edinburgh: T. & T. Clark, 1993), 232–38, 256–79; Casey, *Aramaic Approach*, 64–104.

18. Crossley, *Date*, 98–123, 168–69, 178–81, 200–202.
19. It is of course possible that Luke has retained an earlier context for this saying that Matthew has spread out: see Matt. 11:13 par. Luke 16:16a; Matt. 11:12 par. Luke 16:16b; Matt. 5:32 par. Luke 16:18. Cf. J. M. Robinson, P. Hoffmann, and J. S. Kloppenborg, eds., *The Critical Edition of Q: Synopsis, Including the Gospels of Matthew and Luke, Mark and Thomas, with English, German and French Translations of Q and Thomas* (Leuven: Peeters; Minneapolis: Fortress, 2000), 464–71. None of these sayings in whatever context can be seen as rejecting the biblical law in any way. For this kind of argument, in different ways, see, e.g., Catchpole, *Quest*, 232–38; J. S. Kloppenborg, "Nomos and Ethos in Q," in *Gospel Origins and Christian Beginnings: In Honor of James M. Robinson*, ed. J. E. Goehring, J. T. Sanders, and C. W. Hedrick (Sonoma, CA: Polebridge, 1990), 35–48 (43–46); Tuckett, *Q and the History*, 404–9; Crossley, *Date*, 99–100; 111, 178–82.
20. Crossley, *Date*, 100–104 with bibliography.
21. Ibid., 82–124, 159–205.
22. For Jewish legal parallels see E. P. Sanders, *Jewish Law from the Bible to the Mishnah* (London: SCM; Philadelphia: Trinity Press International, 1990), 93.
23. On this see now J. F. Davis, *Lex Talionis in Early Judaism and the Exhortation of Jesus in Matthew 5.38–42* (London & New York: T. & T. Clark/Continuum, 2005), 55–104.
24. Crossley, *Date*, 103.
25. For a detailed discussion of further legal material particular to Matthew and Luke along these lines see Crossley, *Date*, 98–124, 178–81.
26. Kloppenborg, "Nomos and Ethos," 46–47; cf. J. S. Kloppenborg Verbin, *Excavating Q: The History and Setting of the Sayings Gospel* (Edinburgh: T. & T. Clark, 2000), 153.
27. For details on the more "original" Q passage see, e.g., Schultz, *Spruchquelle*, 96–97; Kloppenborg, "Nomos and Ethos," 38, n. 16; Catchpole, *Quest*, 266–68; Robinson, Hoffmann, and Kloppenborg, *Critical Edition of Q*, 268–73; Casey, *Aramaic Approach*, 78–83.
28. So Casey, *Aramaic Approach*, 80.
29. J. Wellhausen, *Einleitung in die drei ersten Evangelien*, 2d ed. (Berlin: G. Reimer, 1911), 27. This view is defended further by M. Black, *An Aramaic Approach to the Gospels and Acts*, 3d ed. (Oxford: Oxford University Press, 1967), 2, and Casey, *Aramaic Approach*, 22–24, 82.
30. On the problematic nature of the confusing of ד and ז, I owe in particular to a discussion with Diana Edelman. See also P. M. Head and P. J. Williams, "Q Review," *TynBul* 54 (2003): 119–44 (133): "Since *daleth* and *zayin* are not particularly graphically close, the confusion is not quite natural. Neither would the verbs have sounded particularly similar."
31. See, e.g., J. Neusner, "'First Cleanse the Inside': The 'Halakhic' Background of a Controversy Saying," *NTS* 22 (1976): 486–95; Schulz, *Spruchquelle*, 97–99; Tuckett, *Q and the History*, 412–13; Casey, *Aramaic Approach*, 77–83.
32. Kloppenborg, "Nomos and Ethos," 40.

33. For further discussion with one vitriolic debate, see the arguments of Hyam Maccoby and John Poirier. See, e.g., J. C. Poirier, "Why Did the Pharisees Wash their Hands?" *JJS* 47 (1996): 217–33; J. C. Poirier, "Purity beyond the Temple in the Second Temple Era," *JBL* 122 (2003): 247–65; H. Maccoby, "The Law about Liquids: A Rejoinder," *JSNT* 67 (1997): 115–22; H. Maccoby, *Ritual and Morality: The Ritual Purity System and Its Place in Judaism* (Cambridge: Cambridge University Press, 1999). For an important earlier treatment of the rabbinic background to Matt. 23:25–26/Luke 11:38–41, see J. Neusner, "First Cleanse the Inside."

34. Neusner, "First Cleanse the Inside," 488–91.

35. Cf. ibid., 490.

36. H. Maccoby, "The Washing of Cups," *JSNT* 14 (1982): 3–15 (5), followed by Kloppenborg, "Nomos and Ethos," 39; L. E. Vaage, *Galilean Upstarts: Jesus' First Followers according to Q* (Valley Forge, PA: Trinity Press International, 1994), 66–86.

37. E. Hatch and H. A. Redpath, *A Concordance to the Septuagint*, 2d ed. (Grand Rapids: Baker Books, 1998), 502.

38. M. Jastrow, *A Dictionary of the Targumim, the Talmud Babli and Yerushalmi, and the Midrashic Literature* (2 vols.; New York: Pardes, 1950), 1:437–38. On שוק see vol. 2, 1540–41. On the use of שוק elsewhere in Aramaic see Casey, *Aramaic Approach*, 130.

39. T. Muraoka, *Hebrew/Aramaic Index to the Septuagint Keyed to the Hatch-Redpath Concordance* (Grand Rapids: Baker Books, 1998), 15–16.

40. Cf. Crossley, *Date*, 202; cf. 111–23.

41. Maccoby, "Washing," 13, n. 5.

42. Ibid., 7.

43. Kloppenborg, "Nomos and Ethos," 42.

44. Ibid., 42.

45. Ibid.

46. Cf. Philip Blackman on mint: "Any of a genus (menthe) of menthaceous aromatic herbs (family lamiaceoe or menthaceoe), especially garden mint or spearmint (menthe viridis) and peppermint (menthe piperita), used for flavouring and condiments, and medicinally, and for yielding a highly odoriferous oil" (P. Blackman, ed., *Mishnayoth* [7 vols.; London: Mishnah, 1951–1956], 1:497–98).

47. Kloppenborg, "Nomos and Ethos in Q," 42, n. 31.

48. Jastrow, *Dictionary*, vol. 1, 315.

49. Jastrow, *Dictionary*, vol. 2, 905, citing Rashi on *b. Ab. Zar.* 29a.

50. So Casey, *Aramaic Approach*, 73, adding, "Scribes and Pharisees will have tithed it [mint] all the same, whether because they did cultivate it, or because priests in the Temple needed it, and were not helped by the fact that it grew miles away."

51. Kloppenborg, "Nomos and Ethos," 40.

52. Casey, *Aramaic Approach*, 73–74.

53. Cf. Kloppenborg, "Nomos and Ethos," 43.

54. We could also add Matt. 23:28–29/Luke 11:44 to this, particularly if the Matthean version more accurately reflects Q. For a strong argument in favor of something like the Matthean version see Casey, *Aramaic Approach*, 89–92.

55. See further A. Oppenheimer, *The 'Am Ha-aretz: A Study in the Social History of the Jewish People in the Hellenistic-Roman Period* (Leiden: E. J. Brill, 1977), 18–22.

56. Traditionally, of course, the people of the land have been viewed as some kind of poor people oppressed by nasty Pharisees. See especially the important critique in E. P. Sanders, *Jesus and Judaism* (London: SCM; Philadelphia: Fortress, 1985), 174–211. Thankfully there has been some good work done on this subject, in no small part due to Sanders's critique. For a useful overview of the various issues and their relevance for the Gospel tradition, with bibliography, see D. A. Neale, *None but the Sinners: Religious Categories in the Gospel of Luke* (Sheffield: JSOT, 1991), 40–67. Neale also shows with some justification that the "people of the land" were more of a "religious category" than a label for some sort of social underclass.

57. Note also that the Matthean τὸ ἔλιος (Matt. 23:23) is also found in Matthew in the context of a discussion about sinners (Matt. 9:13–14; cf. Sir. 5:6).

58. G. W. E. Nickelsburg, "Riches, The Rich, and God's Judgment in 1 Enoch 92–105 and the Gospel according to Luke," *NTS* 25 (1979): 324–44; J. G. Crossley, "The Damned Rich (Mk 10.17–31)," *ExpT* 116 (2005): 397–401 (400–401).

59. In favor of a Gentile mission in Q see, e.g., R. Uro, *Sheep among the Wolves: A Study of the Mission Instructions of Q* (Helsinki: Suomalainen Tiedeakatemia, 1987), 210–23.

60. In favor of an exclusive Jewish mission, see, e.g., H. Schürmann, *Traditionsgeschichtliche Untersuchungen zu den synoptischen Evangelien* (Düsseldorf: Patmos, 1968), 137–49.

61. See esp. J. Jeremias, *Jesus' Promise to the Nations* (London: SCM, 1958), e.g., 51, 55–57.

62. D. C. Allison, "From East and West, Q 13:28–29: Salvation for the Diaspora," in *The Jesus Tradition in Q* (Harrisburg, PA: Trinity Press International, 1997), 176–91. See also Sanders, *Jesus and Judaism*, 119–20; Catchpole, *Quest*, 306.

63. Catchpole, *Quest*, 280–308.

64. Tuckett, *Q and the History*, 394.

65. On Tyre see G. Theissen, *The Gospels in Context: Social and Political History in the Synoptic Tradition* (Edinburgh: T. & T. Clark, 1992), 72–80; Kloppenborg Verbin, *Excavating Q*, 172–74. See also below. On Sodom see the previous chapter.

66. This argument stands if we include Matt. 11:13/Luke 16:16a; Matt. 11:12/Luke 16:16b; Matt. 5:32/Luke 16:18 as part of the original context. None of these texts provides proper evidence of "anxiety regarding the enduring validity of the Law" as Kloppenborg ("Nomos and Ethos," 46) suggests.

67. Schultz, *Spruchquelle*, 401–2, 244, 306.

68. See further Tuckett, *Q and the History*, 401–2.

69. The Matthean version is presumably the earliest as it has a negative reference to Gentiles that is ironed out in Luke and brought into line with Luke's concern for sinners (cf. Luke 15).

70. Tuckett, *Q and the History*, 402–3.

71. Ibid., 403.

72. P. D. Meyer, "The Gentile Mission in Q," *JBL* 89 (1970): 405–17.

73. On "and beds" in Mark 7:4 being accurate and the original reading, see J. G. Crossley, "Halakah and Mark 7.4: '. . . and beds,'" *JSNT* 25 (2003): 433–47.

74. For detailed discussion of these "traditions" see Crossley, *Date*, 183–93.

75. Ibid., 82–98.

76. Ibid., 183–88; Crossley, "Halakah."

77. Crossley, "Halakah."

78. E.g., H. Hübner, *Das Gesetz in der synoptischen Tradition* (Witten: Luther-Verlag, 1973), 163–64.
79. See esp. R. P. Booth, *Jesus and the Laws of Purity* (Sheffield: JSOT, 1986), 183–84.
80. See G. Alon, *Jews, Judaism and the Classical World: Studies in Jewish History in the Times of the Second Temple and Talmud* (Jerusalem: Magnes, 1977), 210.
81. Poirier, "Pharisees."
82. C. Stettler, "Purity of the Heart in Jesus' Teaching: Mark 7:14–23 Par. as an Expression of Jesus' *Basileia* Ethics," *JTS* 55 (2004): 467–502.
83. E.g., Stettler, "Purity," 494.
84. Ibid., 471–72.
85. L. Fuller, "Review of James G. Crossley, *The Date of Mark's Gospel*," *JGRChJ* 2 (2001–2005): R1–R5 (R5).
86. E. C. Maloney, "Review of James G. Crossley, *The Date of Mark's Gospel*," *CBQ* 67 (2005): 526–27.
87. Ibid., 527.
88. E.g., R. P. Booth, *Jesus and the Laws of Purity: Tradition History and Legal History in Mark* 7 (Sheffield: JSOT, 1986); Poirier, "Why Did the Pharisees Wash Their Hands?"; M. Bockmuehl, *Jewish Law in the Gentile Churches: Halakah and the Beginning of Christian Public Ethics* (Edinburgh: T. & T. Clark, 2000), 1ff.; T. Kazen, *Jesus and Purity Halakah* (Stockholm: Almqvist & Wiksell, 2002), 60–88. These kinds of arguments have also found their way into more popularizing scholarship. Cf. M. D. Hooker, *The Gospel according to St Mark* (London: A. & C. Black, 1991), 178, on Mark 7:15: "To be relevant to the dispute in vv. 1–5, we must assume that the Pharisees believed that cultic impurity could be passed from unwashed hands to food to eater (as has been argued recently by R. P. Booth . . .)."
89. When Maloney does raise his review to the level of argument, he simply misses the point or does not understand what I wrote. He gives some criticism of my Markan analysis claiming my "main premise about Mark's unencumbered presentation of Jesus' legal understanding is not convincing" and that even if I had interpreted Mark 7:19 correctly, Mark's lack of awareness of the problems Jesus' language might create is not necessarily evidence it was written before 45 CE. This is because the Gospel is full of "perplexing problems" such as Jesus' undergoing John's baptism of repentance for the forgiveness of sins, the incompetence of the disciples, wrongly named high priest in 2:26, silence of the women at the end, etc. In such instances Mark is also "corrected" by both later Synoptics (527). But this is irrelevant. Different motivations led to different changes. For example, it is not going too far, surely, to suggest that the tinkering with the details of Jesus' baptism by the evangelists was due to reverence of Jesus. Or that the downplaying of the incompetence of the disciples was due to respect for the disciples in certain areas of early Christianity. Or again, that the silence of the women at the tomb had to be changed to make sure major authorities were present at the resurrection. Or, yet again, that 2:26 was removed because it was deemed a historical/biblical inaccuracy. Irrespective of whether I am right or wrong on Mark, it is clear that the reason why Matthew and Luke would want to portray a law-observant Jesus is because of all the problems over the law in earliest Christianity. Why else would Matthew write Matt. 15:20? Change for this reason is not the same as Matthew and Luke wanting to downplay Jesus' baptism, or to present the disciples in a better light, or making it clear that there were big authorities present at the resurrection, or removing

what they thought was a historical mistake. Moreover, the examples Maloney gives are deliberate "corrections" whereas the examples I gave were making explicit what Mark assumed. Finally, Maloney (526–27) regards my lack of engagement with J. Svartvik, *Mark and Mission: Mark 7.1–23 in Its Narrative and Historical Contexts* (Stockholm: Almqvist & Wiksell, 2000), as "unfortunate." This complaint is extremely difficult to understand, and it is no coincidence (and by now no surprise) that Maloney gives no indication of what details I was supposed to have included. Svartvik dealt with issues such as the historical-critical analysis of Mark 7:15, cultural originality, the haggadic background to evil speech, and approaches to narrative structure with particular reference to the role of crossing the lake in Mark 6–8. All these are important issues in themselves but were different to the questions I was asking, so more engagement than what I gave would have been pointless.

90. For example, see the vigorous critique of scholarly criticisms based on opinion, no argument, condescension, conservative Christian agendas, and comfortable theories in L. L. Grabbe, "'The Comfortable Theory', 'Maximal Conservatism', and Neo-Fundamentalism Revisited," in *Sense and Sensitivity: Essays on Reading the Bible in Memory of Robert Carroll*, ed. A. G. Hunter and P. R. Davies (Sheffield: Sheffield Academic Press, 2002), 174–93, esp. 174–78.

91. For a detailed discussion of the various issues see J. Marcus, *Mark 1–8: A New Translation with Introduction and Commentary* (New York: Doubleday, 2000), 404–515.

92. Cf. esp. Svartvik, *Mark and Mission*.

93. See esp. Theissen, *Gospels in Context*, 72–80.

94. Cf. ibid., 243–45.

95. See, e.g., F. W. Danker, "Mark 8:3," *JBL* 82 (1963): 215–16; B. W. F. van Iersel, "Die wunderbare Speisung und das Abendmahl in der synoptischen Tradition (Mark VI.35–44 par VIII.1–20 par," *NovT* 7 (1964): 167–94; R. A. Guelich, *Mark 1–8:26* (Dallas: Word, 1989), 404; Marcus, *Mark 1–8*, 487. Against this see, e.g., R. H. Gundry, *Mark: A Commentary on His Apology for the Cross* (Grand Rapids: Wm. B. Eerdmans, 1993), 396. Cf. also J. R. Edwards, *The Gospel according to Mark* (Grand Rapids: Wm. B. Eerdmans, 2002), 230: ". . . fits entirely with the austere and rugged geography of the Decapolis."

96. This assertion of the superiority of Jewish ethnicity over against Gentiles who are barely worthy of crumbs from the table (Mark 7:26–27) should be recalled by those scholars who stress the anti-Jewish and pro-Gentile nature of Mark's Gospel.

97. Marcus, *Mark 1–8*, 411. Cf., e.g., Guelich, *Mark 1–8:26*, 343; W. D. Davies and D. C. Allison, *A Critical and Exegetical Commentary on the Gospel according to Saint Matthew VIII–XVIII* (Edinburgh: T. & T. Clark, 1991), 492.

98. Marcus, *Mark 1–8*, 489. Although κόφινος can be used to describe baskets carried by Roman soldiers (Josephus, *J.W.* 3.95; cf. Edwards, *Mark*, 193, n. 41), the combination of Juvenal's language and the different word used in the Gentile feeding give Marcus's argument its force.

99. G. Alon, "The Levitical Uncleanness of Gentiles," in *Jews, Judaism and the Classical World: Studies in Jewish History in the Times of the Second Temple and Talmud* (Jerusalem: Magnes, 1977), 146–89.

100. J. Klawans, "Notions of Gentile Impurity in Ancient Judaism," *Association for Jewish Studies Review* 20 (1995): 285–312; J. Klawans, *Impurity and Sin in Ancient Judaism* (Oxford: Oxford University Press, 2000), 43–60, 134–35.

101. C. E. Hayes, *Gentile Impurities and Jewish Identities: Intermarriage and Conversion from the Bible to the Talmud* (Oxford: Oxford University Press, 2002), 107–44, 199–221.
102. Hayes, *Gentile Impurities*, e.g., 22–34, 53–59, 145–92.
103. Cf. B. Lindars, "'All Foods Clean': Thoughts on Jesus and the Law," in Lindars, ed., *Law and Religion*, 61–71 (62–63, 65–66, 68–69).
104. Marcus, *Mark 1–8*, 464.
105. Cf. M. C. de Boer, "God-fearers in Luke-Acts," in *Luke's Literary Achievement: Collected Essays*, ed. C. M. Tuckett (Sheffield: Sheffield Academic Press, 1995), 50–71.
106. Marcus, *Mark 1–8*, 407.

Chapter 5: Recruitment, Conversion, and Key Shifts in Law Observance

1. L. R. Rambo, *Understanding Religious Conversion* (New Haven, CT: Yale University Press, 1993), 87–88.
2. For an analysis of the various NT texts on conversion see B. R. Gaventa, *From Darkness to Light: Aspects of Conversion in the New Testament* (Philadelphia: Fortress, 1986).
3. R. Stark, *The Rise of Christianity: A Sociologist Reconsiders History* (Princeton, NJ: Princeton University Press, 1996). For an earlier and no less important approach to networks in earliest Christianity see W. A. Meeks, *The First Urban Christians: The Social World of the Apostle Paul*, 2d ed. (New Haven, CT: Yale University Press, 1983, 2003), 27–31. I will return to Meeks below.
4. See especially J. Lofland and R. Stark, "Becoming a World-Saver: A Theory of Conversion to a Deviant Perspective," *American Sociological Review* 30 (1965): 862–75.
5. J. T. Sanders, *Charisma, Converts, Competitors: Societal and Sociological Factors in the Success of Early Christianity* (London, SCM, 2000); J. T. Sanders, "Conversion to Early Christianity," in *Handbook of Early Christianity and the Social Sciences*, ed. A. J. Blasi, P.-A. Turcotte, and J. Duhaime (Walnut Creek, CA: AltaMira, 2002). See also P. A. Harland, "Social Networks and Connections with the Elites in the World of the Early Christians," in Blasi, Turcotte, and Duhaime, eds., *Handbook of Early Christianity*, 385–408 (388–89).
6. Rambo, *Conversion*, 108, with 195–96, n. 9. See also L. R. Rambo and C. E. Farhadian, "Converting: Stages of Religious Change," in *Religious Conversion: Contemporary Practices and Controversies*, ed. C. Lamb and M. D. Bryant (London: Cassell, 1999), 23–34 (30).
7. W. Kox, W. Meeus, and H. 't Hart, "Religious Conversion of Adolescents: Testing the Lofland and Stark Model of Religious Conversion," *Sociological Analysis* 52 (1991): 227–40 (238). Cf. also A. L. Greil and D. R. Rudy, "What Have We Learned from Process Models of Conversion? An Examination of Ten Studies," *Sociological Focus* 17 (1984): 306–23 (316); T. Robbins, *Cults, Converts and Charisma: The Sociology of New Religious Movements* (London: Sage, 1988), 79–88.
8. L. L. Dawson, "Cult Conversions: Controversy and Clarification," in C. Lamb and M. D. Bryant, eds., *Religious Conversion*, 287–315 (287).
9. J. T. Richardson, "Conversion," in *Encyclopedia of Religion and Society*, ed. W. H. Swatos (Walnut Creek, CA: AltaMira, 1998), 119–21 (120).

10. T. E. Klutz, "The Rhetoric of Science in *The Rise of Christianity*: A Response to Rodney Stark's Sociological Account of Christianization," *Journal of Early Christian Studies* 6 (1998): 162–84 (171).

11. H. O. Maier, "Review of *The Rise of Christianity: A Sociologist Reconsiders History* by Rodney Stark," *JTS* 49 (1998): 328–35 (330). Cf. also Stark, *Rise of Christianity*, 21–22, responding to Ronald F. Hock's comment (in a 1986 *SBL* response to Stark) that ancient cities and networks were markedly different from modern cities and networks. But, as Stark and Sanders point out, this only implies difference, and indeed more points of contact within an ancient network, and does not invalidate the theory of Christianity spreading through networks. See Sanders, *Charisma, Converts, Competitors*, 137.

12. Lofland and Stark, "Becoming a World-Saver"; Stark, *Rise of Christianity*, 15–18.

13. Stark, *Rise of Christianity*, 16.

14. Ibid., 17.

15. Ibid., 18.

16. R. Stark and W. S. Bainbridge, "Networks of Faith: Interpersonal Bonds and Recruitment to Cults and Sects," *American Journal of Sociology* 85 (1980): 1376–95 (1379).

17. Stark and Bainbridge, "Networks of Faith," 1380; W. S. Bainbridge, *Satan's Power* (Berkeley: University of California Press, 1978).

18. Compare Dawson, "Cult Conversions," 293: "It may often appear that cults target the lonely or vulnerable because cult involvement is strongly correlated with having fewer and weaker extra-cult ties. . . . This accounts, in part, for the disproportionate representation of adolescents and young adults in NRMs [New Religious Movements]. This segment of the population is simply free of countervailing social and economic commitments."

19. E.g., the number of U.S. Mormons in 1900 was 268,331; in 1947 it was 1,016,170; in 1967 it was 2,614,340; and in 1978 it was 4,180,000.

20. Stark and Bainbridge, "Networks of Faith," 1386.

21. Ibid., 1387.

22. D. A. Snow and C. L. Phillips, "The Lofland-Stark Conversion Model: A Critical Reassessment," *Social Problems* 27 (1980): 430–47 (432).

23. Ibid., 440.

24. Cf. D. Snow, L. Zurcher Jr., and S. Ekland-Olson, "Social Networks and Social Movements: A Microstructural Approach to Differential Recruitment," *American Sociological Review* 45 (1980): 787–801 (790–91): 82 percent of Nichiren Shoshu recruits were from social networks—17 percent by recruitment in public places and 1 percent through the media.

25. Snow and Phillips, "Lofland-Stark Conversion Model," 440.

26. Snow, Zurcher, and Ekland-Olson, "Social Networks and Social Movements," 787–801 (790–91).

27. Ibid., 792.

28. Ibid., 794.

29. This is based on J. S. Judah, *Hare Krishna and the Counterculture* (New York: Wiley, 1974).

30. Snow, Zurcher, and Ekland-Olson, "Social Networks and Social Movements," 795 with n. 12.

31. Ibid., 796. See also the qualifications and positive evaluation of this approach in Robbins, *Cults, Converts and Charisma*, 86–88.

32. Rambo, *Conversion*, 108–13.

33. Ibid., 112. Cf. W. Arens, "Islam and Christianity in Sub-Saharan Africa: Ethnographic Reality of Ideology," *Cahiers d'études africaines* 15 (1975): 443–56.

34. Cf. Robbins, *Cults, Converts and Charisma*, 85: "Social network studies of NRM [New Religious Movement] recruitment are related to the current broader vogue for social network analysis in sociology."

35. For further details of and scholarly debates on these kinds of relationships see, e.g., the following selection: J. A. Barnes, "Class and Committees in a Norwegian Island Parish," *Human Relations* 7 (1954): 39–58; J. C. Mitchell, ed., *Social Networks in Urban Situations* (Manchester: Manchester University Press, 1969); J. Boissevain, *Friends of Friends: Networks, Manipulators and Coalitions* (Oxford: Blackwell, 1974); J. C. Mitchell, "Social Networks," *Annual Review of Anthropology* 3 (1974): 279–99 (288–295); B. Wellman, "Network Analysis: Some Basic Principles," *Sociological Theory* 1 (1983): 155–200; S. Wasserman and K. Faust, *Social Network Analysis: Methods and Applications* (Cambridge: Cambridge University Press, 1994); J. C. Cavendish, M. R. Welch, and D. C. Leege, "A Social Network Theory and Predicators of Religiosity for Black and White Catholics: Evidence of a 'Black Sacred Cosmos'?" *Journal for the Scientific Study of Religion* 37 (1998): 397–410; J. Carrington, J. Scott, and S. Wasserman, eds., *Models and Methods in Social Network Analysis* (New York: Cambridge University Press, 2005). For use of social network analysis in areas of Christian origins see, e.g., J. K. Chow, *Patronage and Power: A Study of Social Networks in Corinth* (Sheffield: JSOT Press, 1992); L. M. White. ed., *Social Networks in the Early Christian Environment: Issues and Methods for Social History* (Atlanta: Scholars Press, 1992); H. Remus, "Voluntary Associations and Networks: Aelius Aristides at the Asklepieion in Pergamum," in *Voluntary Associations in the Graeco-Roman World*, ed. J. S. Kloppenborg and S. G. Wilson (London: Routledge, 1996), 146–75; D. C. Duling, "The Jesus Movement and Social Network Analysis (Part II: The Social Network)," *BTB* 30 (2000): 1–12 (5–10); D. C. Duling, "The Jesus Movement and Social Network Analysis," in *The Social Setting of Jesus and the Gospels*, ed. W. Stegemann, B. Malina, and G. Theissen (Minneapolis: Fortress, 2002), 301–32; Harland, "Social Networks"; P. A. Harland, *Associations, Synagogues, and Congregations: Claiming a Place in Ancient Mediterranean Society* (Minneapolis: Fortress, 2003), 137–60.

36. J. C. Scott, "Protest and Profanation: Agrarian Revolt and the Little Tradition, Part II," *Theory and Society* 4 (1977): 211–46 (220).

37. Lofland and Stark, "Becoming a World-Saver," 864. Cf. "Persons who accepted the truth of the doctrine, but lacked intensive interaction with the core group, remained partisan spectators, who played no active part in the battle to usher in God's kingdom." Ibid., 874.

38. Ibid., 871.

39. I.e., the bearer of the message in the United States: the names were changed in "Becoming a World-Saver" to protect anonymity (862, n. 3).

40. Lofland and Stark, "Becoming a World-Saver," 871.

41. Ibid., 873.

42. Cf. Sanders, *Charisma, Converts, Competitors*, 102: "Most of what Paul writes in all his letters involves the assumption that Christians are in process—that they have become Christians, but that they still need to learn what it means to be Christian, both regards belief . . . and as regards practice." Cf. E. V. Gallagher, "Conversion and Community in Late Antiquity," *Journal of Religion* 73 (1993): 1–15.

43. Lofland and Stark, "Becoming a World-Saver," 873.

44. Compare Philip Harland's work on multiple memberships of different associations in the ancient world, esp. Asia Minor. It is significant that Harland can also discuss the competition for loyalties among associations. See, e.g., P. A. Harland, "Spheres of Contention, Claims of Pre-eminence: Rivalries among Associations in Sardis and Smyrna," in *Religious Rivalries and the Struggle for Success in Sardis and Smyrna*, ed. R. S. Ascough (Waterloo, ON: Wilfrid Laurier University Press, 2005), 53–63, 259–62.

45. J. T. Richardson and M. Stewart, "Conversion Process Models and the Jesus Movement," in *Conversion Careers: In and Out of the New Religions*, ed. J. T. Richardson (Beverly Hills, CA: Sage, 1978), 24–42 (37–38, cf. 41, n. 9).

46. Snow and Phillips, "Lofland-Stark Conversion Model," 441.

47. K. W. Welch, "An Interpersonal Influence Model of Traditional Religious Commitment," *Sociological Quarterly* 22 (1981): 81–92. See also K. W. Welch, "Community Development and Metropolitan Religious Commitment: A Test of Two Competing Models," *Journal for the Scientific Study of Religion* 22 (1983): 167–81.

48. For further empirical details see Welch, "Traditional Religious Commitment," 86–89.

49. Rambo, *Conversion*, 102.

50. Dawson, "Cult Conversions," 309.

51. J. Lofland and N. Skonovd, "Conversion Motifs," *Journal for the Scientific Study of Religion* 20 (1981): 373–85 (380).

52. Kox, Meeus, and 't Hart, "Testing the Lofland and Stark Model," 228.

53. Sanders, *Charisma, Converts, Competitors*, 102, cf. 82.

54. Rambo, *Conversion*, 97; six types are found on 97–99. Cf. S. Kaplan, "The Africanization of Missionary Christianity: History and Typology," *Journal of Religion in Africa* 16 (1986): 166–86.

55. An extremely relevant example would be Diaspora Jews at the time of Christian origins. See esp. J. M. G. Barclay, *Jews in the Mediterranean Diaspora from Alexander to Trajan (323 BCE–117 CE)* (Edinburgh: T. & T. Clark, 1996). Barclay discusses in some detail the varieties of accommodation, acculturation, and assimilation among Mediterranean Jews. For another important use of such approaches with reference to synagogues and Christian congregations, which will be discussed below, see Harland, *Associations, Synagogues, and Congregations*, 195–212.

56. Rambo, *Conversion*, 99–100.

57. Ibid., 101.

58. Ibid., 89. Cf. E. Isichei, "Seven Varieties of Ambiguity: Some Patterns of Igbo Response to Christian Missions," *Journal of Religion in Africa* 3 (1970): 209–27.

59. Rambo, *Conversion*, 94. Cf. H. J. Fisher, "Conversion Reconsidered: Some Historical Aspects of Religious Conversion in Black Africa," *Africa* 43 (1973): 27–40; and "The Juggernaut's Apologia: Conversion to Islam in Black Africa," *Africa* 55 (1985): 153–73.

60. Sanders, *Charisma, Converts, Competitors*, 88.

61. A. L. Epstein, "Gossip, Norms and Social Network," in *Social Networks in Urban Situations*, ed. J. C. Mitchell (Manchester: Manchester University Press, 1969), 117–27. E.g., 125: "The exchange of gossip . . . denotes a certain community of interest: it marks off the 'set' from others of whose intimate affairs they are

ignorant, or which they would consider too unimportant for their concern. Through such gossip is expressed the norms of behaviour specific to the 'set'."

62. Scott, "Agrarian Revolt and the Little Tradition, *Part II*," 221.

63. Ibid., 222.

64. P. A. Harland, "Honouring the Emperor or Assailing the Beast: Participation in Civic Life among Associations (Jewish, Christian and Other) in Asia Minor and the Apocalypse of John," *JSNT* 77 (2000): 99–121 (116–21).

65. Duling, "The Jesus Movement and Network Analysis," 317.

66. Cf. Duling, "The Jesus Movement and Network Analysis," 313, in a different but not wholly incompatible way: "*Generalization*: Larger networks provide possibilities for more interactions, but they also have potential for more interpersonal conflict."

67. S. J. D. Cohen, *The Beginnings of Jewishness: Boundaries, Varieties, Uncertainties* (Berkeley: University of California Press, 1999), 140–74.

68. Meeks, *First Urban Christians*, 27–31.

69. Ibid., 29, referring to R. F. Hock, *The Social Context of Paul's Ministry: Tentmaking and Apostleship* (Philadelphia: Fortress, 1980), 37–42. See also Harland, "Social Networks," 392; and Sanders, *Charisma, Converts, Competitors*, 101: "The fact that he [Paul] had a full-time job, as we should say, and preached at the same time certainly makes the possibility of his networking and talking to small groups more credible, but there is no proof." Cf. also 1 Thess. 2:9; 4:10–12; and Origen, *Cels.* 3.55.

70. Harland, "Social Networks," 389–94. Cf. Sanders, *Charisma, Converts, Competitors*, 139–40 on households and the growth of Mithraism.

71. Harland, "Social Networks," 393–406; Harland, *Associations, Synagogues, and Congregations*, 33–36, 177–264.

72. Harland, *Associations, Synagogues, and Congregations*, 211.

73. As is well known, Gentiles attracted to Judaism and the synagogue are often referred to as "god-fearers." Although this may not have been a technical term in the early decades of Christianity, I see no harm in retaining it in the loose sense of Gentiles with a variety of degrees of attraction to Judaism. So when I refer to "god-fearers" without qualification, it is meant to be taken like this and not as a technical first-century term.

74. See further S. J. D. Cohen, "Respect for Judaism by Gentiles according to Josephus," *HTR* 80 (1987): 409–30.

75. Cf. Josephus, *Ant.* 14.110: "But no one need wonder that there was so much wealth in our temple, for all the Jews throughout the habitable world, and those who worshipped God [σεβομένων τὸν θεόν], even those from Asia and Europe, had been contributing to it for a very long time."

76. For a selection of studies on the "God-fearer" inscription at Aphrodisias, see, e.g., J. Reynolds and R. Tannenbaum, *Jews and God-Fearers at Aphrodisias* (Cambridge: Cambridge Philological Society, 1987); I. Levinskaya, "The Inscription from Aphrodisias and the Problem of God-Fearers," *TynBul* 41 (1990): 312–18; J. Murphy-O'Connor, "Lots of God-Fearers?" *RB* 99 (1992): 418–24; M. Williams, "The Jews and Godfearers Inscription from Aphrodisias," *Historia* 41 (1992): 297–310.

77. Harland, "Honouring the Emperor or Assailing the Beast," 101–21; Harland, *Associations, Synagogues, and Congregations*, 200–210; Harland, "Spheres of Contention," 59–61. See also T. Seland, "Philo and the Clubs and Associations of Alexandria," in Kloppenborg and Wilson, eds., *Voluntary Associations*, 110–27.

78. This is a controversial subject tied up with issues of defining "god-fearers" and the Aphrodisias synagogue inscription. The secondary literature is huge. For a selection, and in addition to the literature on Aphrodisias above, see, e.g., F. Siegert, "Gottesfürchtige und Sympathisanten," *JSJ* 4 (1973): 109–64; A. T. Kraabel, "The Disappearance of the Godfearers," *Numen* 28 (1981): 113–14; M. Wilcox, "The God-fearers in Acts—A Reconstruction," *JSNT* 13 (1981): 102–22; R. S. MacLennan and A. T. Kraabel, "The God-Fearers—A Literary and Theological Invention," in *Diaspora Jews and Judaism. Essays in Honor of, and in Dialogue with, A. Thomas Kraabel*, ed. J. A. Overman and R. S. MacLennan (Atlanta: Scholars, 1992), 131–43; J. M. Lieu, "The Race of God-Fearers," *JTS* 46 (1995): 483–501.

79. Cf. Lieu, "God-Fearers," 483–84, n. 3.

80. S. Fine, "Non-Jews in the Synagogues of Late-Antique Palestine: Rabbinic and Archaeological Evidence," in *Jews, Christians, and Polytheists in the Ancient Synagogue: Cultural Interaction during the Greco-Roman Period*, ed. S. Fine (London: Routledge, 1999), 224–42 (225–31).

81. Meeks, *First Urban Christians*, 75–77.

82. Ibid., 77.

83. N. H. Taylor, "The Social Nature of Conversion in the Early Christian World," in *Modelling Early Christianity: Social Scientific Studies of the New Testament in Its Context*, ed. P. F. Esler (London: Routledge, 1995), 128–36 (133).

84. Cf. J. G. Crossley, *The Date of Mark's Gospel: Insight from the Law in Earliest Christianity* (London: Continuum/T. & T. Clark, 2004), 177–78.

85. Cohen, *Beginnings of Jewishness*, 154.

86. See further P. V. M. Flesher, *Oxen, Women, or Citizens? Slaves in the System of the Mishnah* (Atlanta: Scholars Press, 1988), 139–56.

87. M. Stern, ed., *Greek and Latin Authors on Jews and Judaism* (3 vols.; Jerusalem: Israel Academy of Sciences & Humanities, 1974), 3:64.

88. Cohen, *Beginnings of Jewishness*, 155.

89. For further discussion of this conversion see, e.g., J. Neusner, "The Conversion of Adiabene to Judaism: A New Perspective," *JBL* 83 (1964): 60–66; L. H. Schiffman, "The Conversion of the Royal House of Adiabene in Josephus and Rabbinic Sources," in *Josephus, Judaism, and Christianity*, ed. L. H. Feldman and G. Hata (Detroit: Wayne State University Press, 1987), 293–312; D. Schwartz, "God, Gentiles, and Jewish Law: On Acts 15 and Josephus' Adiabene Narrative," in *Geschichte—Tradition—Reflection: Festschrift für Martin Hengel I: Judentum*, ed. H. Cancik, H. Lichtenberger, and P. Schäfer (Tübingen: Mohr Siebeck, 1996), 263–82.

90. Cf. *Gen. Rab.* 46:10: "Once Monabaz and Izates, the sons of King Ptolemy, were sitting and reading the book of Genesis. When they came to the verse, 'And you shall be circumcised' [Gen. 17:11] one turned his face towards the wall and commenced to weep, and the other turned his face to the wall and commenced to weep. Then each went and had himself circumcised."

91. For further discussion on female converts to Judaism see T. Ilan, *Jewish Women in Greco-Roman Palestine: An Inquiry into Image and Status* (Tübingen: Mohr Siebeck, 1995), 211–14.

92. Cf. Cohen, *Beginnings of Judaism*, 227.

93. Rabbinic literature was set against conversion through marriage if it was done for any other reason than loving God (cf. *y. Qidd.* 4:1, 65b; *b. Yebam.* 24b; *Gerim*

1:7/Minor Tractates 60a). The existence of such a view doubtlessly suggests that convenience conversions never died out. Indeed they never would and never have.

94. For the various political, ethnic, and religious nuances of the "conversion" of the Idumeans see Cohen, *Beginnings of Jewishness*, 17–18, 110–39. For a useful summary of the debated scholarly issues see L. L. Grabbe, *Judaism from Cyrus to Hadrian* (London: SCM, 1992), 328–31. Compare also the actions of Aristobulus when he claimed parts of the lands of the Itureans at the end of the second century BCE. Those who wished to stay had to undertake conversion as far as circumcision and law observance (Josephus, *Ant.* 13.318; Strabo, *Geogr.* 16.2.34). It should be noted that circumcision was popular in the region, and so the Itureans along with Idumeans may already have practiced circumcision prior to incorporation with Judea/Judaism (cf. Philo, *QG* 3.48; Herodotus 2.104.2–4; *Mek.* [Exod. 15]; *b. Yebam.* 71a).

95. This Ptolemy is recorded in a work called *De Adfiniom Vocabulorum Differentia* and usually attributed to Ammonius (Stern, *Greek and Latin Authors*, 1:355).

96. For further discussion see, e.g., P. Richardson, *Herod: King of the Jews and Friend of the Romans* (Columbia: University of South Carolina Press, 1996), 240–61; Cohen, *Beginnings of Jewishness*, 13–24.

97. Cohen, *Beginnings of Jewishness*, 15.

98. There are also attacks on Herod's background in later Christian writings where there are claims recorded that Herod was from Ascalon (Justin, *Trypho* 52) or even that Antipater's father was a slave from the temple of Apollo in Ascalon and that Antipater was captured by Idumeans (Eusebius, *Eccl. Hist.* 1.7.11). Compare also *b. B. Bat.* 3b.

99. "Half-Jew" may carry the force of half-Judean in this instance, so Cohen, *Beginnings of Jewishness*, 18.

Conclusion

1. S. Mitchell, "The Cult of Theos Hypsistos between Pagans, Jews and Christians," in *Pagan Monotheism in Late Antiquity*, ed. P. Athanassiadi and M. Frede (Oxford: Oxford University Press, 1999), 83–148 (148).

2. This is in a book tentatively entitled *Explaining Christian Origins Historically: The First Century* (forthcoming).

Scripture and Ancient Source Index

Author Index

Trotsky, Leon, 7, 8
Tuckett, Christopher, 123, 125–26, 191 n.53,
    201 n.14, 202 nn.17, 19, 31; 204 nn.64,
    68, 70, 71; 207 n.105
Turcotte, P. —A., 187, 190 n.52, 207 n.5

Uhlhorn, G., 182 n.84
Uro, R., 204 n.59

Vaage, L. E., 203 n.36
van Iersel, B. W. F., 206 n.95
Verheyden, J., 201 n.14
Vermes, Geza, 20, 27–29, 30, 32, 33, 131, 178
    n.18, 183 n.103, 185 nn.128, 129, 130,
    131, 132, 133, 134, 135

Wallace-Hadrill, A., 188 nn.16, 19; 189 n.28
Wasserman, S., 209 n.35
Watson, F., 186 n.154
Weber, Max, 16, 20–21, 32

Welch, Kevin W., 152, 210 nn.47, 48
Welch, M. R., 209 n.35
Wellhausen, J., 105, 202 n.29
Wellman, B., 209 n.35
West, M. L., 199 n.6
White, L. M., 209 n.35
Whitelam, Keith W., 189 n.22
Wilcox, M., 212 n.78
Wild, R. A., 201 n.17
Williams, M., 211 n.76
Williams, Peter J., 202 n.30
Wilson, Bryan, 187 n.4
Wilson, S. G., 209 n.35, 211 n.77
Wright, N. T., 2, 25–26, 32, 33, 177 n.3, 185
    nn.121, 123, 125; 192 n.69, 194 n.113,
    196 n.1, 198 nn.37, 39
Würthwein, E., 198 n.33

Zurcher, Louis, 147–48, 208 nn.24, 26, 27,
    28, 30, 31

Subject Index